Pondering in Wonder

Contemplations of a Mountain Contemplative

Barbara Joan Cooke Brocksieck

outskirts
press

Outskirts Press, Inc.
http://www.outskirtspress.com

ISBN: 978-1-9772-3239-7

Outskirts Press and the "OP" logo are trademarks belonging to Outskirts Press, Inc.

PRINTED IN THE UNITED STATES OF AMERICA

FOR

My sons, STEVEN and KEVIN, have watched me ponder all their lives and now have taken some time to read parts of the book and given me lots of encouragement.

Some of the ladies with whom I share a spiritual bond, JOYCE ANDERSON and LISA BINGHAM and at our church, Woodland Life Center in Woodland Park, Colorado, have continually urged me forward to put this book together – among them BERNIE VAYLE, LISA HOEKMAN, and CINDY RUMSEY.

Most of all I thank my husband, HARRY BROCKSIECK. Without him there would be no book. I have a shelf full of journals to do something with some day. I enjoy the writing, but he has done the rest – the search for a publisher, has taken what they have said and turned my stuff into something printable. Harry, you are my hero, my patient and loving business manager, and my guide.

⌒

DEDICATION: For Harry, Steven and Kevin, who have always given me time and space to ponder. Grandson Dylan has been a delightful addition to our lives these last 12 years

A word about "Mountain" Contemplative: It is true that we live at 8500′ in the Colorado Rockies, however, the word "Mountain" refers to Barbara's life in the rarefied air of Moses and Elijah who lived in the mountains of God and who received from Him to share with us.
Harry (Barbara's husband)

The graphics of the book Pondering in Wonder

Notes from Major Elenia Krutusa

Why the font of "Pondering In Wonder" is handwritten?

When I ponder I usually make a handwritten notes or sketches

What are the images?

Olive branch represents restoring - "So much of life so much of God"

Thorn Crown - "...so much of God's work was led me to ponder, to wonder and wonder"

Straw Pieces - "Christ was born as human in a less than rich family ...and laid in straw"

Contents

Acknowledgments

ELENA KATRUTSA, the artist who designed the cover and the art work in the book, was our student at The Salvation Army Institute for Officer Training for Eastern Europe. The school which she attended with her husband, Slava, was then is Helsinki, Finland. They are now stationed with The Salvation Army in Kishinev, Moldova. I am deeply indebted to Elena for her sensitive and creative drawings that capture my intent for each section of these writing.

LUCINDA COOKE, Cindy, my niece, has spent hours reading, editing, suggesting wording, correcting these many words (even enjoying some of them, I hope).

KEN BAILLIE, Commissioner of The Salvation Army and a very good friend and the first to see me as a contemplative, appears to know me well, and I am grateful for his words in the Forward.

Foreword

I met Barbara more than thirty years ago and we have worked in overlapping settings many of the years since. I've gotten to know her well both in Christian ministry and in personal friendships. Indeed, the Baillies and Brocksiecks have sometimes taken vacation trips together. To be asked to write this *Foreword* is an honor and privilege.

Barbara is a natural contemplative. By 'natural' I mean she comes by the practice of contemplation instinctively. She's going to do it because that's who she is. By 'contemplative' I mean she *thinks* about the spiritual life, not just reads about it, or studies it, or lectures about it though she does all that. She goes further, every day thinking seriously about the spiritual life. In her own words she is "meditating, reading, pondering" [p.128]. And she calls all of us to the same, "mainly on the inside – in our thought-life and in our feelings" [p.164]. "The challenge for me," she notes, "is to slow down, look, gaze upon the ordinary, see!" [p.237]. This book is the collected result of her longtime looking, gazing, meditating, reflecting, pondering.

I have none of her gift. I'm the opposite: task-oriented, driven and hurried. But I can read her ponderings and be blessed. Sometimes her thoughts are head-snaps for me: Sure, God rested on the seventh day of Creation [p. 416]. Anyone who reads the Bible knows that. But Barbara goes on to wonder what God did on His rest day! Huhh?! Well, yes, now that she brings it up. But who would have thought of it but a contemplative? There are many such head-snaps.

This book is not a Bible commentary though there are aspects of that. It is not a novel or serial narrative. Not a systematic theology. Not an analysis. Not an essay. It is a collection of meditative musings on the spiritual life, the deeper things of the human, the Christian, experience. So, slow down, sit down and....contemplate.

Ken Baillie, Commissioner
The Salvation Army

PONDERING IN WONDER

*One of my favorite words in the Bible is "ponder." I love the
fact that Mary "treasured up all these things and pondered
them in her heart" (Luke 2:19). The Psalmist also pondered and
calls us to ponder (Psalm 64:9, 111:2, 119:95). Ponder means
to think about something deliberately, carefully, to engage in
contemplation. That pretty much defines how I come to God's
Word and how I think about life. I ponder.*

*Then one year at Christmas I realized that pondering often led
me to wonder, sometimes questioning (I wonder how or why),
sometimes in astonishment or amazement, with curiosity, or
surprise (the Wow factor).*

*Thus, the title of this book. So much of life, so much of God,
so much of God's Word has led me to ponder, to wonder in
all the definitions of that word. May these thoughts from my
ponderings lead you to Ponder in Wonder.*

Dave & Brenda —
Long time special friends!
May all your ponderings
turn to wonder.

Barbara

...my heart, Lord Jesus –
it's kind of
barnlike – not as
clean as a birthplace
should be, but there is
room in my heart
for you.

CONTEMPLATING CHRISTMAS

There are many things to contemplate about Advent, about Christmas, about the people, the events, about what we have done with this season, to this season. It's no wonder that so many books, articles, poems, and stories have been written about it.

It's worth pondering! I pray that my ponderings will bring you blessings, a cause for thought, a moment to laugh or shed a tear, a reason to do your own pondering.

EXAMING CHRISTMAS

THE MEANING OF ADVENT

The dictionary defines advent as the arrival of something momentous, as in the coming or birth of Christ – Jesus, the Son of God was indeed born, something truly momentous. We call the period of four Sundays before Christmas, Advent. The word is from Latin, "to come," Adventus, or coming. In Greek the word is "Parousia," which we commonly use for the Second Coming of Christ. And so today we commemorate his first coming even while we are preparing for his second coming.

The colors associated with Christmas are not red and green, but purple, the royal color, and blue, for hope. When Jesus was about to leave earth he said, "Keep awake, for you do not know on what day your Lord is coming...for the Son of Man is coming at an unexpected hour" (Matthew 24:42). Hope for a royal second coming! The first time he came he was unexpected. A few people were awake then, maybe hoping, but very few anticipating so that when he proved through his teaching and signs that he was the Messiah few believed, especially among those who should have recognized him. Angels visited. A star was in the sky but only the shepherds were seeing the angels and only two or so wise men from far away noticed and followed it.

How ready are we to celebrate Jesus' birth? What will capture our attention this season? How prepared are we for his coming again? It will be something momentous and we will not be able to miss it according to the Bible. Be ready!!

ANTICIPATION
Isaiah 9:1-7

What must it have been like to anticipate Jesus' first coming? Thousands of years of waiting; women hoping against hope that they would be chosen, and yet hoping they wouldn't, too much responsibility! Every Jew was expecting a miraculous experience, though definitely not God coming as a baby, maybe someone who would overthrow all their enemies and restore a theocracy.

Now we anticipate Jesus' coming again, and we try to know the Word so that we don't miss it like they did when he came the first time. What do we anticipate at this season? Blessings of family together; the wonderful, inspiring music; the special church events; and the TV specials. Or maybe some painful losses that leave us lonely or sad. God will speak and we will hear if we listen with our hearts.

We'd really like to anticipate "peace on earth to men on whom his favor rests." Maybe especially peace in Jerusalem and Bethlehem, and of course in Iran and Afghanistan, between Christians and Muslims everywhere, and between Christians in Ireland! May there be peace in places where gangs control people's lives, where children learn hatred and fighting for their "turf."

O God, use your people who are working in these places in this season. Come to them in power, with peace during this Advent. May there be peace in families where there is disagreement keeping them apart. O Prince of Peace, may these people and these places be reminded of who you are and why you came. You can change everything! Come, Lord Jesus! Reign in MY heart, that where I am I will experience and maybe even bring peace.

EXPECTATION
Luke 1:5-25, 39-45, 57-60

Tom Mullen, a Christian humorist and author, reminds us that when the Christmas story took place it was "in the time of King Herod" not in the days of "Ole King Cole, a merry old soul." When Luke wrote his Gospel he carefully placed events in their historical perspective. We are reminded of the chaos in which the Jews were living – "the time of King Herod." Life moved along somewhat normally, but the tension was always there – Roman rule and religious corruption. The Jews still had the temple and a priesthood, questionable as it was. Most Jews felt that their only hope was the overthrow of the Romans, leading to the return of a true theocracy. But God had other plans! He was about to make "all things new" after 400 years of silence.

It began with an angel's temple visit to a priest named Zechariah. He may well have been one of the few priests who was truly holy, "upright in the sight of God, observing all the Lord's commandments and regulations blamelessly." In fact, that describes both him and his wife, Elizabeth (Luke 1:6). Zechariah was in the Holy of Holies when the angel appeared on the "right side of the altar," a beautiful expression of detail. Zechariah had been chosen by lot to burn incense, a treasured opportunity which he took very seriously. He was alone in the presence of God, probably the only time in his life that he could enter that place, and it turned out to be a once-in-a-lifetime experience indeed! And the angel said, "Do not be afraid; your prayer has been heard. Your wife Elizabeth will bear a son, and you are to give him the name John."

I wonder what prayer Zechariah thought of when the angel said, "Your prayer has been heard." At least the angel didn't leave him hanging for long, but went on to say, "Your wife will bear a son" and not an ordinary one, at that – well, of course, he would be extraordinary. They hadn't been able to have children and were now too old! "And you will have joy and many will rejoice. He will be great in the sight of the Lord and be filled with the Spirit even before his birth. He will turn people to God and be in the spirit of Elijah," etc., etc. How could he take all that in? What a message – unbelievable, full of information and hope!

And because he didn't really believe, the angel Gabriel told him he could not talk until it all came true! He couldn't explain to the crowd outside what had happened. He couldn't even tell Elizabeth about it when he got home. He was disciplined by silence because he couldn't believe what he had been told. Maybe the discipline from God was not just to make him realize it really was the truth, but also allowing the message to go from his head to his heart in ways it would not have done had he talked about it.

He would go home and write the message to his beloved Elizabeth and they would wait in expectation and hope for the fulfillment of this unbelievable promise, a promise he would begin to believe because God had given him a sign.

REVELATION
Luke 1:23-25, 39-45, 57, 58

"He went home....Elizabeth conceived....'This is what the Lord has done for me....'" Simple faith, utter trust, and unbelievable things happened. Nine months went by, nine months of silence for Zechariah, nine months of amazing pregnancy for Elizabeth, nine months of wondering anticipation – "What could this mean?" No one else knew about this miracle; no one knew what was going on or what the meaning was; no one, including Zechariah and Elizabeth, had any idea what was next. Even when the angel came to earth again, it was far away in Nazareth and they didn't know, but the truth was about to be revealed after six months of hope and expectation, when Mary came to visit.

Elizabeth had instantaneous insight – the moment she heard Mary's greeting not only did the "child within her" leap for joy, but she was "filled with the Holy Spirit!" So as we begin this new era in spiritual history, two women, Mary and Elizabeth, are filled with the Holy Spirit. Both of them were righteous women who had found favor with God bringing them a special blessing, miraculously birthing children, one old, long past child bearing age, one young and still a virgin. But it was God's time – "when the time was right" (Galatians 4:4), when there were two virtuous women, God broke into history and filled them both with the Holy Spirit, and they bore children, special children – one the forerunner by a few months of the other. Both boys were to proclaim the good news of the Kingdom, the good news of God with us, in the flesh, living in the neighborhood.

Elizabeth recognized a very significant fact about Mary – "She believed that there would be a fulfillment of what was spoken by the Lord" (Luke 1:45). She believed what God said, the Old Testament promises of the Messiah and the message from the angel to her – she believed! Mary also believed that Elizabeth was pregnant as the angel had told her. She was a woman of intense, deep faith who lived by her commitment to being the servant, the handmaid of the Lord.

I wonder if Mary returned to Nazareth just before John was born, and why then? If Luke's months are accurate Elizabeth would have been 9 months pregnant when Mary left. It was long enough that Mary was settled in her soul about the coming events for Elizabeth and herself and had decided what she would do regarding Joseph and her marriage.

Elizabeth's time had come and she bore a son. Her neighbors recognized that it was God showing his mercy to her that brought this about and they rejoiced with her. They knew that Zechariah and Elizabeth were blameless and righteous and continued to be. This might have been a community of priestly families, good people, and they joined Elizabeth in her joy when John was born – amazed and rejoicing in God's grace.

Lord, I believe! Help me to live like it! Elizabeth experienced the fulfillment of the promised Holy Spirit within her. She would die, I think, soon after John's birth, but her faithfulness, her righteousness, her belief was "rewarded" by this early filling by the Spirit who would be her companion, her strength, her joy through the remaining years of her life. I believe she passed all that on to her son, who became known as John, the Baptist, the forerunner of Jesus, who prepared the way of the Lord.

LOOKING AHEAD –
Luke 1:76-79

It seems to me that the first part of Zechariah's prophecy (1:67-75) is his reflection on Mary's visit and the revelation Elizabeth had when she realized that Mary was carrying in her womb the Messiah. "God has redeemed his people; he has raised up a mighty savior – Hallelujah! – he is the fulfillment of the Old Testament prophecy; he has shown the promised mercy and remembered his covenant with Abraham" [a covenant of faith], a covenant which says that when we are rescued from our enemies we can "serve him without fear in righteousness and holiness before him all our days." I don't know if Zechariah was thinking of "enemies" in terms of political enemies or spiritual enemies. It is so much broader, bigger, universal, for all men when we recognize that our real enemy is Satan and his armies so that no matter who we are, where we live, who may appear for or against us, our enemy is Satan and God rescues us from his attacks. When we learn that we are rescued and have been redeemed, then we can live in victory, "without fear in holiness and righteousness before him all our days."

Zechariah turns his thoughts, his prophecy, to the baby boy he holds in his arms, his own son whom he has named John. He knows this tiny infant will be a prophet who will go before the Lord to prepare his way. It seems to me that we have much the same task. We each are preparing the way in people's lives for God to do his work. We are not the Savior, but we can be the ones who open people's heart to the possibility of receiving the Savior.

"By the tender mercy of God, the dawn from on high will break upon us." He knew that his son was to be the forerunner of the Messiah. John would give "knowledge of salvation to his people by the forgiveness of their sins because of the tender mercies of God."

We don't meet these two wonderful people again in Scripture. We'll have to wait until heaven to get the rest of the story.

THE SILENCE IS OVER
Luke 1:57-75

Elizabeth and Zechariah knew what their son's name was to be – John. The neighbors were sure they would name him after his dad. After all they should have someone to carry on the family name. But no, Elizabeth said, it's John, and they turned to Zechariah who still could not speak. He wrote the name John – did he write it in big bold letters? When I am like Elizabeth, "upright in the sight of God, observing all the Lord's commandments and regulations blamelessly," I have no idea what prayers God will answer or how he will do it, but I can be sure that my prayer has been heard, and God is at work.

The neighbors are stunned – a miracle birth, a strange choice of names – and suddenly Zechariah can talk. Just you watch, it all seems to say!! But first listen to how Zechariah praises God. You'll get a clue you should remember! When John leaves home later to begin his ministry, do those neighbors remember this day? Do they remember what Zechariah said? Do they go to hear him? Do they believe?

As we read Zechariah's "song" we can't help but think that he had spent nine silent months pondering the angel's message to him and inwardly composing his thoughts for this moment. He had rehearsed the prophecies and realized that in this son of his was the promised prophet who would precede the promised Savior who had been in the womb of Mary when she visited. (I wonder how he related to the two women during that three month visit. He is not mentioned at all.) Now he is "Filled with the

Holy Spirit" as was Elizabeth earlier. Was it a permanent filling for them?

He refers to some of those prophecies, some of which would soon be fulfilled. "God has come and has redeemed his people" (vs. 68). And will save them from their enemies. The purpose of the rescue, the salvation, was to allow his people to serve God "without fear, in holiness and righteousness" (vs. 75). Zechariah knew that John was not the Savior but was the one sent to prepare the way.

What a task lay ahead for John! It was more than Zechariah knew and different from anything he would have planned for his only son. He said that John "would give knowledge of salvation...by the forgiveness of their sins" (Luke 77-78). John would later announce the very things his father had said, "The Kingdom is coming among you, right into your neighborhood, to knock on your door. It will be because the 'tender mercy' of God will break upon you, the light will come to those in darkness and in the shadow of death – no more darkness or fear or dread – and you will be guided into the way of peace. Get ready!!" (Luke 1:76-79, BB Paraphrase)

Neither you nor I are the Savior either, but we are the preparers of the way, who by our words and actions help people see Jesus – "That by our good works others may give glory to your Father in heaven" (Matt. 5:16).

MARY

"Blue and gold aline
Purity breathless awaits
In trembling stillness. "
Barrie Shepherd

This simple haiku poem describes simply and succinctly the arrival and the announcement of the angel Gabriel to Mary.

The words of the angel must have seemed strange because Mary asked, "How can this be?" However, when the angel said, "Nothing will be impossible with God!" She was ready for whatever lay ahead!

Two words that I think describe Mary's reaction are "perplexed" and "pondered." If only we could wait in purity for what God has to tell us when he comes to us in our daily lives. If only we could be still long enough for him to speak. Yes, we may be perplexed by what we hear or feel or see, but we, like Mary, can ponder, think about, remember. When we are perplexed by what is going on around us, the way through to enough understanding to accept God's way is to ponder. Mary did that throughout her life – at the arrival of the shepherds, when Jesus was 12, when she came with her other sons to see Jesus and as messages reached her of what he was doing and where he was going, when she joined him in Jerusalem and witnessed with great grief his crucifixion – she pondered. She seemed to know that there was more to understand, not necessarily now, but when the time was right. And so she was able to say, out of "trembling stillness," "Behold the handmaid of the Lord; let it be to me according to your word" – embracing the will of God, whatever it might mean!

So, no matter what questions doubts, fears, ponderings we might have, may we say, "May it be to me according to your word," pondering in trembling stillness.

CONSIDERATION
Luke 1:26-38

"Greetings, favored one! The Lord is with you." Think about that one for a moment!! You look up from the meal you are preparing, the email you are writing, the laundry you are folding, and there stands an angel - that much you know by the way he shines. And he calls you "favored." Gabriel (we know his name because Luke tells us) doesn't give Mary long to ponder what is going on. He gets right to his message – first, "Do not be afraid, Mary (nice touch, using her name), you have found favor with God." And then without pause he gets to the core of his message. "You will be with child and give birth to a son, and you are to give him the name Jesus. He will be great and will be called the Son of the Most High. The Lord God will give him the throne of his father David, and he will reign over the house of Jacob forever; his kingdom will never end."

Did Mary take all that in during those few moments of the telling? Did she realize that he was talking about the Messiah? Were these the words that every Jewish girl wanted, longed to hear, or were they a shock, an introduction to an unknown? Was she simply submissive to Gabriel, a messenger from GOD, ready to do whatever God had planned for her to do?

"How can this be since I am a virgin?" – Ah yes, the practical side of a very lofty message, a woman's question, not doubting, just practical. And the angel gave her a practical answer. "The Holy Spirit will come upon you. And the power of the Most High will overshadow you. (What could that mean? How did it feel? When did it happen? Mary didn't talk about that when Luke came to interview her for his book.) Therefore the child will be HOLY. He will be called SON OF GOD. Elizabeth, your relative, has conceived – yes, in her old age. Nothing is impossible with God – not Elizabeth's pregnancy or yours, Mary!"

Mary must have been overwhelmed, to say the least. Was she afraid, shaking, astonished, amazed, wondering, awestruck? Do not be afraid! How many times in the ensuing months did she replay that scene in her mind? But, at the moment, she simply said, "Here I am, the servant of the Lord; let it be with me according to your word." Simply put she said, "Okay."

How about us? God doesn't have any tasks like this one for us today, but he does have work for us to do for him. It may be making a phone call or witnessing to a grouchy neighbor; it may be saying something to make things right in a situation or helping out with the kids' programs at church. It may be simple or overwhelming, but when God wants us to do his will, he is ready to work with us and through us to accomplish his work in our world. "Here I am, the handmaid of the Lord. Let it be to me according to your will." O Lord, may it be so!

CONTEMPLATION
Luke 1:38, 46-56

Martin Luther is quoted as interpreting Luke 1:38 in this way –

"I am only the workshop in which you operate, God. Let it be to me according to your word."

This is my prayer – May I be your workshop, not like Mary, but may you be spiritually formed within me, O Lord, until I bear your likeness in all I say and do! May my soul magnify you, make you large, as I glorify you in my everyday living! I rejoice in you who came to be my savior and my Lord - God coming in the flesh to do what I, what all humankind, every living soul could not do for ourselves. You looked with favor on ME, saw in me something you valued and made me your very own. You have done great things for me. You are holy and yet you love me, live in me, walk with me, encourage me, guide me, strengthen me – do all the things I need including disciplining me, molding me into your likeness. Be formed in me this day, O Lord.

When Mary visited Elizabeth she again spoke eloquently in what we call the Magnificat. "My soul magnifies the Lord and my spirit rejoices in God my Savior." To "Magnify" means, 1. To extol, laud, or 2. To make larger. (Webster's College Dictionary) We've gotten so "scientific" we don't always connect "Magnify" with its original meaning. Mary's song, her "magnificat" was to extol, laud, praise God in a very personal way, so much so that God is magnified, "extolled, lauded, made larger" before others as well.

Can this "magnificat" be my song?

My soul magnifies, lauds and praises you,
    And my spirit rejoices in you, my Savior.
You have looked on me with favor, blessing me
    In so many ways, marvelous ways.
You, the Mighty One, have done great things for me,
    And holy is your name.
Your mercy is for those who fear you
    From generation to generation.
You have shown strength with your arm;
    You have scattered the proud;
You have brought down the powerful from their thrones;
    You have lifted up the lowly;
You have filled the hungry with good things;
    You have sent the rich away empty.
You have helped your servants, your disciples,
    In remembrance of your mercy.
According to the promises you have made!!

And you keep on doing it. It was not just long ago, and it is
not in fairy tales, but in my life. No matter how things may
seem at any moment, you will scatter, bring down, lift up,
fill, and help according to your mercy and your holiness.
May it be to me according to your will. I am your servant,
your handmaid.

WHAT A HERITAGE
Matthew 1:18-24, 1:1-16

God let Joseph work through a plan before telling him his plan. Joseph concluded that the best way to help Mary avoid public disgrace was to divorce her quietly. How well did he know the Scriptures? Isaiah had foretold that "The virgin will be with child and will give birth to a son, and they will call him Immanuel, which means, 'God with us.'" Did he think of that? Did he realize that his Mary could be the one chosen? Did he think of his own limitations of being asked to raise such a child, the Messiah? Whatever his thoughts might have been, he chose the best HUMAN plan to protect and not disgrace her.

Then the dream! An angel appeared who addressed him by name and by lineage, reminding him that though they lived in Nazareth he was of the house of David which was Bethlehem, and so he was eligible to be in the line of the Messiah. How did it happen that after so many years of not having a descendant of David on the throne, these two obscure and very ordinary people in Nazareth would have lived such exemplary lives that they were chosen by God to be the earthly parents of His Son? When we examine Jesus' genealogy in Matthew 1, we find a host of wonderful and not so wonderful, in fact even some evil, people. However, by God's grace and grace alone we find the kingly line coming to a carpenter shop in Nazareth, far away from the Royal city.

That genealogy in Matthew reveals the royal line did not come through Saul, the first king, but from Abraham through David who was related to shepherds and farmers like Boaz, Ruth's husband, men who lived on and worked the land. The women who are mentioned are both good and bad, as if to say to us that birth and genealogy do not control who we become. Even the kings were both good and bad, some very bad, but each generation makes its own choices and decisions. God works through us, in spite of us, and with us, whatever it takes, however long it takes to fulfill his purpose. And so the line comes to Mary and Joseph; a line that looks an awful lot like yours and mine, full of all kinds of people. But God was in it, preparing the generation into which Jesus was born – Son of God and Son of Man! He is the Son of Man - descendant of Abraham, the faith line; the son of David, the royal line. He is the Son of God, born of the Holy Spirit, born and given, a child born, a Son given. Hallelujah!

YOUR SON WILL SAVE

"…an angel of the Lord appeared to him in a dream and said, 'Joseph, son of David, do not be afraid to take Mary home as your wife, because what is conceived in her is from the Holy Spirit. She will give birth to a son, and you are to give him the name Jesus, because he will SAVE HIS PEOPLE FROM THEIR SINS.'" (Matthew 1:20-21)

Did Joseph wonder how this salvation of God's people from their sins would be accomplished? When Joseph was dying, which we assume he did sometime after Jesus was 12 and before Jesus began his ministry, did he and Mary discuss what lay ahead for Jesus and for her? They had a hint at the temple dedication (Luke 2:21-38). What Simeon said was mostly positive, but he ended by turning to Mary with these words – "And a sword will pierce your own soul too." Did they understand then?

Joseph always looks protective in the manger scenes we display at Christmastime. He did protect them after Jesus' birth and through the journey to and from Egypt, but the time came when Jesus turned away any protection offered to him and he went as a lamb to the slaughter to save his people from their sins. Even if Joseph had been alive, he could not have protected Jesus. "He came to save his people from their sins" by the means God had chosen – the perfect sacrifice, THE LAMB OF GOD. "He is the atoning sacrifice for our sins and not for ours only but for the sins of the whole World" (I John 2:2).

"When Joseph woke up, he did what the angel of the Lord

had commanded him." Sometimes we need to wake up, to just get at it, whatever it is that God calls us to do. He is with us and what he wants us to do can be done. Sometimes it's a miracle but usually it's ordinary, but if we delay or refuse we miss his will, done in his way, by us. Wake up and....

JOSEPH, THE SILENT ONE

Joseph really does take a back seat in the Christmas narrative. And yet he is an important person! Trusting, caring, silent, obedient, protective. Only a man like him, chosen by God who knows every human heart, could have been the man he was in these circumstances. What courage it took to "fear not," to believe that the child Mary was carrying was indeed from the Holy Spirit!! Call him Jesus, the angel said, for he will save his people, whoever and wherever they are, from their sins.

Matthew refers us back to Isaiah's prophecy, reminding us that it is a virgin who was to conceive God's son for only as God's son could he be Immanuel, God is with us. So Joseph, who is the silent, stoic figure in the story of Jesus' birth, does God's will, foster father to the Son of God!

When all I can do is stand by and watch in wonder at what God is doing and wonder what might happen next, help me to do so with faith and courage and hope.

"When Joseph awoke from sleep he did as the angel of the Lord had commanded him; he took her as his wife...." He saved her from humiliation and disgrace; he gave her dignity and worth. God always knows, as he knew then, how to make his will, his story unfold, choosing the right person for each responsibility and bringing glory to himself. It is true, as the poet John Milton said, "They also serve who only stand and wait." Joseph was ready; ready to protect, support, respond to Mary's needs and the needs of his infant son. Joseph named him Jesus, just as the angel had instructed him. He heard the words, "He will save his people from their sins," but he had no idea what that would mean, for him, for Mary, for this baby in the womb.

WHAT WERE THEY THINKING?

When Luke came to Mary asking her to look back on that night, I think what we have is what she remembered. It's almost as if she had forgotten the specific location – "she laid him in a manger." The important thing was that they were in the right town, Bethlehem, orchestrated by God via the government of the day ordering a registration. Mary was probably too weary from the trip on a donkey, in too much pain from labor to think much about where they were or how could it be that God's own son was coming into the world in a barn.

If Joseph had bad thoughts about what God was doing, I don't think he would have shared them with Mary. How helpless he must have felt if he was like most husbands – trusting God, but worried; sure of their past dreams and visions, but wondering, questioning. God sent confirmation of those dreams and visions by the only group of people who wouldn't be afraid or turned off by going to a stable. They didn't just show up. They were sent by an angel, a host of angels. That confirmation of shepherds and angels was just what Mary and Joseph needed to assure them that all was well. Strange as it seemed, the son of God, the Son of God, really was born in a barn!

God doesn't always provide what we think is even adequate, but he always provides enough – for Mary and Joseph that was a clean, warm, dry place – and angels!

SHEPHERDING

Being a shepherd is a quiet occupation, without a lot of hustle and bustle, though always on the alert for danger. Sometimes the only noise was the baaing of the sheep. Such circumstances gave time for quiet meditation, for writing psalms of praise to God, like David did, and what a treasury we have thanks to his time with the sheep. Angels would find an audience for their announcement, not too distracted to hear, humble enough to believe, curious enough to go and see, excitable enough to tell their story to any who would hear.

The night after the angels came was dark, no angel visitation, but they had much to ponder for they had seen and heard most extraordinary things. What happened to them in the years after this eventful night? Were some of them still shepherding when Jesus became the Lamb of God who by his death took away the sins of the world? Did they witness his death? Did they still see in their mind's eye the baby in the manger, wrapped in cloths, that somehow made him look like a lamb?

SIGNIFICANT WORDS TO THE SHEPHERDS
Luke 8-20

The shepherds somehow realized the significance of every word the angel said.

"Do not be afraid!" Yeah! Right!

"I bring you good news" – Okay, the angel is not here to punish or condemn us.

"...of great joy" – There hasn't been much joy in Israel under the Roman oppression or the Jewish religious leaders.

"...which will be for all people" – So it's not just for us, but it does include us. (I doubt if they thought about the fact that they were the first to hear.)

"Today..." – a specific time; "...in the town of David," – a specific place nearby; "has been born..." a human baby; "...to you..." did they catch that – "to YOU"? "...a Savior..." – hmmm, what could that mean, a Savior from what? "...who is Christ the Lord." Christ, the Messiah, the one we've been waiting for, praying for, has come!!

"This shall be a sign..." When we need a sign God gives one! And they needed one. "You will find the baby wrapped in cloths and lying in a manger." Wait, we get the baby wrapped in cloths, just like any other baby would be, but lying in a manger? Did they realize that meant that they could go to see him? He wasn't in the palace in Jerusalem or even in an inn. He must be in a stable and his bed was a manger. They had no idea at this point how blessed, how extraordinary, how privileged they were! A whole choir of angels interrupted any questions they might have had. And then it was over, this great visitation from heaven, this one angel who came with good news, and then "a great company of the heavenly host" praising God in song.

How did they react? They decided "to go and see this thing that has happened." I wonder where the stable was – maybe on their edge of town, or did they have to go right through town to the other side? Did they wonder where everyone else was? After all, this was the best news anyone had heard for centuries, and it had been announced by an angel. There had been a bright light, bright enough to be seen for miles. "A great company of the heavenly host" had sung a great anthem; surely someone else had seen and heard all this.

But it seemed that no one had! The town was full for the census, but no one seemed to be aware of the great news they had heard. That didn't stop them. "They found Mary and Joseph, and the baby who was lying in the manger" just like the angel had said. Ken Gire says, "Lying there amid the straw, with white cloths wound tightly around him, he looked to them like a newborn lamb." (Moments with the Savior, p. 36)

They left there and went into town and told everyone what they had seen and heard. Everyone was amazed, but did anyone go see? Was anyone curious or did anyone believe? Maybe a concerned mother or grandmother or two, some children – and things haven't changed in 2,000 years.

THINGS TO COME
Luke 2:25-38

Simeon was "looking forward to the consolation of Israel" and "It had been revealed to him by the Holy Spirit that he would not see death until he had seen the Lord's Messiah."

Anna had the same kind of experience and when she saw Jesus she "began to praise God, to speak about the child to all who were looking for the redemption of Jerusalem."

Both of them saw in Jesus the answer to their prayers as revealed by the Holy Spirit. Simeon was content to die now, be "dismissed in peace" as the Spirit had promised him for he "had seen the Lord's Messiah." Anna, as old as she was, witnessed with enthusiasm. How did those around them react? Did they listen to Simeon's exclamation and further prophecy or was that more private? Did some listen to Anna's witness and believe – was she the second evangelist after the shepherds?

Simeon recognized Jesus as the "salvation which God had prepared for all people and a light of revelation to the Gentiles" and glory to the Jews. Then he said to Mary, "People will respond positively and negatively to your child as he grows." I can imagine it would be true even in childhood and teen years if children then are like children are now. "Inner thoughts will be revealed!" I can see that happening in playmates and friends. "How did he know that?" And Mary remembered through the years Simeon's saying to her, "...and a sword will pierce your own soul too."

In the midst of all the excitement – angels and shepherds, finding a home, adjusting to a new life – came this word which Mary was to remember years later, maybe along the way on occasion, maybe when she visited him and certainly when the crucifixion occurred. Not a pleasant prophecy to hold on to but one to remember, to prepare for, to ponder even though she didn't know how it would happen or when. I don't think it squelched her joy. She knew her child was special, in fact, God's own Son which may have made her wonder how real this could be. "Mary, did you know?"

DEDICATED

"Every firstborn male shall be designated as holy to the Lord." (Exodus 13:2, Luke 2:23) It was the law of Moses and yet it was ironic that this child, the very son of God, should be "designated as holy." There is no doubt that he was holy, but Mary and Joseph were faithful Jews. On the 8th day they had circumcised the child and named him Jesus as they had been instructed by the angel, and now they brought him to the Temple to be presented to God and dedicated to God's service. If we believe that Jesus is truly and properly God and truly and properly man, we might say, "God presented himself to himself, dedicated to and by himself." I wonder how much that baby was observing then? Of course, as a true and proper man he could not observe much at this stage of his life, but then we don't know much about how or what babies, a month or so old, can think or observe, probably more than we can imagine, and there's no doubt that Jesus was extraordinary!

His Heavenly Father was, no doubt, watching from heaven and receiving the dedication being made by Mary and Joseph. What a scene! Dedication time for the ordinary parent is done, by us, to let the world and God know that we are bringing our children to God and that we are promising to do our best to raise them in God's ways, teaching them God's truths, helping them find the Way that they should go. We also know that each will keep his or her free will – they are truly and properly human. Even Mary's other children "born of the will of Joseph," were no doubt dedicated by Mary and Joseph, and yet chose to go their own way. We know that their son, James, eventually believed and became head of the church, but we don't have a record of the others. They may have found it "impossible" to give up their Jewishness or they could have done worse. Mary went to live with the disciple John after Jesus' death, not with any of her other children – male or female. They had all been dedicated to God in the Jewish tradition. Dedication is done by the parents; the child who becomes an adult is still "free" to choose his or her own way. We can only do our best in teaching them, loving them, praying for them, and letting them go.

WHERE IS HE?
Matthew 2:1-12

In Matthew 2:3 there is an interesting phrase – "When King Herod heard this [that the Magi were searching for one who was born king of the Jews], he was disturbed, and all Jerusalem with him." The Magi must have caused quite a stir when they entered the city. They would have come through one of the gates and stopped to ask where the baby king had been born. No one there knew anything about a new baby king, but they would have directed this unusual assemblage of outstanding men through the narrow streets towards Herod's palace, the logical place for a king to be born. Those who overheard the question must have wondered why they hadn't heard about the new baby – was something wrong with the baby; why is it such a secret?

Herod was disturbed for other reasons. A new king of the Jews that he hadn't heard about was a threat to him. He didn't have a clue about who Christ would really be, even though he was the one who called him the Christ when he enquired of his chief priests. What he knew was that whoever had brought these men to Jerusalem was a threat to him.

These Magi explained that they had come to "worship him!" Of all things, a new born king to be worshipped! What an odd way to describe their quest; what an odd someone to look for? Would these men have gotten into the palace if they hadn't been different? We don't know anything more about them except that they were from the east, possibly having in their possession some of the prophecies about the king who was to come, prophecies left behind when the Israelites had been in captivity in Babylon or Assyria. Now they had seen what was prophesied through a star and they had followed it, maybe for as long as two years, determined to worship this new king of the Jews.

Do you suppose that some who saw or heard the Magi remembered this incident later, when Jesus was 12 or 30 or 32 years old and remembered these men and what they had asked? I don't believe that God would have wasted this visit or allowed it only to cause of the murder of Bethlehem's children.

Herod did reveal to them the answer to their question. They had arrived publicly, but I wonder if he snuck them out of town. He certainly didn't want a crowd following them and discovering this new king of the Jews. He got all the possible information from them and sent them off in the direction of Bethlehem.

"And the star went ahead of them until it stopped over the place where the child was. When they saw the star they were overjoyed." Why hadn't they followed the star all the way? Had they traveled mostly at night, but when they got near Jerusalem, the capitol city, they decided to go into town by day and couldn't see that the star was not over that city. Their road may well have passed through Jerusalem, but the star wasn't over Jerusalem.

Where is God leading you? Don't stop until you get there!!

HERE HE IS!
Matthew 2:10-13

"When they saw the star, they were overjoyed. On coming into the house, they saw the child...and they bowed down and worshipped him." When the Magi looked up again as they left Jerusalem, they saw the star and it led them to their destination, right to Jesus. When they walked into the house they knew they were in the right place and they immediately bowed down and worshipped him, not them - not mother and child, but him. They were not fooled by the palace even though it had seemed the obvious place. They recognized the real Jesus and they worshipped him. How far they had come! How long they had traveled! And they worshipped. It was worth the trip. I'm hoping to meet them in eternity and hear the rest of the story!

Then, and only then, did "they open their treasures and present him with gifts." It seems to me that there's a lesson here - first worship and then gifts. No, we aren't going to "worship" those to whom we give gifts nor will we expect anything like that from them, but without that pause to say to someone, "I treasure you; I value you," the gift could be meaningless. The real value is in the person not the gift and we and they need to see that. The Magi had brought wonderful gifts that would be fit for a king. They did not know how they would be used by this peasant family, but they were very useful in helping them with the journey ahead, to Egypt so that they would avoid Herod's vengeance. Joseph was warned in a dream to escape to Egypt and stay there until he was told to go home.

The Magi also had a dream. I wonder if all the Magi, however many there were, had the same dream or only their leader. Whatever may have been the case, they believed the dream more than they believed Herod. Had they detected Herod's insincerity or had they learned to trust in dreams and signs more than in people?

These are very interesting people who make a brief appearance on the Biblical scene and then disappear. What happened to them? Were they changed when they returned to their eastern homes? Will we see them in eternity? Are they smiling at us now as they look on our nativity scenes, seeing themselves as we imagine them? They worshipped and then presented him gifts, wonderful, expensive, helpful gifts.

"What can I give him? I'll give him my heart."

CHAOS AND PEACE

Many years ago on the CBS program "Sunday Morning" one of the commentators took us backstage at Radio City Music Hall during their big Christmas production – remember, the Rockettes? Backstage was a hectic scene of chaos as giant scene changes were made, live animals roamed about waiting their entrance with their minders, flying "reindeer" were tested to make sure that everything was in order for their flight, hundreds of cast members playing multiple parts rushed to and fro, changing costume, hurrying to their next entry point.

The audience out front was responding with excitement and cheering and clapping as each scene unfolded. Children giggled; adults exclaimed over the amazing things happening on stage.

Then suddenly backstage everything became quiet. The audience settled down and the curtain opened on a cutaway barn complete with animals, stall and a manger. Mary and Joseph appeared in peaceful silence on the left, shepherd and Magi moved in from the right, and an angel hovered peacefully above it all. Strains of "Silent Night" reached deep into the audience and quiet and peace settled over all.

At the manger, no matter what the chaos might be around it, there is peace. May we focus on Jesus, come among us to bring peace, in the midst of whatever may be going on in our world during this season.

LIGHT – A WORD FOR CHRISTMAS

"Light is sown as seed for the righteous." We will always be able to see the way to go, but we will not always see far ahead; so we may at times move ahead just one step at a time. The light always springs up at the right time, like a car's headlights on a dark night. The points of light might not always be obvious; so we need to be alert – they are always there (John 1; I John 1).

When we lived in Finland the contrast between light and darkness was very evident! During the Christmas season, it was very dark. The sun might peek over the horizon at 10 a.m., but it would set again at 2 p.m. and we seldom saw it because the season was very cloudy. Snow, however, helped to brighten the landscape, and in all those northern countries it is the Season of Light. Everyone lights their home brightly; there are candles in every window; stores use lots of light decorations; city streets are bright with light.

But we also traveled to Russia during the Christmas season, to St. Petersburg and to Moscow; and there, it was dark. Christmas had been shut down. For the Russian Orthodox Church Christmas is a time of prayer and fasting and the celebration, such as it was, occurred on January 7. The government decreed that New Years Eve and Day was the time for lots of light and celebration. There were no Christmas decorations, no lights in homes or stores to indicate that this was a special time of year, a time to celebrate the greatest of earthly events. In the year 2000, the mayor of Moscow decreed that every store should have at least a string of lights, and we began to see some paltry efforts to bring lights, a tree outside of a hotel where westerners stayed, a few lights on the main shopping street, but the reason was not clear – just lights.

When Deitrich Bonhoeffer was in a German prison for his faith in 1943, he wrote this – "Just when everything is bearing down on us to such an extent that we can scarcely withstand it, the Christmas message comes to tell us that all our ideas are wrong – that what we take as evil and dark is really good and light because it comes from God. Our eyes are at fault; that is all. God is in the manger, wealth in poverty, light in darkness, succor in abandonment." God is in the darkness with us to make it light because he is light!

The Origin of Light, Light itself, the Shekinah Glory became human in order to lead the way to the place of eternal Light. Jesus came to give light to those who were "sitting in darkness and in the shadow of death, to guide our feet into the way of peace." He gives light, he is light, to overcome darkness so that we can see the way of peace. He penetrates every and any darkness, whether the darkness of blindness or a prison cell, of loneliness and depression, of illness or poverty, of sin! He came for that purpose; he dawns on our lives with a great yet gentle illumination that changes everything. Things are no longer obscure, hidden, uncertain. There is light!

"Wonderful Counselor, Mighty God among us;
Everlasting Father, Prince who rules in peace;
To us a son is born; to us a son is given;
For those who walk in darkness, the Light has come"
Chick Yuill SASB # 133

The Word and the Light

"In the beginning was the Word/God/Creator/One" (John 1:1). That incomprehensible Being who Jesus always was, who he always is, who he always will be, the Word spoke; the Word speaks; we can hear the Word through the written Word, through God's Holy Spirit, through other people, through dreams – like those in the Christmas stories. God designs those hearings for each of us in the way we can best "hear." "Word" speaks of communication, intimacy, oneness, yet separateness. Words have always been spoken. God spoke in the very beginning and there was light, and in his perfect timing man invented the written word, and we can be so glad that we live now when the written word is so accessible, when the written word is available in so many ways and forms. Jesus is the Word.

He is also Life and Light. "What came into being was life and the life was the light of all people" (John 1:4). The Word brought life into being so that we who are his creations could live in the light. "The light shines in the darkness and darkness did not overcome it" (John 1:5). Light was his first creation and while he made daytime and nighttime there is always light and it cannot be overcome by darkness. Day and night are for our convenience! He, as light, also cannot be overcome! Oh, there is the darkness of sin in the world, but it cannot overcome or even overwhelm God's light. It always shines in and through those who love him.

REALITY OF CHRISTMAS

There must be hundreds, even thousands of poems, essays, articles, plays, short stories, even whole books about what happened that first Christmas.

In the Christmas pageant the innkeeper can be a really ornery guy, ready to send the couple away, but the child who is playing the simple part of the innkeeper calls to them as they turn away – "Wait, you can have my room."

Or the dad who is filling in as a wise man is suddenly struck by the majesty of the moment as he walks down the aisle carrying a gold covered box and when he reaches the manger he falls on his knees in wonder.

There are the idealized, immaculate manger scenes on our mantles and the more realistic renditions with smelly, unruly animals and rustic stables on church lawns. We attempt to show truth as we want it to be or render it as closely as our human minds can comprehend it, our city minds, our minds that conjure "holy" and "silent" when it was really unkempt and noisy.

I doubt if there was much about Bethlehem with its soldiers and census takers and hundreds of David's descendants converging on the place to make it attractive. The bare bones verses in Luke 2 are realistic, stark, in-your-face facts. God says, "Add all you want; use your imagination, but never lose sight of the fact that Jesus, my Son, was born in a barn and laid in a manger for a cradle, and for a good reason." Isaiah's prophecies said it would be a tough life from the beginning – no room! Jesus, son of God, humbled himself from the beginning – a barn, a manger! That's the reality of Christmas. We can all come here, with all our noise and confusion, with all our unholiness and sin and we find Jesus waiting to quiet the voices of condemnation and confusion, waiting to create in us a clean heart where he can willingly and gladly dwell and make and keep us holy!!

It's overcrowded with stuff, Lord; too much, too many, noisy and full of confusion, but please, come to my heart, Lord Jesus – it's kind of barnlike – not as clean as a birthplace should be, but there is room in my heart for you. I promise to work with you to make it your dwelling place and it will become holy!

WHEN

The child is born, and I think it was at that moment when the angel burst in upon the shepherds and the star appeared in the sky! Men were doing their jobs on night duty, whether in a field near Bethlehem or on a rooftop far away.

The shepherds near Bethlehem were watching their flocks, not expecting anything out of the ordinary, alert to the sounds of the night, looking around with protective eyes through the darkness, up at the stars which were bright on this clear night.

Off in another land there may have been more of an expectancy, a search for a new star, but that's what they did every night. And in that other land "his star appeared in the east."

These appearances were not like the quiet visits to Zechariah, Mary, and Joseph. This was a burst of light and glory, a shout of triumph in the midst of a flock of sheep, a new brilliance in the sky in the form of a beckoning star.

There came upon both shepherd and Magi a sense of urgency – we must go and see. Did they all get it or were some frightened by this revelation? Was there a quick touch of the older shepherd on the shoulder of a younger, of the ancient Magi on the arm of the newer member of their group? How "religious" were they? It seems that they all knew what the angel was talking about, what the star meant.

The shepherds went immediately to nearby Bethlehem to see. The Magi gathered what they needed for a much longer journey, maybe even a two-year journey. But they each went to see, to stand in awe before this miracle of God, this Immanuel.

REFLECTION
Luke 2:17, 18

"All who heard it were amazed at what the shepherds told them." I imagine Bethlehem coming awake that morning and those shepherds stopping everyone they saw and excitedly telling them about the baby and the angels. When their shift ended, they went home and told their families. But who believed them? Did others go to see the baby? Amazement can lead to different responses – curiosity surely, thoughtfulness, belief or disbelief, jealousy maybe, new respect for shepherds, awe and wonder, questions. Which response have we experienced this CHRISTmas season?

We need to be like Mary – treasuring and pondering. We've heard these stories over and over through the years. We've attended Christmas Eve services, read the stories from Luke and Matthew, participated in pageants and memorized lines, treasured them in our hearts, told them to children and grandchildren. And again this year, we have pondered anew and the Spirit has given us some new thoughts to ponder.

The Gospel of John says, "He came unto his own and his own did not receive him" (John 1:11). The very world that he made did not know him. His own people, his chosen ones, the ones he had rescued time and again, the ones who admired Abraham and Moses and David, his ancestors, were so far away from the truth and the real law, that by the time he came they did not accept him. And yet there were those who did know and accept him. The shepherds, the Magi who were Gentiles, Anna and Simeon who were waiting and waiting, and others throughout the Gospels and eventually around the world – and you and me! We can become the very children of God through Jesus. He never forced anyone to see and believe, but he has given us all the "power to become the children of God" by believing in his name (John 1:12).

Mountaintop experiences end; visions and dreams cease; extraordinary moments pass; babies grow up; we go back to work, and everyday living begins again. What we do after those moments of inspiration or ecstasy is what really makes a difference in our lives and the lives of others.

MERRY CHRISTMAS

When Jesus is born in us we dare to say, "Merry Christmas." Without him it is just another date on the calendar, maybe a family get together with gifts and food, but what do we celebrate? He is the baby born this day. It's his birthday, the Messiah, the one who grew up to become the Savior of the world through his death for our salvation and the Lord through his resurrection.

My Lord, what a morning! As the sun rose and Bethlehem awoke to another busy day of census taking and ordinary life, the shepherds, who didn't venture into town very much, were telling everyone about the baby in the inn's stable and about the angels who had told them about him. People were amazed - but what did they do about it? Mary, bless her, kept these things – the birth, the shepherd's visit with their story of the angels – in her heart and pondered them, pondered them for the next 30 years, probably reflecting on them for confirmation of what she had experienced as she watched her son grow up, go through popularity to rejection, finally to death and ultimate resurrection. These early events could well have been a gift to her from God helping her remember – God is able.

POEMS OF CHRISTMAS

PONDER AND WONDER AND WONDER

"Mary kept all these things and pondered them in her heart."

Mary had the right idea.
Christmas events need a lot of pondering.
Mary must have pondered why she was birthing the Son of
God
in a stable of all places. What a wonder!
Mary must have pondered
why their first visitors were shepherds,
fresh from the fields with a story of angels.
What a wonder!

We cannot begin to capture the scene –
oh we've tried with all kinds of manger scenes,
none very realistic!

But what we need to do is ponder with Luke what it was
really like And pondering will lead to wondering as in
discovering, questioning – How, why, where, these people,
this place, those angels, that star?
Which leads us to wondering as in adoration,
becoming like the shepherds
like the wisemen, bowing in adoration, in awe.

O come let us adore him. He is Christ the Lord!!

THE RIGHT PLACE

"The church must be sumptuous and magnificent
to compensate
for the vulgarity and poverty of the place and poverty
where the Eternal Word chose to be born."
If only her majesty had been in charge!!
But wait a minute.
Someone greater than her majesty was in charge.
God was!! And look what he chose!
I wonder if Mary had questions that night in that stable –
"What went wrong?"
"Was it me? Or Joseph?"
"Did the Roman census throw your plan off?"
"A cave/stable, Lord, for your son?"
"Are you sure?"
Your answer – "I chose this place.
"This smelly, fly ridden, worn place.
"I was anxious to be born here among the animals."
Yes, Lord, so much is so ugly and yet so beautiful;
So real and yet so full of love.
A place where shepherds could come
Straight from the field, just as they were.
Where we can come, just as we are.
It's the right place.

WHY NOW?

We really don't know when Jesus was born.
We sing about "the deep, cold winter,
"Snow lay on the ground."
The date, December 25th, was chosen by early church fathers
In the northern hemisphere,
During the darkest season of the year.
He came as the Light that shines in the darkness
Whatever our darkness might be.
Maybe those church fathers realized that –
They saw the Light,
And deliberately chose the dark time.
Maybe that's why we who live here
Use so much light to celebrate Christ's coming.
All the lights can be symbolic of The Light,
The light that shines on our darkness,
Our despair,
Our grief,
Our sadness,
Our depression,
Our trial,
Our strife,
Our fear.
What can we do with darkness?
Have you ever tried to sweep darkness out the door?
Only light can get rid of darkness!
Only He who is The Light can bring The Light to whatever
is darkness in our lives.

"I am the Light of the world.
He who follows me will not walk in darkness
But will have the Light of Life" (John 8:12).

WHERE WOULD YOU BE BORN TODAY?

In a housing project in Chicago?
In the slums of Calcutta?
In a rundown trailer park in small town USA?
In a tent among the homeless in the forest?
Under a bridge?
At a homeless shelter?
In the bus station?
Wherever the prophecy said for your mom and dad to go.
Wherever shepherds or cowboys,
Or garbage collectors
Or day laborers
Or the unemployed would go just as they are
When they heard the angel's message.
Angels? Yes, angels.
They always go with important words -
To people who will hear them,
To people who need to hear Good News
And respond.

WHAT DO I SEE AT CHRISTMAS?

"Love all lovely, love divine"
Love that said, "I'm willing...
Willing to be a baby,
Willing to be cradled in a manger,
Willing to be held by my mother,
Willing to be protected by a carpenter.
Love that was God – God in a manger!
And having seen, what do I do?
How do I go home from the manger?
Not the way I came, back through Jerusalem,
the way it used to be.
I will walk with this Man
who was God on the road of life.
I will go the way of the Man
who became the Savior on the Cross.
I will walk the way of love, loving as he loved, "I'm willing
Willing to do your will,
Willing to be your person,
Willing to go the way of love, following you."
I need the Cross to save me, but the manger convinces me!

WHAT WONDROUS LOVE IS THIS?

He came to the world
And the world said, "Who are you?"
He came to his own
And they rejected him.
He had made the world!
How could they not know him?
He had created his own special people!
How could they reject him?
Were they afraid?
Did they build walls?
What will the Triune God do?
Is there any hope?
They talk it over –
They could reject the people, but they did not!
God had, in fact, a God-sized solution,
A rescue plan,
A second chance,
A way to release an enormous love!
I overhear them talking about a horrible sacrifice –
Could they do it?
Would the Son of the Trinity do it -
Shed his own blood for their souls?

And I realize I am the subject of their loving conversation –
They, he, did it for me!
"What wondrous love is this, O my soul."

IF ONLY....

"Do you ever wish Christmas would just go away?" she
asked.
A store clerk who had heard
Too many Christmas songs over and over,
Too many complaints about this and that.
Too many rude comments as impatient customers waited
impatiently in line.
"Do you ever wish Christmas would just go away?" he
asked.
A father tiring of the endless list greeting him each
evening,
Too many Christmas specials on TV,
Too many arguments over ....
If only we would all concentrate on Jesus' coming
And less on Santa's coming.
If only we would listen for the angels in our midst
And less for all the other calls and cries and demands.
If only we would look up and see the star
And less the distracting lights and gaudy decorations.
If only we would pause to see you, the Babe in the manger,
And less the Santas, elves, and reindeer.
If only....

HOME FOR CHRISTMAS

Home for Christmas – kind of what everyone dreams
about -
The perfect place to be at the perfect time.
The perfect decorations, the perfect gifts under the tree.
The perfect everything!
And how about when we arrive in Heaven?
You have promised that we will receive the best gift ever!
We will experience full salvation!
We will look on your very face.
That's the gift that was bought at an enormous cost!
And it's the gift reserved in Heaven for all who believe!
It will be like, well, getting home for Christmas!!

CHRISTMAS GIFTS

I've spent a lot of time –
Asking what would please each one,
Choosing what I think would be best from their list,
Ordering from the best web site,
Purchasing what I have to trudge to the stores to find,
Wrapping them in the right paper or putting them in the
right bag.
I bet you have too! For family, for friends!
The Magi, those Wisemen, did that too.
They chose gold,
Frankincense,
Myrrh,
Rather strange gifts for a new baby -
Fit for a King.
Christmas is still a celebration of Jesus' birthday.
He is still alive, every year.
Did you, did I, think of what we could give him?
Did I ask him, choose, order, purchase, wrap a gift for Jesus?
The wisemen presented their gifts,
But first they worshipped, presenting themselves as part of
their gift.
Those strange baby gifts would be useful to his family.
And that's all we too can give him still – ourselves in
worship.
All we have,
All we are,
So that he can use us
However he might choose
In service for the world he loves.

JUST FOR KIDS!

Kids make the most wonderful manger scene!
They are so cute, maybe especially when there's a real baby
in the "manger."
Kids dressed in bathrobes, crooked haloes,
Shepherds wandering down the aisle
Waving at Mom and Grandpa.
Wisemen with headdresses askew;
Carrying boxes wrapped in gold paper.
Joseph standing beside the manger,
Poking the shepherd who came up to stand next to him.
Mary staring in rapt fascination
At this real baby who seems to smile at her.
Kids love the real story of Christmas,
Love to be chosen to be a character for the scene in church;
Love to move the characters in the scene at home –
Until they are distracted by their Christmas list
Or another ad on TV telling them what they want for
Christmas.
Occasionally adults are chosen to create the manger scene.
Occasionally an adult shepherd will arrive with a live sheep.
Occasionally an adult wiseman will dress in finery, carry a
gold-wrapped box, even leading a live camel.
Occasionally an adult Joseph will stand guard over Mary
and the Baby.
Occasionally an adult Mary will gaze in wonder at her own
Baby, hopefully asleep in the manger.
And God has something to say to all those who create the
scene,
And God has something to say to all who watch.
Listen!

THE NAMES OF JESUS
Matthew 2:1-12

Matthew calls him Jesus and the child.
The Magi call him "King of the Jews."
Herod amazingly asks the chief priests and teachers,
"Where is the CHRIST to be born."
And when Herod makes his report to the Magi, he asks
them to search for the "child."
The prophecy to which the teachers refer
calls him ruler and shepherd.
King, ruler, shepherd, Jesus, child, Christ.
Human and divine,
fulfillment of prophecy – the Messiah.

Everything we needed him to be is revealed these names.
And Herod thought he could get rid of him!!

I WONDER

I wonder how long it took Mary and Joseph to travel from
Nazareth to Bethlehem.
I wonder how comfortable, or uncomfortable, it was for a
very pregnant Mary to ride on a donkey all that way.
I wonder if they went prepared to birth Jesus on the way
or did they think they'd get back in time.
I wonder what Joseph thought when Bethlehem finally
came into view.
I wonder how he reacted as Mary began to have normal
labor pains.
I wonder how many doors he pounded on before a kindly
innkeeper offered a stall in his barn.
I wonder how long it was from the time they went to the
stable until Jesus was born.
I wonder how much Joseph had to clean up before the
baby started coming.
I wonder how much help Joseph was during the birth.
I wonder how long Mary was in labor.
I wonder; I ponder; I feel, but mostly I celebrate!
The reality is you were born,
a human baby, in a Bethlehem barn,
far from home,
in order to become the Savior of the world –
and of me.

GREAT FAITH; GREAT JOY!

Two words that describe Christmas for the Christian -
FAITH AND JOY!
Mary had faith in what the angel said.
She may have been apprehensive, but she believed.
Joseph had faith in the dream God gave him.
He may have been apprehensive, but he believed.
Did they feel much joy on the way to Bethlehem?
Did they feel much joy when they went to the stable?
But their faith was rewarded with joy when Jesus was born,
And their faith was rewarded with joy when the shepherds
told their story.
The shepherds weren't experiencing much joy
Out in the fields keeping watch on the night shift,
In the dark, maybe cold, maybe wet night.
But they did have faith in the angel's message of good news
of great joy
And their faith was rewarded with joy.
When they saw the Babe they went out glorifying and
praising God.
The wisemen probably didn't have a joy-filled ride
Through the desert at night on their camels,
Or on arriving in Jerusalem and being told, "No king here."
But they had faith in the prophecy they had discovered -
The new star announced a new king of the Jews.
And they saw the star again as they left Jerusalem
And they rejoiced with exceeding great joy.
And so it would seem that great faith will be rewarded
with great joy - for you and for me.

HE COULD HAVE

He could have come to any place;
He chose to come to Bethlehem.
He could have come in any form;
He chose to come as a baby.
He could have had a palace;
He chose a barn.
He could have had announcements sent to all the world
dignitaries;
He chose shepherds.
He could have had a queen as mom;
He chose a girl child not yet a bride.
He could have had a royal name;
He chose the common Joshua.
He could have had a handsome face;
He chose one no one would notice.
He could have been raised amid intellectuals;
He chose a town from which nothing good ever came.
He could have….
But he chose, instead, to be what everyone needed.

LAST NIGHT LONG AGO

(Thoughts on Christmas morning)
Last night long ago angels sang to shepherds
And told them you were born -
And they believed.
Last night long ago Magi saw a star unlike any other star
And it told them you were born -
And they believed.
Last night long ago Mary felt the pains of childbirth
And Joseph knelt beside her to help -
And you were born
And they believed.
O come to my heart, Lord Jesus,
Be born in me today.
I believe!

THERE MUST HAVE BEEN A CHILD THERE

There must have been a child there
That first Christmas.
Who would it have been?
A young shepherd in training who had heard the angels?
The innkeeper's curious child who heard the baby's first cry?
An urchin from the street hiding in the warm stable?
We have made Christmas a child's holiday –
Santa with his elves and reindeer, including Rudolph,
Many presents for them according to the latest TV ad.
But there must have been a child there that first Christmas.
Did he or she have any idea who was lying in the manger?
No!
Did he or she have any idea who this mom and dad were?
No!
Did he or she have any idea what this baby would become?
No!
Would he or she ever forget this night, this silent, holy night?
No!
Maybe he or she would see Jesus as an adult,
Walking the streets of Jerusalem,
Healing a blind beggar,
Teaching in the Temple,
And would he remember and somehow know?
Would he bow in worship, awe, and wonder
Like the shepherds did in the stable so long ago?
There must have been a child there!

WORSHIP FIRST

Wisemen, Magi (whatever they were),
Strange men from the east (wherever that was),
Following a star (however that could be),
Showing up at the door of a simple home
In a little town,
Far removed from the elegance of the palace
Far removed from the noise and bustle of the big city.
But this is where the star had led them
This humble home, this little town,
This ordinary couple, this new baby.
Somehow, though, they were sure,
With a God-given certainty,
That they were in the right place.
They came into the house;
They saw the Child with his mother
And they fell to the ground,
These magi, these strangers,
And they worshipped him.
And they presented to him gifts -
Gold, frankincense and myrrh.
And having been warned in a dream from God
Not to return to Herod,
They went home another way –
Pondering, wondering, and in a state of wonder.

LAST TIME – NEXT TIME

Last time you came in humility;
Next time you will come in glory.
Last time you came to a manger in a barn;
Next time you will come in a cloud.
Last time you were seen by two humble servants and a
bunch of shepherds;
Next time you will be seen by every eye.
Last time you came as a baby, Son of man, servant,
ransom;
Next time you will come as King of Kings, Lord of Lords,
the Almighty.
Last time you came to save your people from their sins;
Next time you will come to take your people home.
Last time you were visited by Magi, maybe kings from the
east;
Next time all the tribes of the earth will bow before you.
Last time you came as God's only begotten son;
Next time you will come as Firstborn from the dead.
Last time you came in solitude;
Next time you will come and appear before everyone.
Last time you worked as a carpenter;
Next time you will reign as King of Kings and Lord of
Lords.

ALONE AT CHRISTMAS

Or so it seems –
Widowed – recently or maybe many Christmases ago.
Bereaved of a child – and that's who Christmas is all about.
Memories bring tears!

Some can't get home for Christmas –
Servicemen and women, missionaries, hospital or nursing
home bound patients.
Some choose not to be home for Christmas – lost to family.
But Jesus is Emmanuel; he can be with us -
We need never be alone.
Fill the gaps, Lord.

AND WHAT ABOUT TOMORROW?

All too soon the decorations will be put away;
All too soon the carols will be silent;
All too soon the toys will be played with (and broken?);
All too soon the new clothes will be put away;
All too soon the new tools will become old ones.
Life will return to "normal."
But You will still be our Emmanuel, our God with us.
The same yesterday, long before this year's Christmas, or
even the first one.
The same today, whatever the circumstances of today may
be -
The same forever, and into all eternity.
That's something to celebrate, today and tomorrow!

DAD

When our boys were born – 40 or 50 years ago –
All Dad could do was pace the waiting room floor,
To wonder and try not to worry,
And wait for someone to come with news.
Today Dad is allowed, even encouraged,
to be there in the birthing room.
"Breathe!"
Hold Mom's hand, wipe her brow.
Joseph wasn't just there,
Encouraging, holding her hand.
He may have been her "midwife."
And then, while the shepherds came and went
The wise men came and went
And Joseph stood there, simply stood there.
What crossed this new Dad's mind as he stood there?
Did he stand by with pride, proud of Mary and this new
child who was not even his?
Did he stand by in fear of what might lie ahead for all of
them?
Did he stand by in awe and wonder at the fulfillment of
the prophecy he's been told?
Did he stand by and wonder how this wee baby thing
could save the world?
He had done his part.
He got them to Bethlehem.
He got Mary to a safe place.
He had cleaned it up the best he could.
"And she brought forth her first born son."
And he just stood there, simply stood there
In the background

"Foster father of the Son of God."
Sometimes I am wise enough to stand there, simply stand
there
And gaze in wonder at the manger.
And contemplate and ponder.
There is peace here, rest for soul and body
There is hope here for the spirit – and joy.
Let me stand there, simply stand there,
And be blessed.

DID YOU HEAR THAT?

I'd really like to hear the angels sing –
And I think I do, often, at Christmas.
As the carols are played in the background in stores,
As the choirs break into song in unexpected places,
As the children sing around the manger during their
program at church,
As we sing "Silent Night" sitting on the floor in Frank and
Bernie's home,
As I turn up the CD of the "Hallelujah Chorus."
As long as I'm not looking for wings and haloes, I hear
them.
As long as I'm listening for the Good News, I hear them.
As long as I'm caught up in adoring and wondering, I hear
them.
They still sing, "Glory to God in the highest."
And then add, "And on earth peace among men of good
will.'
I wonder, Do you hear them too?

"It came upon a midnight clear, that glorious song of old."
Listen!!

DON'T MISS THE LIGHT

There are lights all over the place at Christmas –
Tree lights in the living room,
Candles in the windows
Spotlights on the manger scene,
Spotlights on Santa,
Rudolph's nose on the foggy Christmas Eve,
Strings of lights on the deck and porch,
around the windows and up the tallest of evergreens,
and around the trunks of aspens.
"Even street lights blink a bright red and green." It was
light that announced your birth - The angel shone a great
light all around as he spoke; The wisemen saw a great star
and followed it; And in the stable and later in the house
Candles and lanterns shone their light So that any who
came, Shepherds and wise men, anyone, Could see the
baby who came to be The LIGHT OF THE WORLD! Don't
let those other lights distract you! It's all about Jesus! So
that any who came Could see the baby who came to be The
LIGHT OF THE WORLD!
Don't let those other lights distract you!
It's all about Jesus!

LISTEN

Listen for the angels.
They are all around and might show up anywhere.
They have a special message just for you, or maybe for all
mankind.

Listen to the music
To the words of the traditional carols or a song you've
never heard before.
I'd avoid "Grandma got run over by a reindeer."

Listen with your heart
To your neighbor, a family member, a friend, the store
clerk.
They may have a message for you or be in need of a
prayer from you.

Listen in your quiet place.
To the Scripture, The story, a poem, any story.
You haven't heard it all yet as it moves from your head to
your heart.

Listen, just listen! You might hear angels!!

MY LORD, WHAT A MORNING!

My Lord, what a morning!
There's a baby lying in a manger!
There's a mother wondering at this wee thing!
There's a father alert to the needs of these two precious
people!
My Lord, what a morning!
There are shepherds on the night watch!
There's an angel and the glory of the Lord shining all
around!
There's a whole host of angels singing about peace and
good will!
There are shepherds running through town with news of
great joy for all the people. My Lord, what a morning!
There really is a baby lying in a manger and he is Christ
the Lord.
There are shepherds kneeling in awe and wonder.
There are shepherd running through town with news of
great joy for all the people.
My Lord, what a morning!

NO ONE STAYED

The shepherds listened and hurried to find the stable
And the Baby just as the angel had said,
But they didn't stay.
Couldn't they have turned that stable into a shrine,
A place where everyone could come to see -
The "Savior who is Christ the Lord."
Couldn't they have fixed it up, cleaned it out -
You know, kept the atmosphere, minus the flies and
manure
Put up new boards.
But they didn't stay.
They made known what had been told them
They returned to their sheep glorifying and praising God
For all they had heard and seen.

Three disciples went up a high mountain with Jesus
And he was transfigured before them, joined by Moses
and Elijah
But they didn't stay.
Oh, they wanted to.
Peter wanted to build three tabernacles,
Make a shrine for them
Where others could come to see this miracle.
They could all stay right there and be safe.
But they couldn't stay
A voice from heaven said,
"This is my beloved son; listen to HIM!"
They weren't even allowed to tell their fellow disciples
What they had heard and seen.
No one stayed!

Sometimes it's time to move on -
To be obedient, whatever our next appointed task might be.
Whether to get back to work or not,
It will be to glorify and praise God.

NO ROOM

And that's all there was to it, according to Luke.
The rest we don't know.
Was the innkeeper heartless, without compassion,
No concern, except for the money?
Did he want to keep his one remaining room ready
In case a "more distinguished guest" appeared.
I prefer to think he really didn't have another spot.
Maybe he'd already given up his own bed
And was sleeping on a couch in the office.
He saw a need and offered the stable.
It was warm, safe, private.
Not ideal under the circumstances.
Luke didn't make a big deal of it.
"There was no room for them in the inn."
No big deal – that's just how it was.
Today, Lord, there's room in my heart for you.
You're in charge of cleaning and making up the room,
For the joy, love, peace you long to bring.
Come into my heart, Lord Jesus.

PONDER and WONDER

"Mary kept all these things and pondered them in her heart."
Mary had the right idea – ponder!
We cannot begin to capture the scene, but we can ponder it.
We can ponder until we begin to wonder -
How, why, these people, this place, those angels, that star, where?
And that leads to wonder, as in adore, awe.
And we become like shepherds, like wisemen bowing in awe; we can't help it!
"O Come let us adore him, Christ the Lord."

REALITY

In the midst of all the colorful lights and beautiful
decorations;
Alongside the holiday dinners and parties,
Mixed in with the wonder and warmth of the season,
There are still people dying,
Kids taking drugs,
Homes burning,
Floods happening.
Even Christmas cannot wipe out those bleak realities,
The ugly events that disrupt out lives.
Hang on, Friends!
Jesus is still Emmanuel, God with us through them all.
He was, is still, born to save.

THE APPLICATION

Where were you born? In a Bethlehem stable
What is your hometown? A no-account village called
Nazareth
Where did you live? I've never had a place to lay my head
Where did you die? On a Roman Cross near Jerusalem
Where were you buried? In a borrowed tomb
Where are you now? On a throne in glory, building
mansions for all those who believe in me.

THE MESSAGE

How did the shepherds react to the message from the
angel?
The immediate response was, "Let's go and see."
But did they all respond that way or
Were there skeptics among them?
Those who said, "A baby? What good is a baby?
"You go ahead; I'll watch the sheep.
"Laying in a manger! Some parents they must be."
"He'll never amount to much and come to a bad end
anyway!"
How do you react to the message from the angel,
from the pastor?
It would seem that the immediate response for a few is,
"I'm going to see."
But it would seem that there are many skeptics.
Those who say, "How ridiculous!
"I know the story – He was called the Son of God,
"But no god would become a baby and be placed in a
manger."
"His parents were delusional at best.
And look what happened to him in the end. He died!
He was crucified, for heaven's sake!"
How do I react to the message today, from the Scripture,
from the pastor?
"I am going to see. I going to the stable;
"I'm going all the way in where I can see him, experience
him.
"I'm going to walk with him in the highways and the
byways,
"Learn from him how to live,

"How to find peace and joy,
"How to treat others with kindness and respect.
"I will even go with him to die, if necessary!"
That's how I react!

THOUGHTS ON CHRISTMAS MORNING

Last night long ago angels sang to shepherds
And told them you were born
And they believed.
Last night long ago Magi saw a star unlike any star
They had ever seen
And it told them you were born
And they believed.
Last night long ago Mary felt the pains of childbirth
And Joseph knelt beside her to help bring you into the
world
And you were born
And they believed.
O come to my heart, Lord Jesus,
Be born in me today.
I believe!
Yes, unto us is born this day a Savior who Christ, Lord.
We believe.

STORIES FOR CHRISTMAS

⌒

THAT DONKEY

This is a story that I read many years ago in an English Salvation Army War Cry. I have since lost the original and have adapted it over and over again.

Once there lived in the town of Bethlehem an old donkey. His name had long ago been forgotten, but he was always referred to as "That Donkey." He was old and had stepped into so many holes that he was quite lame in his left rear leg. The only time he was useful was when there was no other animal left in the barn, but someone needed something carried somewhere and they would say, "Well, I guess I'll have to use That Donkey." He would always work hard, but it was never good enough and he would be beaten with a stick and though exhausted from the effort would keep going until the job was done.

One night after everyone was settled in the cave/barn for the night a very strange thing happened. A man and a woman came into the stable and chased a lazy cow out of its stall. The man cleaned the stall, found some fresh straw and made a sort of bed for the woman. The animals, who had settled down for the night, were very unhappy at the disturbance and quickly went back to sleep, but That Donkey watched the curious happenings. When the couple seemed to be settled, he crept into his corner and also went back to sleep. Deep into the night the animals were awakened by a strange noise. The cows and sheep began to moo and bah until the strange noise stopped, but That Donkey, knowing the noise came from where the man and woman were, crept close and saw a most amazing sight. There, lying in the stall's manger was a tiny human figure. That Donkey had never seen anything like it in his life. He looked at the woman who was sitting beside the manger and she smiled at him, seeming to invite him to come closer to see the baby. He felt a warm glow deep all over as he gazed down at the wee little thing.

After a few moments he moved away, not wanting to disturb the mother and her beautiful child. But this time instead of moving as far away from drafts, the door, the holes in the stable walls, he moved right up into one of the holes that was close to where the baby was lying. He pushed that old left rear leg right into the hole and thought to himself, "I have to keep that baby warm. He is very special. We've never had such an event happen in our home before. I want these people to remember this as a very special, warm place." He could feel the cold and the ache coming into his old bones, but he eventually fell asleep.

The next morning the animals hurried up and out of the barn to be fed. As usual that donkey planned to be the last one out. He knew he didn't deserve as much food as those who would work hard that day. He stretched out his good front legs and then his right rear leg and felt pretty good. But he still had to move that left rear leg which he had pushed into the hole to keep the draft from the baby. He looked over at the mother and baby. She was holding the baby close to her heart, but when she looked at That Donkey she smiled at him as if she knew what he had done. He felt that warm-all-over feeling again and tentatively moved his left rear leg. Much to his surprise it moved without any pain or stiffness. In fact, it was as if it had never been sore at all. Then he began to move easily around the stable, stopping by the stall where the mother and baby were. Then he trotted out the door and around the barnyard, once, twice, three times in utter amazement. The stable boy from the inn was just coming with another bucket of oats and when he saw That Donkey he was amazed. He called to those who were getting their animals ready for the day's work. "Look," he cried. Look at that donkey. Look at him trot. Good Trot."

And from that day on that donkey's name was "Good Trot." Amazing things can happen in stables, or wherever Jesus is.

DON'T STOP

Another magazine from which I have received many blessings, and stories to tell, is ALIVE NOW! published by the Upper Room. The following thoughts are based on a seed from an article read there long ago, used, refined, and reused.

The stars looked much the same as they had every other night the Magi had studied them, when suddenly they became aware of a new star which appeared in the east. They were sure they had read about such an appearance and for some reason had kept the thought in the back of their minds over the years. They were impressed enough by the new star that they searched through the ancient scrolls which had been left by some captives who had lived in the land many years before. There it was – the star would signal the birth of a new king, born to the Jews. He was not to be an ordinary king, but one to be worshipped as well as honored. They must go and see this new king and worship him.

And so they began their journey, trudging eastward, led by the star which seemed to move with them through the night sky, leading them to the place where the new king would be. They traveled by night, resting during the heat of the day, making their way wherever the star guided them.

One morning as daylight began to creep over the horizon they could see the city of Jerusalem just ahead. The light of the star had begun to dim in the morning light, but they were sure that the place where the King of the Jews would be born would be Jerusalem. They decided to press on, sure there would be great excitement in the city. However, when they asked at the gate where the palace was so that they could see the newborn king of the Jews, no one knew anything about such a birth. In fact, those they asked seemed frightened by the idea; what could it mean? Did the present king know and was keeping it a secret for some reason? What would the occupying Romans think? Were they headed for revolt or even war?

Eventually word reached Herod, and he was greatly disturbed! He called the Magi in for a consultation and asked the Jewish scholars to discover if they could confirm the Magis' claim. "Yes," they said, "A new king would be born in Bethlehem." After he had found out from the Magi when the star had appeared, Herod sent the Magi on their way, asking them to come back and report to him so that he could "go and worship him also."

The Magi went on their way, and "the star which they had seen in the east went ahead of them until it stopped over the place where the child was. When they saw the star, they were overjoyed. On coming to the house, they saw the child with his mother Mary, and they bowed down and worshipped him."

Of course, Jerusalem was the place where the King of the Jews would be born. It was morning; the star had dimmed and it looked as if had stopped right there. But it hadn't! It appeared to be right, but it wasn't.

Where does God want you to be? Where is the place he wants to use you? Where is the place where you can best worship him? Don't stop until you get there!!

BORN IN A BARN

When I was in college and for many years afterward I subscribed to <u>His Magazine</u> *from Intervarsity Christian Fellowship. One of my well-worn thoughts came from that magazine. It has changed and developed over time as God has blessed me and used these words to bring others to him.*

Over the years I have collected several manger scenes, my favorite Christmas "decoration," each of which brings special memories. Our first such scene was the one we bought when we were first married. Anticipating that we would one day have children, we bought one we knew they would be able to use themselves, placing the figures, moving them about, telling the story. Over the years we had others given to us, from simple creations from our time in Russia, to the very lovely creations purchased by special people.

While we were with The Salvation Army in Detroit, we attended the Army church in Royal Oak. The women's group there had a weekly ceramics program. I had admired a beautiful manger scene one of them had created; blue and white, like the Delft china from Holland. I was determined to make one of my own, even though I have not one handicraft bone in my body. During the spring of the next year I began to make my manger scene. I started with a shepherd and was feeling quite proud of my accomplishment when I was told that I had used the wrong paint and would have to scrub it off. That just about ended my career. But I did it and proceeded to finish one shepherd, one wiseman, Mary and Joseph and the baby. But that was enough.

About two years later we moved from Detroit and at our farewell picnic, the ladies presented me with the rest of the figures from that wonderful manger scene, all done correctly! We now display it on our mantel in our retirement home.

But wait – "While they were there, the time came for the baby to be born and she gave birth to her firstborn, a son. She wrapped him in cloths and placed him in a manger, because there was no room for them in the inn." Jesus was born in a barn!! There were no flowing robes of blue and white; the shepherds who had been on night shift in the fields came just as they were. It was much later that the wisemen even appeared. About the only authentic looking things in the scene is the angel, and we have only one.

I'm sure Joseph had cleaned out a stall and found fresh straw for the manger. No doubt Mary had brought along the swaddling cloth just in case, but other than that, it was a barn. The smells, the sounds, the worn boards where the animals had scratched their backs over the years were barn things. But into that place, just as it was, Jesus came.

And so he comes to us, just as we are! There are some things we can do – recognize our need of him, repent. But we can't finish the job without his help. We'll never be right, never be perfect for his coming, and so he comes to be born in us, just as we are and it is he who makes us clean, makes us holy, makes the place and the time a holy place, a holy time.

"O come to my heart, Lord Jesus; there is room in my heart for thee."

THOUGHTS OF CHRISTMAS

CHRISTMAS EVE

On Christmas Eve I hear an echo of an age-old question – "Why is this night different from every other night?" The question is usually asked at Passover, "Why is this night different from every other night," but somehow I think it fits this night even better. The answer, relevant to every December 25 for the Christian, is this - "Christ is born in Bethlehem!" If you listen with your heart you will hear the angels sing. If you look with your spiritual eyes you will see the star rise in the east. If you rest in him you will know his peace on your piece of the earth and in your heart, and you will sense his good will poured out on your soul. This night is different from every other night! Glory to the new-born King. It's time to celebrate! It's time to ponder!

What angel can the grace explain?

The very God is very man,
By love paternal given!
Begins the uncreated word,
Born is the everlasting Word,
Who made both earth and Heaven!!
(From Advent with Charles Wesley, p. 68)

And so Christmas Day dawns.

MARY

The angels called her the "favored one, the Lord is with you. You have found favor with God." Mary called herself "the bond slave, the handmade of the Lord.

My soul exalts the Lord and my spirit has rejoiced in God, my Savior."

FEAR

"Do not be afraid, Zechariah."
"Do not be afraid, Mary."
"Do not be afraid, Shepherds."
What does one feel when an angel appears?

CHRISTMAS WORDS

Joy

Light

Merry

Ponder

Celebration

Expectation

Anticipation

Might and Mercy

Manure and Majesty

ADD
YOUR
OWN!

CHRISTMAS WORSHIP

Do homage and worship mean the same thing? Was the wise men's "homage" as real, as "worshipful" as the shepherds'? The wisemen were certainly persistent! A long journey, the wrong place, where the dickens is Bethlehem anyway? But they kept going, following the Star "until it stopped over the place where the young child was. He was now in a "house" with Mary his mother, and "they knelt before him and paid him homage."

I'm glad they found a house, Mary and Joseph! Traveling back to Nazareth was out of the question, and we have no idea how much time had passed since the baby was born – a young child might imply, at the very least, not a newborn. He was circumcised at 8 days, and Mary was purified after another 33 days; so they would have had to stay in Jerusalem/ Bethlehem for just over a month before heading home.

I think all those rituals were complete when the wise men showed up. Significantly they had brought gifts with them – expensive ones that were probably more meaningful than they knew – not gifts that one would ordinarily give to a child, but maybe the kinds of gifts one would choose for royalty, for the King of the Jews, to be added to the treasury. But in this case the kinds of things that would save his life – all arranged by God. God sent the wisemen home another way, one that did not take them through Jerusalem so they would not have to take any news to Herod.

Obedient to a star – God does speak in such a variety of ways. We must be alert to hearing him, knowing the Scripture, ready no matter what, ready to be obedient, ready to worship.

Wesley Christmas hymns

Among the books I enjoy reading at Christmastime is a compilation of Charles Wesley's hymns, written for Advent and Christmas reflection and celebration by Paul Wesley Chilcote.

One which I have learned to love is one I have never sung or even heard, full of questions, full of the story as the Magi, and now we, might tell it.

Where is the holy, heaven-born child?
Heir of the everlasting throne?
Who heaven and earth hath reconciled,
And God and man rejoined in one?
Shall we of earthly kings inquire?
To courts or palaces repair?

Shall learning show the sinner's friend,
Or scribes a sight of Christ afford?
Us to his natal place they send,
But never go to seek the Lord.

We search the outward church in vain,
They cannot him we seek declare,
They have not found the Son of man,
Or known the sacred name they bear.

Then let us turn no more aside,

But use the light himself imparts,
His Spirit is our surest guide,
His Spirit glimmering in our heart.

We are so blessed to live in the Age of the Holy Spirit who reveals to us the answers to all our questions as we feed on the Word of God, the Scriptures, and listen to his inward voice teaching and interpreting his every word, the Word, to us. "His Spirit is our surest guide." He is our Immanuel!

ASTONISHED
BY EASTER

I am writing these thoughts during the strangest Easter season we have ever experienced. We have been in lock down with no opportunity for corporate worship and yet we have known the presence of the Risen Christ in ways we've never experienced before. All of these meditations and poems were written pre-Covid-19. I wonder if they would be different now. I have some ideas to share in the future! In the meantime, ponder these.

EXAMINING EASTER

⁓

PALM SUNDAY THOUGHTS – Mark 11:1

"The Lord needs it." And the people let the disciples take the colt (or the colt and the donkey as Matthew suggests) when they promised to return it. The disciples used their cloaks for a saddle and others threw their cloaks onto the road and branches were spread as a pathway over which the donkey and Jesus would walk. The shouting began, "Hosanna!" they cried. "Blessed is he who comes in the name of the Lord!" Did they mean "save"? That's what Hosanna means - or was it just a note of praise for this one who had raised Lazarus from the dead among other miracles. Many of that crowd who had gathered in Jerusalem from all over Israel might have seen and heard him through the years of his ministry.

We like this story – people praising Jesus, crowds escorting him into Jerusalem, victory just ahead over the Romans' oppression, putting the religious leaders in their places. This is good! But what happened next? Mark says he went into the city, looked around the temple, and left for Bethany where he was to spend the night. What happened to the crowd? Did the disciples return the donkey? So many questions enter our minds as we considered "the rest of the story" which we do not have. But we do know that Jesus was fulfilling Old Testament prophecy from Zechariah 9:9.

And we can return to the initial statement, "The Lord needs it," and contemplate for a moment how that happened and what implications there are in that statement for us. Had Jesus made the arrangements for that particular donkey ahead of time? Or was it just a reaction to the LORD, whoever he was, needing it?

What is Jesus saying to us? What does he need that we have that could be of use to him and his Kingdom today? A song says, "I have not much to give thee, Lord, for that great love which made thee mine. I have not much to give thee, Lord, but all I have is thine!" (Salvation Army Song Book(SASB) #570) All I have is thine! It's up to him how he will use what we give him. How in the world can he use the little I have? Or maybe our reaction is no, I need this, but when we think of his GREAT LOVE which sent him to the Cross, we cannot help but give him ALL. Maybe as we get into the rest of the story, we will see what he gave more clearly and why we cannot help but give him ALL.

PASSOVER WITH FRIENDS AND FAMILY

Evidently none of the disciples of Jesus had family coming to the Passover Feast so the plan was that Jesus would celebrate the Feast with the 12 disciples so they asked him where they were to prepare it. He seems to have made arrangements for the guest room in a house and the disciples would find it by following a man carrying a jar of water, normally a woman's task so they would know whom to follow. There would be several things to prepare – the correctly prepared lamb, the salt water, the herbs, the eggs, the unleavened bread so that when Jesus and the other disciples arrived at sunset everything would be ready.

While they were eating, enjoying the celebration and remembering what it was all about, Jesus interrupted their conversation with an astonishing statement. "One of you will betray me – one who is eating with me." Looks of horror may have crossed their faces, looks of astonishment, after all no one was eating with them except those who had walked with him for three years, now eating in intimate fellowship. Where did that statement come from? Mark says, "They were saddened." Maybe they were and should have been horrified. They all knew some of them had said some wrong things; others had doubted him, questioned his methods; some of those things are recorded, but I imagine that some were not. What was going through each of their minds? "Surely not I!"

What would cause anyone then or now to betray Jesus? Fear for my very life or the life of my loved one, maybe my friends, not money! Judas may have done it for money or he may have done it in hopes of forcing Jesus' hand to step up and overthrow Rome or the religious rulers. But at that Last Supper Jesus said it was going to happen and there was nothing that could stop it. How could it? "One of you 12 who dips bread into the bowl with me." – someone sitting beside him? And no one noticed! Would they have tried to stop him? Could they have stopped him? Probably not.... But then no one saw it.

And the meal continued. I wonder what the disciples were thinking. Were they having a good time celebrating that long ago deliverance from Egypt? Were they remembering the great Palm Sunday parade? Did they worry and wonder about what would happen as a result of his cleansing the temple? Did they talk about the miracle of the fig tree? Did they ask questions or did they just enjoy the evening?

In the normal course of their shared meal, Jesus broke the bread as the head of the household normally would have done, and he passed it to the disciples. "Take it; this is my body." He did the same at the right time with the cup from which they all drank. "This is the blood of the new covenant, poured out for many." I doubt if the disciples caught the significance of those words. It probably took some reflection for them to realize he was again announcing his death. Whether he ever thought it would become ceremonial beyond the once a year Passover which they might continue to commemorate, I don't know. It is, I think, intended in the yearly Eastertime when we as Christians remember the original Passover and then Christ's sacrifice, in church with fellow believers or in our home as the Jews did and still do. Remember! "I will not drink again of the vine until I drink it anew in the Kingdom of God." Did they get it? Did they realize that the end was very near for him?

Scripture records that they sang a hymn and went to the Mount of Olives. Maybe they weren't so busy celebrating by now. Maybe they were more solemn as they walked. Did they notice that Judas had not rejoined them? Jesus wanted them and us to remember and this can be the remembering function of communion, but not a ritual whose intent we forget. Communion is so much more – it is a deep fellowship that we often share at a meal, conversation at a deeper level, even Bible Studies can be communion.

IN THE GARDEN

On the way to the Garden of Gethsemane, Jesus made another announcement that must have shaken them to their core – "You will all fall away. I will strike the shepherd and the sheep will scatter." Jesus was quoting from Zechariah 13:7 and then he added, "But after I have risen, I will go ahead of you into Galilee." Another prophecy that will soon be fulfilled, like the resurrection, but did they hear him. Peter's reaction was, "Even if all the rest fall away, I will not!" Peter was focused on falling away, not on the next sentence. Then came the real blow for him – "Today, yes this very night, you, yourself will disown me three times." Of course Peter says he won't; in fact "Even if I have to die with you I will never disown you, and all the others agreed." I think Jesus must have looked at them sadly, knowing that what they promised they would not be able to do.

Betrayed, abandoned, denied, on his way to pray to his Father who will not stop what is going to happen, knowing Jesus came into the world to do the one thing you could not do in Heaven – to die!!

When Judas left the meal, Scripture tells us, it was night! How significant is that? It was night. I'm sure the Passover Meal was long and so the evening had turned to night. Now as they walk along the way to the Garden it is night. The Garden is a lovely spot across the valley from Jerusalem and up the other side to a grove of olive trees with their leaves lit by the stars, glistening in their reflection.

"Sit here while I pray." He took Peter, James, and John

deeper into the garden. These three must have noticed that he was becoming more deeply distressed. He asked them to keep watch. He told them that his soul was overwhelmed with sorrow "to the point of death." What could that mean? He went on a bit further to pray alone. Could they hear him? Did that bother them, that he was so overwhelmed? I wonder what his sorrow was over – I'm not sure it was just what lay ahead for him. Maybe sorrow over the reactions of the disciples, sorrow of the world's sins, sorrow over my sins all of which were the cause of what lay ahead. He knew it was inevitable. But he was also human; he wanted someone to be with him, someone to be human with him, to stand by him. It was a very human event, and those disciples just fell asleep, even the three who were nearby. All he asked for was one hour. "Falling asleep" could lead to falling into temptation. He warned them!! Their spirits were willing but their flesh was weak – and so is mine, ours, far too often. Sometimes we fall asleep, sometimes we succumb to laziness or to doing the easy thing or to boredom. Jesus had warned them to be alert, to be watchful, to be on guard, and here they are sleeping. Three times, but they couldn't do it!

"Enough! It's too late now. The hour has come. The Son of Man is betrayed into the hands of sinners. Come on; let's go! The betrayer has arrived." Would it have been any different if they had stayed awake? Maybe not as far as events go – maybe less guilt on their part, maybe a stronger Peter, maybe Jesus would have been comforted. We would have missed some crucial lessons.

DEFENSE
Matthew 26:57-68, 27:11-26

The Sanhedrin, the Jewish High Council, was looking for damning evidence that would give them an excuse to kill Jesus, but only false witnesses came forward. Some came with his supposed claim that he would destroy the manmade temple, the center of Jewish worship, and then rebuild it in three days, and not use any human labor to do it. The high priest came at him when he didn't respond to the accusations.

Then the priest said to him, "Are you the Christ, the son of the Blessed One?" Now he spoke – "I am," Jesus replied. He did not need to defend himself against false accusations, but when the truth was spoken he acknowledged it. But the Sanhedrin could not, would not accept it. "This is blasphemy," they declared and condemned Jesus as worthy of death. They did not want to believe him. They were the authorities and they loved it! To think Jesus could be who he said he was put him in a position over them. Then they would be the ones condemned in their fancy dress and superiority and Jesus in his homespun garment. Authority and power can be deadly enemies in the wrong hands.

When the Sanhedrin failed to find sufficient evidence to condemn Jesus, they took him to the Roman governor, Pilate, whose first question was, "Are you the king of the Jews?" "Yes," Jesus replied, "It is as you say." The chief priest began to recite the long list of accusations, hoping to name one that would convince Pilate to kill Jesus. Pilate, like the chief priest, wondered why Jesus didn't answer them. Again, there was no need to defend himself against false accusations, but he did acknowledge the truth. Pilate could find no fault with Jesus. He was even willing to let him go and thinking that the crowd would agree with him, offered to do so, but the crowd cried out, "No, release Barabbas!" How strange! Barabbas was a known criminal, rightly tried and condemned, but the crowd cried out more loudly, "We want Barabbas!" Pilate was a weak man, but he had authority. However, he listened to the crowd when he asked, "What shall I do with Jesus?" He may well have been astonished when the crowd yelled back, "Crucify him!" In his weakness Pilate could only see rebellion on the part of this mob if he didn't give them what they wanted; so he released Barabbas to them and had Jesus beaten and turned over to be crucified.

The Sanhedrin was conniving; the disciples were weak; Pilate had no leadership; the crowd was easily manipulated. Jesus was silent and willing to give his life for those he loved. He refused to be humiliated, even when the soldiers mocked him, put a purple robe on him and made a crown of thorn branches for him, but he went humbly to do what the Father had asked him to do – to die for the sins of the whole world, the sins of all time before and after him, your sins and mine.

THE CRUCIFIXION

"And they crucified him!" That's all the description we get of the crucifixion. Were they there, those who wrote the story later? They knew what a crucifixion was like, a somewhat normal way to execute someone, but none of the Gospel writers describes the process. We learn the horrors of it from historians, from commentaries, and we are horrified. We have been spared from ever seeing one, and it is hard for us to imagine how horrid it must have been. The brevity of the actual act may speak of the truth that the more significant event was yet to come. This is not the end of the story!!

In a three-hour span Jesus was the sacrifice for the sins of the world – only he could have done it and he did! The soldiers distributed his clothes among themselves, another common practice. Thieves were crucified on either side of him. There was a sign over his head – King of the Jews. Those who passed by hurled insults at him. Priests and scholars mocked him. For three hours he listened to the insults, the mocking, the words intended to humiliate him. And Jesus stayed there and died. That death meant salvation for the world. He didn't come down from the Cross, even though he could have. Instead he came up from the grave. He didn't save himself; he saved you, me, the world. He didn't do it so they would believe, he did it so that those who believe in his death and resurrection could live!

In that three-hour span darkness covered the land. The end was near, or so it seemed! Jesus spoke several times, crying out near the end, "My God, my God, why have you forsaken me?" The bystanders thought he was calling for Elijah. He was offered drugged wine to drink. "Now let's see if Elijah will come to take him down," they said. But instead he breathed his last breath with a loud cry and he died. He did not hallucinate; he just "gave up the ghost," as some say. The really dramatic events as recorded by Mark are glorious – the huge but dusty old curtain of the temple was torn in two from top to bottom – a most significant event! Now all men have access to God, Father, Son and Holy Spirit – the barrier was/is gone – no need for a Moses or the prophets or priests to intercede for us. We now have our own access to God – wonderful, amazing, glorious, in all circumstances, everywhere! God is with us. He is Spirit and we worship him in Spirit and in truth as he promised the Samaritan woman at the well. Did God reach down from glory and with his own two "hands" rip the temple curtain separating us from him? Or did he send a lightning bolt to start the tear? Was that the moment when it just tore from having hung there for so long? God's timing is perfect.

The centurion, the leader of the Roman legion charged with overseeing this gruesome event, heard Jesus cry out with a strong voice, not the voice of a weak man in the throes of death and agony, and that centurion said, "This man was the Son of God." What he might have meant exactly we don't know, but he knew that this man was the Son of God. We wonder what happened to him afterward. Did he change his mind and repent?

Some women were watching, women who had cared for Jesus, meeting his physical needs and believing in him. They were probably unsure of the meaning of all that was happening, but they remained till the end – ah, the faithfulness of women! May we be among them! From a distance, watching, caring still, enduring, helpless, hopeful, wondering, pondering. How long did they stay? Two of them, Mary of Magdala and Mary the mother of Joses observed where he was buried, planning to return with spices on Sunday. There is the sense of great sadness, loss of hope – Jesus is dead! But that's not the end of the story!!

IT'S NOT OVER YET!!

As the preacher said, "It's Friday, but Sunday's coming!"
In this era, the emphasis on Friday has been lost. It used
to be that schools and many businesses closed on what we
still call "Good Friday." Not today. But we who believe
in Jesus, in the power of the Cross need to reflect on the
marvel of the crucifixion, the wonder of our salvation won
on that day, but we also remember that it's not over yet. We
have a "silent Saturday" to ponder. We also remember that
Sunday is coming. The truth is He lives!!

It's interesting that Mark's story (Mark 16:8) ends with the
women trembling and afraid as they fled from the empty
tomb saying nothing to anyone. How would I have reacted,
going just after sunrise to anoint Jesus' body, finding the
stone rolled away, no soldiers or other humans nearby, just
a "young man dressed in a white robe" sitting on the right
side of the tomb. He told them not to be alarmed. Yeah, right!
He said to them, "He is risen! See where he lay! Go and
tell the disciples and Peter. He'll meet you in Galilee." But
according to the next verse (without the added paragraph),
they were just afraid. Why were they so afraid? Did they
think they may have imagined the whole thing? Did they
fear telling anyone for their own safety?

If verses 1-8 were all the earliest Christians had would it
have been enough? Verse 11 says when the disciples heard
from Mary Magdeline they did not believe or were at least
skeptical. (Whoever finished Mark's story was at least
honest.) When the two on the road to Emmaus came back
to Jerusalem with their story, they were not believed either.

But when Jesus appeared to the 10 they had to believe!! And so do I! It is their witness and the other resurrection appearances, the witness of generations of people who fully believe and those in my own generation, and the fact that I know "he lives; he lives within my heart!!" He is risen; He is risen indeed!!

THOUGHTS FOR HOLY WEEK
From John's Gospel

Jesus knew what was going to happen and he did everything he could to prepare the disciples for the events that lay ahead. We are blessed to have the record of events and words, and we have time to ponder them in our preparation for Good Friday and Easter. Let the Holy Spirit reveal truths to you that will prepare you for what lies ahead in your life. Allow the Spirit to show you who you really are so that you can become the person you can be in Christ.

John 12:12-16

Five days before Jesus was to die, he entered Jerusalem on what we call Palm Sunday. He was greatly acclaimed by the crowd that gathered, shouting, "Hosanna! Blessed is he who comes in the name of the Lord!" This event was the fulfillment of prophecy – "Your king is coming, seated on a donkey's colt." (Zechariah 9:9) But John says that it wasn't until Jesus was glorified that the disciples realized that these things were written in the Old Testament about him. They needed to see that he was fulfilling prophecy, but with all that was going on at the time, they didn't realize it. Too much went on even in the next week for them to "get it."

How good it is for us to have and to know the Holy Spirit who guides us through the unknown and who helps us remember and understand. There is not a guarantee that we will always understand, but when we need to, we will. If we read the other Gospels we realize that John did not remember or record all the details that the others did, but he records the way in which the event impacted him and what was important for those to whom he was writing. We need to learn to see what God is doing every day, the daily and the special events of life, so that we can recall them when the time is right under the direction of the Holy Spirit.

Lord, help me to see, to record, to remember events, your Word, and to rightly interpret both.

John 12:20-26

Selwyn Hughes has suggested in his devotional book that the second great temptation that Jesus faced was when the Greeks wanted him to come with them, to go "now to the Gentiles," to get out of Jerusalem at this critical hour and possibly avoid being crucified. However, what Jesus said to Andrew and Philip to whom the Greeks had spoken, clarifies his motives and the costs and rewards of doing what has to be done God's way. He says, "The hour has come for the Son of Man to be glorified." Then he goes on to explain that "a grain of wheat must fall into the ground and die." If we stop there, it certainly doesn't sound like glorification. But if we go on we can see that "death" of the grain of wheat results in many seeds for the future. Jesus would not go to the Greeks at this moment but his death would open the door for all Greeks, all Gentiles, to come to him. He would not only die, he would be glorified! The next week would not look like glorification. It would look like death, but the end is not yet.

Did the disciples, particularly Andrew and Philip, understand? It's not a new idea; and Jesus went on to explain in verses 25 and 26. It had to be repeated to them and will be again and again in this last week. I think we, in our day, need it repeated for us as well. We do not like the idea of suffering and death, of being buried, but we need to see Jesus for who he was and for the decisions he had to make, the temptations he had to overcome, and let him prepare us for the days ahead.

Jesus, thank you for going the way of death so that my sins could be forgiven, so that you could be glorified.

John 12:20-26

A seed must die to what it is now in order to become what God created it to be – so much more than what it is! Hoarding seed does no good; keeping it until planting time is okay, but then each seed must die in order to produce, to become what it was intended to be.

"He who loves his [present life as a seed] will lose it, and who [is willing to give it up and die to the seed life] in this world will keep it [his new life through eternity]." This new life means serving Christ and serving Christ means following him, and if we follow him, we will be where he is – even now when we can't see him on earth. He is with us and "My Father will honor you." WOW! But we've got to be willing to give up what we are to become what God has created us to be. We can't become more without giving up, dying to what confines us now. For every individual that looks different but the process is the same.

Lord, I don't want to stay an unfruitful seed. Make me aware of what has to die in me in order to become all that you want me to be. Make me willing to go to death to become the best I can be.

John 12:27-29

Following his statement about the hour in which he will be glorified and his metaphor of the seed which must die, Jesus declares, "Now my heart is troubled, and what shall I say? 'Father, save me from this hour'? No, it is for this very reason I came to this hour. Father, glorify your name!"

He seems to be anticipating the Garden of Gethsemane. He is making his choice – dying or asking for some means of being saved. He makes a definite decision to choose the path intended for him. "No," he says, "for this purpose I came to this hour!" What resolve! He knows the plan and right to the end he will keep his commitment to save the world, us, me, by his death. He finishes this statement with a further choice – "Father, glorify your name!"

How will I do that today? How will I "glorify your name?" I can do that by wise use of my time, my money, my talent, my gifts, being a good steward of all he has given me. I can do that by speaking his name at the right time and place as a witness. Where will I be today and how can I do that? Where have I been and have I done that?

Jesus must have been greatly encouraged, humanly speaking, when the voice from Heaven said, "I have both glorified it (through your life) and will glorify it again (through your death)". What more could we want in our lives than to be the instrument through which God's name can be glorified!?!

Lord, help me to give you all the glory and praise, never to allow pride or selfishness, to want the glory for myself, only for you. Father, glorify your name in and through me today.

John 13:1-17

This is a story, an event that bears thoughtful and careful reading and re-reading, putting myself in the picture, imagining where I would be sitting, hearing Jesus speak, watching what he does, thinking about how I would react.

A major portion of the preparation for the disciples occurs in the upper room at what we call the Last Supper, when Jesus celebrated the Passover with them. We do not have a record of many times when Jesus explained what he had done or said to the disciples, but within this event he gives an explanation. He didn't want them to miss the point.

He often treats us in the same way. He has given us the "ear of a disciple." We have the same privileges they had, the same kind of information, the same opportunity to search for truth and meaning in the text, the same explanation of the text. And we have the Holy Spirit as our teacher, something they did not yet have.

You trust us, Lord. While you were with the disciples some may have asked questions in private and I'm sure we don't have every explanation you gave. But we do have the Spirit to help us understand. Thank you!

John 13:8 - "If I do not wash you, you have no part with me!"

The importance of keeping clean, of daily washing, of submitting to his bathing of what is soiled, of recognizing when I have failed in doing his will - keep it up and soon I am dirty all over, maybe backsliding is the right word and then the result is having no part with Jesus! It was a humbling experience, having their feet washed by Jesus, but he longs for us as well as Peter and the others to be thoroughly clean and he will do whatever it takes, always providing the means by which we can be clean. It is always available. In his first letter John says it this way - "The blood of Jesus keeps on cleansing us from all sin." (I John 1:9)

I wonder how Peter felt after this - not humiliated but humbled (Jesus never humiliates!). Jesus' explanation would have helped him recognize further needs in himself - maybe ones he was still pondering during the next few hours, needs which he saw vividly when he denied Jesus. He knew he was not clean all over all the time, needing to have his "feet" washed. Would Jesus do it again?

Lord, you are so patient with me, showing me, reminding me, guarding me, making ways of escape, forgiving me, cleansing me, keeping me clean. Thank you for not giving up on me! I submit to you today; I delight to do your will, O my God!

John 13:8

"Footwashing" in Jesus' day was a needed ritual every

time one entered a home, especially for a meal – hot and dusty feet that wore only sandals needed to be washed. The implication, of course, is that we need to be cleansed of whatever sin, whatever mistake has soiled us every day, but I think it can also be the continual cleansing that happens as we live in his presence and allow his blood to wash away the sin as it occurs, realizing and confessing, of course, but also learning over time to see the temptation and not yield to it. This is the work of the Holy Spirit in us and our practicing his presence.

I wonder if footwashing is an illustration of what we should do at the end of each day, either alone in God's presence or with someone with whom we are accountable. We ask Jesus to help us see ourselves as he sees us or ask a trusted friend, spiritual companion to help us review our actions and words so that we can see beyond our own observations and see through Jesus' eyes. We may need some cleansing - and sometimes, maybe even often, we will see things about which to rejoice, to celebrate.

Lord, help me see myself as you see me. Wash me, cleanse me today, that I might be whiter than snow!

John 13:17

"Remember" is one of my favorite Bible words, and I think one of Jesus' favorite words. He really wanted the disciples to remember, but oh how often they forgot – how often we forget. I wonder how often he said to them during their three years together, "If you know these things [that's really good; keep them in your memory], but blessed are you if you do them." So there has to be another step beyond remembering. Having knowledge is good, but the blessing comes when we remember and DO the lesson learned from the incident, the story, when we apply the teaching to our daily lives. Doing what people need done for them is what Jesus said – if it's washing feet, wash feet; if it's cleaning up a mess, clean it up; if it's listening, listen; if it's praying with a friend, pray; if it's carrying out the garbage or babysitting or helping with dishes, or... just do it.

Lord, you set an example for us by doing the lowliest of tasks, a task done only by a servant. Make me like you, Lord, a servant doing what needs to be done. You were practical without embarrassing, kind and helpful, showing us how to live.

Three times in chapters 12 and 13 Jesus says that believing him, seeing him, receiving him means that we also believe the one who sent him, see the one who sent him, receive the one who sent him. (12:14, 12:45, 13:20) When Jesus came, all of God came. As the Holy Spirit dwells in us, all of God dwells in us.

But right after that third statement John tells us that Jesus "was troubled in Spirit." I think he was aware of Judas' plans and intentions. Judas believed, but did he receive the truth as Jesus taught the truth? Did he live out the truth he was taught? Jesus' insights into Judas troubled Jesus. He seems to have tried to give Judas one more opportunity by telling him that he knew of Judas' plan. But Judas was convinced he had the better plan. Jesus knew that even having washed his feet, one of the disciples (or more?) was still not completely clean.

I wonder how Judas felt when Jesus washed his feet. Maybe he saw it as confirmation of his own disturbing thoughts – "No Messiah would ever do something like this. He's got to learn to be strong, a kingly conqueror, not a wimpy servant." People today have that same feeling about God. If he's really God he would keep bad things from happening. He would take over, punish evil, reward good. People still look for a conqueror, but not a conqueror over sin in their lives.

If I had been there when Jesus gave the bread to Judas right after he declared that the one who took the bread from him was the one who would betray him, would I have realized the depth of that action? We know this was the last meal Jesus would ever eat with them, a very symbolic Passover, but the disciples didn't recognize that yet. John places a lot of significance on the receiving of the bread and maybe with hindsight during the intervening years before he wrote his Gospel, he saw things in a new light. I wonder if that was the moment, the moment he took the bread from Jesus, when Satan entered Judas. Judas went out immediately; it was night – how significant is that?!?

Lord, I don't know what I would do if I were in Judas' place. I do know that you will be with me, and therefore I can remain faithful if the time comes when I have a temptation like Judas' to betray you – You will be with me and that's all, and that's enough!!

"In the same way I have loved you, you love one another."
13:35 (Message) Jesus is talking with the eleven remaining
disciples. I think He knew that they would not have the
capacity to love Judas so completely.

How did Jesus love them? He saw what they could become;
he taught them; he kept them with him on that three-year
camping trip; he rebuked and corrected them; he took
care of or saw that their needs were met; he explained and
discussed with them – I wish I knew what they talked about
around the campfire. And now here is his last command to
them – "love each other in the same way that I have loved
you." There is no greater challenge to our Christian life than
to live this way towards his other disciples, his intimate
circle. Can I suggest that there ought to be 11 people I love
in this way – not family, but fellow believers? He didn't say
this to a general group, only to the final 11. What is there
about his love that makes it different from what he might
have said to his other followers? Or is this a command he
needed to give them because he would soon be leaving them
and they would be choosing a new form for their group and
in that process they would need to love one another or the
world would not believe that they were his disciples. Jesus
is not talking about dying for each other, I don't think. He's
talking about loving each other in the every day ways in
which he has loved them.

I expect it might be the disputes without love in the church
that have caused more people to go away from the church
than any other cause. If we want to win people for Christ,
our task is lift him up in a way that will draw all men to
him, and it must be done in love, with love for one another

or we become so involved in the disputes that we forget about Christ; we stop lifting him up and get caught up in other things. Jesus had one purpose – to glorify the Father. He kept to that purpose even in loving the disciples. Loving was part of living out the purpose.

I wonder about the break that has been created by starting a new chapter of John here. Chapter divisions were included to help people read the word with more clarity, but I wonder. Maybe Jesus continued talking to Peter – "You will deny me three times. Let not your heart be troubled." Then turning to the others, including all who were left in the Upper Room, "You believe in God, believe also in me." Then Thomas, a usually quiet disciple, asks, "How can we know the way?" The disciples want to know what's going on. They are willing to stick with him. But their unspoken thoughts may have been, "What you're saying is very frustrating, Lord! We don't know where you're going and how can we know the way if we don't know the where?

We humans have such a need to know, a fear of the unknown; it almost paralyzes us. But throughout Scripture we read of people who did amazing things without knowing the what or when or how – Abraham – "Go to a land that I will show you"; Mary – "You will bear a son after the Holy Ghost is come upon you"; now Jesus – "I go to prepare a place for you." It's seems to me that is not just about a place in Heaven but in the every day things of life. He is always there before us. Things are always ready.

John 14:6-7

What is the relationship between Jesus and the Father, these two persons who are God, one God? In this verse he says,

He is the way to the Father.

He is "like" the Father – to know one is to know the other. To see and know Jesus is to see and know the Father.

Jesus was in the Father and Father was in Jesus.

Jesus' authority was the Father.

Jesus' works were done, not by him but by the Father.

Jesus is not the Father, but they are one. Soon he will talk about the Holy Spirit and there will be three in one. How much did the disciples understand of all this, how much can we understand? I can't understand because I'm human, but I can have faith and believe without understanding. My faith believes what Jesus says.

If Jesus needed to speak with the authority of the Father, how much more do I need to rely on him for all I say and do. Jesus has just said that he is in the Father, we are in him, and he is in us; so if I remember that, there is no need to sin, or to say or do anything that is not his will. Can I ever get to that place?

And how much do I believe of verses 12-14? The works he does we can do! In fact, greater works than these because he will be with the Father!! Whatever we ask in his name he will do; ask anything in his name and he'll do it! What we can do; what we can ask. What does this mean to me; what is he saying to me here and now. We are part of a ministry wherever we are, a ministry to preach the Word, to feed the hungry, clothe the naked, heal the sick through adequate nutrition, medical clinics, education, financial assistance; releasing the captive from prison with the Good News.

If I combine these verses with Jesus' mission statement from Isaiah and his description of the judgment in Matthew 25:34-36, I see what he meant – food, drink, lodging, clothing, visiting the sick and those in prison, preaching the Gospel to the poor, healing the brokenhearted, proclaiming liberty to captives, sight to the blind, freeing those who are oppressed, proclaiming the acceptable year of the Lord. The sheer number of Christians combined with increasing technology and transportation makes it humanly possible to do much of this. Yet it often seems more than is humanly possible to do. Combine what we can do with technology and what we can do with faith and prayer and there are no limits.

And we know that while Jesus did feed 5,000, he did not feed every hungry person in Israel. He healed "all who came to him," but he did not heal every sick person. He raised two from the dead, but only 2. But we can do so much more than we do. Does lack of faith limit resources? Lack of prayer? Do we not communicate need as we should?

The next paragraph gives us a clue as to how we can do more than he did. First, our responsibility is to keep his commandments – basically, love God and love our neighbor. As we do this he will "pray" the Father and the Father will send another Helper (Comforter, Paraclete, Spirit of Truth) to dwell in us. That Spirit comes to dwell in us, to show us what to do and how to do it, where to find resources, how to communicate, how to pray. Maybe we can paraphrase the verses this way – As you keep my commandments, I will ask the Father to send the Spirit into your life to help you do greater things than I have done and to guide your prayers so they will be answered.

Lord, keep my eyes and ears open so that I will know what you are doing and can become part of your work in my world today.

John 14:18 says, "I will not leave you orphans." What a wonderful promise! It takes me back to chapters 1 and 3 where Jesus says we are born spiritually by the will of God and now he says that because the Father is in him, we should recognize that the Father will be in the Holy Spirit and so will he – "I will come to you" – the Trinity, the Three-in-one. What more could we ask? Our Helper comes fully equipped and dwells in us. There is no need for us to sin; we don't have to pray prayers that cannot be answered; we don't have to do wrong things because the Spirit of Truth is in us.

I'm sure that the disciples did not begin to realize all that he was saying as he said it. I probably have not plumbed the depths of the meaning even after meditating, reading, pondering these words many times. Nor have I appropriated all the truth that is here. We are indwelt by God – alone but never lonely, never helpless, able to discern Truth. We are children of the King of Kings, indwelt by the Holy Spirit, gifted and able to be all he wants us to be.

Understanding the roles of the Holy Spirit, recognizing what He does and does not do is important to my being what I can be in Christ. Jesus said to the disciples, "I'm telling you these things now, but when the Spirit comes he will teach you and remind you of everything I've said." As I understand it, the Spirit worked in the authors of Scripture to remind them of what Jesus said and in that process taught them what it meant and today he does the same thing with us. The words on the page do not become the inspired Word of God for me until I let the Spirit teach me their truth and their meaning.

Then he helps me remember them and use them as I need them in daily life. We have the words to read. They had him to hear, but not everyone who heard would understand what he said until they allowed the Spirit to work in them. Likewise as we read and study the Word, we need the inspiration of the Spirit to work in us. Then it becomes the Word of God to us. "He will teach you all things and bring all things to your remembrance" (John 16:12-13).

"My peace I leave with you, my peace I give to you, not as the world gives." I don't think the disciples experienced that peace over the next few days. It's Thursday. They will experience the crucifixion on Friday – peace? I don't think so! They will grieve and wonder on Saturday – peace? I doubt it. They will celebrate and wonder and ponder on Sunday – but peace? I think peace may not have settled into their hearts and minds until Pentecost and the coming of the Holy Spirit. Maybe then they remembered his promise of his peace being given to them.

It's always here – his peace. I can be in it or I can step out of it. "Let not your heart be troubled...or afraid" – two opposites of peace which should alert me quickly that I have stepped out of his peace. "At peace" I can listen and respond rather than react. "At peace" I can talk with, have fellowship with someone who causes me to fear, whatever it is that I fear. "At peace" whatever may be going on around me does not disturb my inner sense of his presence. Why let anything control my emotions instead of letting peace be my main focus? Peace isn't the absence of war or even of conflict or disagreement. We will never all agree on some things; change is often needed and not everyone sees it, so disagreements arise. But in the midst of all these things peace can rule my heart, and if it rules enough hearts, compromise and consensus can rule the situation. Lives can be saved, changed for the better. But it has to be his peace. Peace that the world gives is fragile, doesn't last long, causes secretive and underground things to go on. "Peace at any price" is not Christ's motto. His is "peace at the cost of my life for you."

Holy Spirit, remind me today that I have been given the gift of peace and joy and abundant life. Jesus said so and I believe it.

John 18:1

Part of the Passover meal included the singing of a hymn, possibly Psalm 116 – worth taking some time to read and ponder in light of the Passover and the coming events in Jesus' life. "And when they had sung a hymn they went out to the Mount of Olives" (Matthew 26:30, Mark 14:26). I wonder what was going through the minds of the eleven as they got up from the table, gathered their belongings, chatted among themselves, checked on the cleanup, clattered down the stairs in their sandals, somewhat quiet sensing Jesus' mood, subdued in the silence of the night, the streets empty because everyone was home eating their Passover meal. When they were walking in a group Jesus began talking again as they walked along. The significance of much that had happened had escaped them. But some may have been thinking about the foot washing or something Jesus had said about betrayal or love or being with him somewhere or about the Holy Spirit or about peace. Did anyone notice that Judas was gone? But then again he would know where they were going and would catch up with them there.

What would I have thought about without the insight I have now? Lord, sometimes, like you, we have to move on. "Let us leave." How hard was that for you? You alone knew this was the "last supper" you would share with your disciples and you had shared far more than a significant meal! There was so much of you in the meal if they had only been able to see it. But the time had come; you needed to move on. You had more to share and somehow John captured more of it – the vine and the branches, bearing fruit, the work of the Holy Spirit, the joy that would come later when it would be complete. Did any of them get it? You gave them a lot to ponder! Help me to ponder and reach for understanding as I am guided by your Spirit, as I make this walk to the Mount of Olives with you.

John 15:1-11

"I am the true vine and my Father is the gardener. He cuts off every branch in me that bears no fruit, while every branch that does bear fruit he prunes so that it will be even more fruitful" (15:1-2). Useless branches are cut off; branches that are bearing fruit are pruned so that they can bear more and better fruit. Both hurt! There is nothing dead on a fruit bearing branch, but some seemingly good parts are cut back in order for the nourishment to go into the fruit making it bigger, sweeter, a more productive branch. If a branch is to bear fruit it must stay on the vine – something the vine cannot decide. When we are on the vine, we must expect to be pruned, and God knows just how and where to cut. It will be painful but the result is glorious! Sometimes he prunes without our "consent" – a friend leaves, a relative dies, we move, something is taken from our lives. At other times he says, "This has to go," and we choose to let him take it or we hang on to it. He does help us see why "it" needs to go and we can give it willingly, recognizing that the results will be for his glory. Jesus does tell us that the results of being in him and being "pruned" will include receiving whatever we ask for (15:7) and bearing much fruit (15:8) thereby letting others know that we are his disciples and glorifying our Father.

Three times Jesus says that we must abide in him and he in us (vss. 4 and 5) or as in verse 7 "my words abide in you." That's the way it is with a branch of a vine, a branch on a tree. The branch is attached to the tree, part of the tree. It can be cut from the tree, but as long as it is part of the tree it is in the tree and the tree is in it as the sap, the life-giving nutrients flow into it. There is a sense in which Jesus says he is dependent on us for "fruit." The growth of his kingdom is in the branches as they grow and produce fruit. The branches are dependent on him for the ability to do that. We have an interdependent, adult relationship with him.

Remaining in him, the Vine, in order to receive the benefits like having his joy or receiving our desires is not manipulation; it is consequences. He is stating a "natural law" illustrated by the vine and branches. In 15:7 he promises that "whatever you wish, will be given you." It will be the result of your abiding and keeping his word. In 15:11 he promises that "your joy may be complete." You already have my joy and here's how to keep it and make it full, just as you have my peace. Both are my gifts to you.

John 15:12-17

And now Jesus final commandment – "Remain in my love. Love one another as I have loved you."

(15:9, 12) Jesus had loved them and trained them; loved them and knew their faults; loved them and corrected them; loved them and understood them; loved them and died for them. He was their friend ready to die for them as their friend. He had told them what he was doing so they were not his servants. He told them all the things he had heard from his Father, so they knew they were his friends. And me, you – yes, he died for us, even while we were yet sinners, certainly not yet friends. He died for all, for everyone, giving us a chance to be his friends which leads us to eternal life in him.

It seems that most if not all of the commandments about love are about loving God or each other, our fellow Christian brothers and sisters. Is he reminding us and them to do that because he knows it will very hard to do consistently – for some Christians to love other Christians, some fellow church-goers to love others in the same church? Love and forgiveness become the test of our obedience to his final command.

John 16:1-15

And now comes the secret to being able to do as he has commanded us. But I ask again, did the disciples understand what he was saying? Jesus kept pressing the fact that he was leaving. By chapter 16 the disciples are no longer asking where he is going, and he recognizes their sorrow. They didn't have any experience on which to base their hope. I'm not sure any parallel is adequate – how does one prepare for a separation like this? Jesus tried to help them cope – "It is to your advantage that I go away; for if I do not go away, the Counselor will not come to you." (John 16:7) So often in my walk with Christ I misread events seeing them as bad, only to find that the bad, the worst was to my advantage. What a God!! It often takes time for a "tragedy" to become a "comedy," a difficulty to show itself as a blessing, a disadvantage to appear as an advantage, but "all things really do work together for those who love God...."

16:8-10 puzzles me – let's see if I can think this through with the help of the Expositor's Commentary. "When he [the Spirit] comes, he will convict the world of guilt in regard to sin and righteousness and judgment." The Commentary (p. 157) suggests that the Spirit "enforces the standard...of righteousness" which is the means by which sin is revealed.

Jesus' return to Heaven, to the Father, proved finally and completely that he is the righteous One, perfect in all his life, the definition of righteousness (rather than the law as the definition). Then regarding judgment the commentary says the contrast is between the self-will and rebellion of Satan and the obedience and love of Christ – the Cross being the complete, the utter condemnation and defeat of Satan – perfect tense; it's over – Satan is judged, condemned, sentenced! The Holy Spirit's task then is to convict the world, help them, make them see their guilt.

Jesus stops at this point with the disciples and says they can't bear any more. He appears to leave them with an incomplete story – they are convicted, see their guilt, now what? The next step is accepting, believing in Jesus as the Son of God who will be with the Father, victorious over Satan who is now judged and condemned. But Jesus isn't done with them – "I still have many things to say to you, but you cannot bear them now." He isn't done with them. Sometimes that is very frustrating because I know I haven't learned everything yet. I have been tested and I will be tested, and when I've passed this test there will be another. But I couldn't begin to learn it all at once. God, the Holy Spirit, knows how much to give at a time. He is my teacher and I know it's worth listening. I know I can be more Christlike. Some things I wonder if I'll ever learn! Sometimes I think maybe I don't know how to pass the test. But the Spirit is the guide into all truth, and he will teach me all I need to know. Learning from him is an ongoing process. He will help me see and understand Christ in all his beauty and perfection as an example for me to strive towards in myself.

My frustration comes when I can't understand or when I am in pain. Lord, I know I keep failing the tests. Do I need to learn more patience when I don't understand? Do I need to live with pain, finding strength in my weakness? Lord, help me, test me; Spirit, remind me, guide me! Show me how to live victoriously, righteously with the circumstances that are not going to change.

John 16:16-33

Is there any other more instantaneous change of emotion than is promised by the resurrection? Jesus said, "I will see you again and your heart will rejoice, and no one will take away your joy. In that day you will no longer ask me anything. I tell you the truth, my Father will give you whatever you ask in my name. Until now you have not asked for anything in my name. Ask and you will receive, and your joy will be complete" (John 16:19-25). Jesus compares it with the pain of childbirth followed by the joy that a child has been born. In both experiences sorrow is changed to joy, pain to peace, tears to laughter, but it is sequential. The salvation experience follows the same pattern – sorrow for sin, release bringing joy, then learning that prayer is answered. Sanctification can be seen in the same way – the longing for a clean heart which brings sorrow, the joy when the Spirit cleanses, and, amazingly, the new prayer relationship, a presence relationship rather than just an asking relationship.

Maybe your pattern, like mine, is similar to what Jesus predicts in verses 31-33. I believe with great conviction, but something happens and I forget my belief, let down, give in and lose, not by belief, not my faith, but my works don't prove my faith. Realizing it, I return to him and find peace and know that Jesus has overcome the world. I look at what happened and discover why I forgot, what caused me to let down, why I acted as I did. I am so grateful that he restores peace, that he sits with me to help me understand my weakness and failings. I think he leaves me with some weaknesses so that I can and will gain my strength from him. I can even learn to "be of good cheer" in the midst of weakness because I can hold onto the fact that he has overcome the world and can surely overcome my weaknesses and, when I am in him, can be strong.

John 17

What a wonderful prayer is recorded in John 17. Jesus prays for himself, for his disciples, and for you and me. I found it interesting to see what he said to his Father about himself – "I have glorified You on earth" – vs. 4;" I have finished the work you gave me to do" – vs. 4; "I have manifested your name: - vs. 6; "I kept them (those you gave me) in your name" – vs. 12; "I have given them your word" – vs. 14; : I have sent them into the world as you sent me" – vs. 18; "I have given them the glory you gave me" – vs. 22; "I have known you" – vs. 25; "I have declared to them your name" – vs. 26.

Our tasks in the world are similar. God has brought people into our lives and we can turn them to Jesus who receives them to himself and he makes them into more than I can help them to be. Lord, may I glorify you today and complete this day's work. May I keep those to whom I minister close to you and to your word, declaring and showing your glory. May I see you in them also. May I answer your prayer in all I do.

I am interested in Jesus' use of the word "glorify" in this chapter. "Glorify your Son, that your Son may glorify you." Vs. 1; "I have brought you glory on earth by completing the work you gave me to do." - vs. 4; "And now, Father, glorify me in your presence with the glory I had with you before the world began." - vs. 5; "All I have is yours, and all you have is mine. And glory has come to me though them (the disciples)." - vs. 10; "I have given them the glory that you gave me, that they may be one as we are one." - vs. 22; "Father, I want those you have given me to be with me where I am, and to see my glory, the glory you have given me because you loved me before the creation of the world." - vs. 24.

There is no selfishness in Jesus' desire for God to glorify him - it is so that the Father will be glorified. His earthly task was to glorify God and he did it, and he did it perfectly. As One, Father and Son are now glorified together. Jesus asks that the glory be as they had "before the world was." I wonder what that was like, something beyond our imagination!

When the prayer turns to the disciples, Jesus says, "I am glorified in them." Lord, are you glorified in me? Those disciples were not perfect yet, and yet you use the present tense in this statement. Maybe I can glorify you even through my imperfections. You gave them your glory in order to make them one with you and the Father, and you want me to be one with you and with others in the Family, the Body. Our Oneness may be less than complete because we members are not perfect but it's a marvelous Oneness in you that is complete when we are united in you. Thinking of those with whom I feel oneness fills me with joy today, Lord!

Relationships are important in chapter 17. There is the Father/Son relationship which he himself has with his Father – a relationship which is mutual, each bringing glory to the other. There is the Jesus/disciples/Father relationship – God gave them to Jesus and now they are mutually "owned" by both Father and Son. Then there is the Father/Son/disciple/all who believe relationship – all who believe and will believe through the disciples word may become one "in us."

Love is a dominant theme as he comes near the end. The unity of God and all the disciples will prove to the world that God loves us as much as he loves Jesus (vs. 22) – can you believe it?!? And Jesus' final promise is that he will continue to declare the name of the Father to us that his (God's) love and Jesus himself may be in us.

When Jesus prays for the first disciples (and, I think, for us who believe through the witness of the disciples, even 2000 years later) in verses 11-19, he indicates the basic needs that they will have as they go on without him. "Keep them, protect them that they may be one as we are; Keep them from the evil one" (protection from evil for the purpose of unity). "That they may have my full measure of joy fulfilled in themselves" and "Sanctify them by your truth" (provision).

When he prays for us, those who will believe, he prays that all believers will be one (underline)partnership(/underline) so that the world may believe that God sent Jesus. And his final prayer is that we who have received Jesus will be with him where he is going and be able then to see his glory. He promises to continue making God known to us so that God's love will be in us and that he, himself, will be in us. We can be one with him, one with the Father, one with all the disciples in all ages. This is how the world will know that Jesus came from God. He came to reveal God to us, full of grace and truth. It is impossible to know where Jesus ended and God began – they were so one. That same kind of oneness is ours when we, like Jesus, fully surrender to God's will and are kept in the center of that will. It is only possible because the Father loves us so much. And it is by his love and our oneness that we will be able to complete the tasks of doing even "greater things" than Jesus did.

This love relationship is purposeful. It supports us as we do his work of bringing the world to him. He loves the people, everyone of us. However, he loves us so much that he has given us free will that lets us choose whether or not we want to love and serve him. When we do and we are then filled with his love, this full, complete love "as he loved Jesus," we are empowered to be like Jesus. We are holy; we have perfect love.

Lord, I "know" this as a fact. I still can hardly believe it! But I want to live it so please keep reminding me. Here is the truth – God loves me as he loved Jesus. That love is in me. It is perfect love. It is holiness. Fill me today with your perfect love!

John 18:1-11

Dinner is over. Jesus and the disciples have moved to the Garden, the olive grove where he often met with his disciples and where Judas knew he would be. He does not run or hide; he knew he would be found. When Jesus saw them coming, he went to meet them. "Who is it you want?" "Jesus of Nazareth," they replied. "I am he," Jesus said, and they drew back and fell to the ground. "I really am he. If you are looking for me, then let these men go." He will do EVERYTHING his Father has given him to do. "I am he!" How bad a sin is betrayal? Is it worse than denial or murder or gossip? How evil was Judas? One gospel says Satan entered him. Did Satan stay? Judas committed suicide. Could he be forgiven? Is Judas the "ultimate" prodigal son? How did Jesus treat Judas as he came closer to what Jesus knew he would do? He seemed to keep giving him ways out. John made a blanket statement in 13:1 – "Having loved his own who were in the world [which meant all the disciples, I think], he now showed them the full extent of his love." And then he washed their feet, including Judas's. His loving heart must have ached for him then, as it did now in the Garden. As for the other disciples, Jesus was determined not to lose any of them.

Lord, you were so willing to go all the way, even through betrayal to death because you knew what the result would be – it was for me, yes, even me! How you love us, even the Judases among us. Help me to see what you can do with me and with those I work with, allowing them to make mistakes, but never giving up on them.

Jesus obviously was aware of the plan for his arrest, maybe even chose it. He didn't have to come to Jerusalem; he didn't have to go to the Garden; he didn't have to stand there and say, "I am he." The twelve disciples with but two swords among them could not have rescued him and he knew it. Peter tried, but that kind of aid he did not need or want. He knew that his time had come. In three short years, he had done everything that his Father had given him to do except this one last thing and that required his arrest.

I think I empathize with Peter when he denied Jesus, maybe even especially the third time. John says that one who questioned him then (18:25) was a relative of the man whose ear Peter had cut off. He was scared! His thinking may have been that if they were going to kill Jesus, surely they would do something to his disciples, but at least he was there, maybe not as close as John who went in with Jesus, but there nonetheless.

On the other hand, he who had been bold so many other times, speaking up when others were silent, stepping out when others only watched, now denies any relationship with Jesus. I am reminded of I Corinthians 10:1-13 where Paul reviews Old Testament examples of people who were like Peter. He ends with a warning and a promise – "Let him who thinks he stands, take heed lest he fall. No temptation has seized you except what is common to man. And God is faithful; he will not let you be tempted beyond what you can bear. But when you are tempted, he will also provide a way out so that you can stand up under it." It is so simple to say, "I don't know him; nope, not me; you must have me confused with someone else." Or by silence – if no one asks, no one will know. But I also know that I don't have to deny; there is a way of escape because God is faithful! Even if I can't think of a "way of escape," or know it could turn out to be the way Jesus went – but what an escape that would be – straight into the arms of Jesus. Examples in our age include people like Dietrich Bonhoffer, - imprisoned, tortured, faithful even unto death or release, willing to suffer for the Master.

May I be bold for you today, Jesus. You remind us in your word that there will be temptation. When it comes, help me remember that and know that you have given me all I need to see me through the temptations that come my way, escape from every temptation and strength in every circumstance. How I praise you!!

Scripture is full of warnings and promises. It seems to me that if I don't heed the warnings, the promises have less meaning. Did Peter forget the warnings and so forget the promises? I think it takes a long walk in intimate relationship with you to become aware of the warnings and the promises that work together to prepare us for the twists and turns on the journey. The song, "Jesus, the very thought of thee with sweetness fills my breast," needs time to become a reality. There is sort of a "Darby and Joan" feel to it – an awe, a comfort, a love, a companionship, a being together in fellowship, complete fulfillment just in presence.

Of course, that is not the end of the story. There are mock trials over the next day, beatings, denial, sentencing, crucifixion, burial – all of which are more familiar. Yes, there are things to learn, but Sunday is coming. Hope isn't far away. Keep on believing!!

POEMS FOR EASTER

⌒

HOW TO GIVE

A Holy Week Event – Luke 21:1-4
Jesus sat watching the temple crowd.
> There wasn't a service;
> They were just visiting –
>> Some, no doubt, came to worship,
>> To spend some time in God's presence,
>> To bring an offering of grain or an animal
>>> So much ritual, so much blood
>>> sacrifice.
>> Some came for show
>> To be seen by others,
>> To present an offering as elaborate and
>> costly as possible,
>>> So much ritual, so much show.

But then out of the corner of his eye,
> A poor widow quietly dropped two cents into the
> box.
> Others had stepped back and thrown in their
> offering –
>> Clattering and clanging as it fell.
> Both had given to God - or so it seemed.
>> They gave out of their wealth -
>>> Maybe even 10%, the required
>>> amount
>>> They still had enough, even plenty.
>> She gave all she had –
>>> All she had!

She now had nothing but God to depend on.

I remember a dramatic presentation of this story.
> The crowd was in church on a Sunday –
> The offering time came and many danced from
> their seats to the front
>> To present their offering with great flourish
> And then a child stood and turned his pockets
> inside out.
>> There was nothing in them.
>> But he took the offering plate
>>> And simply stood in it.
>>>> He gave all he had –
>>>> All he had!!

What do I give? What can I give?
> I think of attitude –
> Will I have enough or is there enough joy in giving?
> Will anyone notice or is anonymity the right attitude?
> Can I still be independent or do I want to be
> dependent on God?
> Will I worry or can I know peace no matter what I
> give?
> There are so many who give so much –
>> Who take time to teach children or a Bible
>> Class or Yoga.
>> Who give up vacation to go on a mission trip
>> without compensation.
>> Who pay their own expenses to serve others.
>> Who give above and beyond a regular
>> contribution for a special project.
>> And yet few give out of their poverty,

All they have,
Their last two cents, if Jesus asks it of them.
Depending totally on God
Because he has asked them to give all.

We need wisdom;
We need faith;
We need courage;
We need graciousness;
We need to give – all!!

ARRESTED

A crowd armed with swords and clubs
sent from the chief priests,
a greeting of "Rabbi" meaning teacher,
a kiss from a disciple –
and suddenly Jesus is seized and arrested.
The crowd must have included soldiers and officials that
could make the arrest.
The other disciples came running,
and one of them cut off the ear of a high priest's servant.
Jesus reached up and healed the ear.
"I'm not here to lead a rebellion.
Why have you come as if I were?
I've been with you every day in the temple.
But Scripture must be fulfilled."
And at that even the soldiers drew back
and fell to the ground.

What were the disciples to do? They all fled.

And how about me?
Where do I see myself in this part of the story?
Would I have cheered when someone cut off the servant's
ear?
Would I have been relieved when Jesus healed him?
Would I have even cut off the servant's ear?
Would I have come running or run the other way?
Would I have fled when it looked like the end?
Would I have followed at a distance, like John?
Would I have remembered what Jesus had said, that this
was inevitable?

Would I have remembered other things he said, something about rising again?

Startled, scared, bold, rebuked, frightened enough to fulfill his words-
They all abandoned Jesus to his mission,
what must at the moment have seemed his fate.
I don't want to be among those who flee in times of danger,
Nor do I want to be a martyr.
What would you do?

THE DENIAL

Peter had been warned –
"You will deny me three times before the cock crows."
But he did follow Jesus, right into the courtyard of the high
priest
And he sat with the guards, warming himself by their fire.
What was he thinking? Was he plotting a rescue?
Did he just want to know what was going on?
Would Jesus need something that he could get for him?
Did he just want to be nearby,
to give Jesus or himself comfort?
Twice a servant girl recognized him as having been with
Jesus
And twice he denied it.
He moved to the gate where a guard suggested
he knew Peter,
recognized him as a Galilean.
Peter cursed and swore!
And then the cock crowed and Peter remembered.
I can imagine him stumbling from that courtyard,
out through the gate.
Weeping in remorse, he realized he was doing exactly
what Jesus had said he would do.
I can get quite upset with Peter.
How could he deny knowing Jesus?
But then I have to ask myself,
"Have I denied knowing you, Lord?
Have I been in a situation where the easy thing to do
would be to say I don't know you?

"No, I'm not part of that church.

I want to be your friend; so, no, I don't know him.
I want to be in this place where Jesus wouldn't come; so,
no, I don't know him.
I like reading this stuff,
watching that stuff on TV,
going to this kind of movie;
so, no, I don't know him."
I forget;
I revert;
I am guilty;
I repent;
I am forgiven
though at times I carry the guilt like Peter did,
for several days or weeks.
I need so many reminders, Lord –
of sins and of forgiveness,
of grace and mercy, of love,
but also that you always provide a way of escape.
I do not have to sin against you;
I do not have to deny you.

I wonder, was the servant girl interested in Jesus.
Here was Peter's opportunity to say something
to her about him.
I wonder, was the guard curious about Jesus.
Did Peter, nervous as he was, miss a chance
to tell them about him?
Peter cursed and then broke down and wept.
Why was he cursing himself –
For even being there?
For denying?

For not speaking up?
For seeing himself as a coward?
For not being able to own his relationship with you?
Jesus knew his heart, his motivation.
Jesus knew he would fail but
Jesus also knew that Peter could change his mind
afterwards,
would repent,
would help his brothers.

I will fail, and you know it,
and you will redeem my failure.
Redeem it so completely that I, too, will be able to help my
"brothers" and my sisters.
Oh, may it be so!!

WHERE WERE THEY?

There was a crowd there yelling, "Crucify him!"
Who were they?
Who was there?
Who was missing?
Was there no one with any influence to save?
No one to speak on your behalf.
Where were the disciples?
Where were the people you'd healed?
Where were those who had responded to your teaching?
Or were they there and just silent,
There and scared, intimidated by the crowd?
There and unheard over the noise?
Was there no one who knew who you were?
No one who really loved you?
No one who was committed to following you?
No one whose life had been changed?
Why? Where were they? Had hope run out?
Where was I?

"AND THEY CRUCIFIED HIM"

We've never seen a crucifixion
Except in the movies or on TV
Or read about them
in commentaries or novels
And we are horrified!
Even the Gospel writers don't tell us much –
Simply "they crucified him."
But they knew what it was like –
They had seen them and they didn't want to see another.
Only John and a few faithful women were there.
Three hours he hung, suspended between heaven and earth.
The soldiers shared his clothes and cast lots
for his seamless robe.
Thieves were hung on either side of him.
A sign was posted above him, "King of the Jews."
Insults were hurled at him by those who passed by.
Priests and scholars mocked him.
He was thirsty but refused
the drugs they offered.
He spoke some words,
Words of forgiveness,
Words of comfort and caring.
But basically, He just hung there;
He could have come down, but he just hung there.
And then he cried out with a loud voice -
"It is finished."
And he died.
That death meant salvation for the world!
He didn't save himself; he saved you and me.
He didn't do it so "they" would believe; he did it so that

all who believe could be saved.
He didn't have to do it;
He did it because he loved the world he had created.
He did the one thing he could not do in Heaven – He died!
He didn't come down from the Cross;
he came up from the grave.
But that's another story.
Stay tuned!!

WAIT

The Pieta, a lovely, loving statue
Carved by Michelangelo
Of Mary holding the crucified, dead Christ.
What was she thinking as she held him?
Was this the end?
Was she taking last moments with his broken body?
Was she waiting to see what would happen next?
You never know in God's world!
I am waiting, Lord, unsure yet hopeful,
Uncertain of myself yet sure of you.
You've got something in mind,
Something already at work.
Where will it lead?
How will it affect me?
You never know in God's world!

SILENT SATURDAY

"He's dead," the centurion on duty declared;
It was about 3:00 in the afternoon on Friday.
"We can't leave him there," his followers exclaimed.
"I have a tomb; I will take responsibility,"
said Joseph of Arimethea.
And so began the gruesome task
Of getting permission,
Of taking him down,
Of carrying him from Golgotha,
Of placing him in the borrowed tomb,
Of rolling the stone into place,
Of leaving him there -
All before sundown, before the Sabbath began.
No time for a funeral or a memorial service -
Maybe that would come later.
No time for mourning or to properly prepare his body -
The women would come back on Sunday.

Where were the disciples, the eleven?
Maybe John, to whom Jesus had entrusted his mother,
Had taken her away from this place of death.
Imagine her grief!
But two men, neither of whom was an apostle,
Assumed the awful task of burying Jesus,
As some women watched and followed –
They needed to know.

And where would I have been?
Hiding, fearful of getting involved?
Standing at a distance with the women?

Watching Joseph and Nicodemus?
Helping them carry the body?
Rolling the stone into place?

Saturday, the Sabbath, sundown to sundown
A day of rest,
A day of worship,
A day of gathering in the temple or synagogue,
Were they all together hiding out?
Did they discuss the happenings of yesterday,
of how he was treated?
Did they reflect on Jesus' teachings?
Did they remember that he had said he would rise again?
Did anyone express hope?

IT'S SUNDAY!!

Yes, it's Sunday – time to take the spices to the tomb.
Mary Magdalene, Mary, Salome leave just after sunrise
"Who will move the stone?" they wonder.
But someone already has – what does that mean?
They went into the rock hewn tomb and there sat a young
man,
Dressed in white,
Sitting on the right side.
He couldn't have moved the stone; it was huge.
They were alarmed.
"Don't be alarmed! Jesus, the Nazarene, who was crucified,
is risen.
"He is not here, as you can see.
"See the place where they laid him."
Mary knew the place, the exact place where they had laid
him
She'd been with them, there, and now he isn't there.
"Go, tell his disciples, and Peter, that he is going to Galilee.
There you will see him, just as he told you."
The women were stunned, amazed, incredulous.
Did they remember the promises Jesus had made,
Especially the one about rising on the third day?
Had the men even told them what Jesus had said about
rising?
Or did they just run away, flee the tomb and say nothing as
the Gospel of Mark suggests.

I prefer a different ending –
as the other three Gospels tell it.
Mary Magdalene ran back and told Peter and John.

They also came running, but saw no one –
they were slow to believe
In fact, they left Mary crying at the tomb.
And Jesus came to her, revealed himself to her,
and she believed.

Two disciples headed out to Emmaus, walking along,
talking about what had happened.
Jesus came and walked with them,
but they didn't recognize him,
Until they stopped for the night and he revealed himself
when he broke bread.
Their hearts burned within them and they believed.

The eleven were gathered in hiding sharing their grief
When Jesus walked through the wall and said,
"Peace be with you."
Hard to believe, but he showed them his wounds;
he ate some fish;
And they believed.

He met 8 of the disciples in Galilee and they shared
breakfast
on the seashore.
Later Jesus appeared to 500 at one time.
It takes a lot of seeing to believe.

And I, I have not "seen" him alive. And, yes, I believe!
And you ask, "How do you know he is alive?"
"You ask me how I know he lives?
He lives within my heart."

AWED BY THE HOLY SPIRIT

It seems to me that when Jesus left the world, the disciples really thought they were about to be plunged back into the darkness of Roman rule and religious bigotry. But the Holy Spirit came to keep the Light bright, a Light that would shine on and on and on, a Light that we have within us, that we hold out for all to see. Ponder his Light shining through you. Keep it bright!!

LEAD ME, MAKE ME, GIVE ME

Holy Spirit, lead me -
Lead me beside still waters where I can listen to you,
hear your voice;
Lead me in paths of righteousness where I can do right
things;
Lead me where you want me to go, being obedient to your
will;
Lead me into life, yes, Life Everlasting then,
but life abundant now;
Lead me to holiness, living a godly life
that pleases you and me, too;
Lead me gently because sometimes I rebel against force,
but never or seldom against gentleness;
Lead me in triumphal procession in this world,
spreading everywhere the fragrant aroma of Christ.

Holy Spirit, make me –
Make me what I ought to be, like Jesus;
Make me able to accomplish today what you have for me
to do;
Make me a "fisher of men" or a shepherd of your flock
or whatever I am to be;
Make me "fit to be they dwelling," cleaning out
every secret closet of my soul;
Make me content with who I am and what I have;
Make me glad so that I can sing your praises;
Make me whole, wholly thine,
and, in fact, holy as you work in me today.

Holy Spirit, give me –

Give me a robe of righteousness indicating that I am yours;
Give me peace like a river, even when the world,
even my world, is chaotic;
Give me "daily bread" not just "mine" but show me
how to give to others;
Give me songs in the night whatever, whenever, wherever
I am;
Give me power to live the holy life that I am capable of in
you;
Give me courage to step out to new things
as well as things I know I can do;
Give me grace, that amazing grace that can save me
and keep me and make me what I can be in you.

GIFT OF LIFE

We who are children of light are not "different" by what we do or do not do, though our behavior should be different and distinctive. It is mainly on the inside – in our thought-life and in our feelings - that we are different. Our thoughts dwell on what is good (Psalm 4:8) and our dominant feeling is love, for ourselves as well as for others. Life is a gift from God and what is difficult is allowed by God. Joy and peace, however, are dominant. God believes in me!!

DESIRES

If what I desire is contrary to God's will, he will gradually change my desire. What do I desire today? Where is my focus? Do those desires focus on me and what I want or even need? Or do they focus on God's kingdom and his righteousness as Jesus suggested they should? Does God need to change, modify, uproot my desires?

I really want to have enough significant things to do. Is "significant" a good word, a godly word or will he want me to do mundane things, rather than what I might think are significant things? Is it my desire to develop a good relationship with whomever I encounter? To love my family so that I have more knowledge and insight to know how to do and say what is best. To have a clean house. To write emails that are meaningful and will bless. To choose things to do what will honor God throughout the day. To keep focused on God's kingdom and his righteousness.

BRING ON THE LIGHT

Isaiah. 9:2-7 – Because these verses refer to a coming king for the Jews, then my cry today is, "Do it again, Lord!" Send us a ruler with your authority and power who will fix things! On the other hand, I know that the verses are a prophecy of Jesus' coming and in a sense of his coming again in order for the prophecy to be completed. I see its fulfillment in Jesus who came as the Light to dispel the darkness, not just in the nation, but in individuals and communities who turn to you, who repent, change their minds after hearing your word. You bring joy, freedom and peace in place of grief, bondage, conflict and war. So many live in a "land of deep darkness," but on each one light can shine as they hear your word, as we tell them about you! Slums in the U.S. or in India, the bush in Africa, an oppressive marriage or work environment, places of slavery, human trafficking – no joy, no peace! But the Light is great, it is very bright. It can be seen as I carry the Light of Life wherever I go. "On them has the light shined."

AWARENESS

Awareness of God, of his presence, is becoming ever more consistent for me. I see him in events and I am aware of him as I move through my day – aware of him quieting my heart, exciting my spirit, teaching and reminding me how to react, how to control my racing thoughts and emotions and replace them with new ones. Some day I'd like to be able to say with Theresa of Avila, "There is nothing in me that is not God; my 'me' is God.'" Of course I have to understand what that means for me. I guess I come back to "what would Jesus do if he were I" because I am the "me" he created and that won't change, but what he keeps working on is making my actions and reactions my thoughts and words, my emotions and ideas more in tune with his will – a consciousness even in my sub-conscience of God, his Spirit, his guidance in my everyday living. It is so freeing to know that he has a "perfect me" in his mind, and I can be conscious of being that me! "My 'me' is God" – rightly understood and lived out.

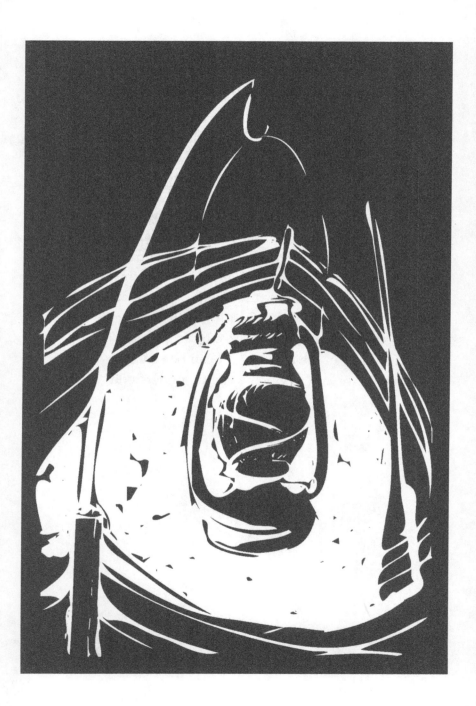

CONSIDERING DISCIPLESHIP

What did Jesus mean when he said, "Follow me?" It's different than what we do when we follow the waitress to our restaurant table. It's more than we are when we become "believers." That's just the beginning of our journey. It has taken me years of listening to the Holy Spirit, discovering what discipleship really is and what he wants to do with me at the various times of my life to get further up and further into understanding where he wants me to be. May these ponderings lead you in your walk with him.

EXAMINING DISCIPLESHIP
LISTEN, WAIT, HOPE:
Isaiah 9:1

"But there is no gloom for those who were in anguish," because you will "make glorious" the land where you walk!" These people, the disciples of Isaiah and Isaiah himself, could only wait and hope. They never saw or heard God, but they did wait and hope. Sometimes that's all we can do too – whatever our prayer might be. We can accept the circumstances. God knows every need; he has the answers and how to get to them. Wait and hope, focused on God. Do not call conspiracy all that "they" call conspiracy! Do not fear what "they" fear! God and God alone is our hope – who is like him? And his way is holy!!

Isaiah 28:23

Keep listening and pay attention! God teaches how to plant – don't keep on harrowing!! – and how to harvest – use the right equipment! He is wonderful in counsel and excellent in wisdom. He teaches me how to do things correctly, when to do what and how, when to stop and wait, what to plant when and where and how, when to stop and wait. The Dutch have developed new farming methods – indoors, LED lighting, controlled temperature, organic pesticides, and it ends in a huge crop. I'm sure it is wisdom from God, proven through experimentation, and successful, as it spreads around the world. "God teaches them!" They are well instructed! Thank you for counsel and wisdom in the things we need to know, including our daily lives.

Isaiah 41:1

"Listen to me in silence!" – just listen, listen to the end without interruption! It was important for the Israelites to listen to all God had to say in Chapter 41 because he has warnings and directions and hope to give, but unless they are silent they will not hear the end. They might not realize that they are precious, loved, honored in God's sight. They might miss the words, "Don't be afraid for I am with you." "By flood and flame surrounded I still my way pursue; nor shall I be confounded with glory with in my view. Still Christ is my salvation – what can I covet more? SASB #361 I fear no condemnation; my Father's wrath is o'er." I can be calm in the midst of anything, my heart in tune with him. He can give me the ability to think, to pray, to pursue my way until I come out safely on the other side, one way or another. "Do not fear for I am with you!"

TEMPTATION

"You will hear a voice behind you saying, 'This is the way; walk in it.'" (Isaiah 30:21)

"No temptation has seized you except what is common to man. And God is faithful; he will not let you be tempted beyond what you can bear. But when you are tempted, he will also provide a way out so that you can stand up under it." (I Corinthians 10:13)

I want to claim these promises today! There is nothing that can tempt me that I am not able to overcome by escaping it by the means God provides. How good he is to provide that escape, which is never hard to find if I choose to find it! The choice then is mine to take it. The testing, the temptation can be part of the process of growth for me. I see areas that need refining, places where I succumb to old ways that I ought to have overcome, or thought I had given up. There are times when I feel I have given them up, ways I no longer give in to temptation, and then how I praise you! I have had an addiction – an addiction to selfishness and I praise God for, at least, a partial victory – aware that I must still watch out. When I think I am standing firm, I must be careful that I don't fall (I Corinthians 10:12). May I see and take God's way of escape for me when I am tempted to still be selfish.

Complacency: Isaiah 32:9-15

Being complacent and too at ease in the midst of spiritual warfare in not good! The women of Isaiah's day were warned that in a year everything would be gone "until a spirit from on high is poured out on us..." Complacency is ignoring, doing nothing about the evil we see in ourselves and in others, in situations around us. At times my cry is, "But what can I do?" I know I can pray and rest in the Lord and wait and sometimes and in some situations that's what I should do. The Lord might guide me to do something, say something in other situations. Then I need the courage to do or say what he would say if he were I.

Isaiah goes on to say that justice and righteousness will come from on high and there will come peace, quietness, and trust. "The effect of righteousness will be peace," which is available to every human heart now, "and the result of righteousness will be quiet and trust," also available to every heart now! God's blessings are for now, not just for Heaven; they are known only to the heart of the believer, but they can be seen as a witness to the world. They are our present experiences if we are among the righteous, when we receive them through Jesus. If we lived under persecution we might see them as "yet-to-be," and we must be careful not to take the peace, quiet, and trust for granted. There are and always will be trials and challenges, but the fact remains that in Christ we still have all we need to live at peace and in security now.

SHEDDING LIGHT: Isaiah 60

"Arise, shine for your light has come." Can you see it? Can you feel it? "The glory of the Lord has risen on you." There may be darkness in lots of places, but the Lord will arise on you. Christians always bring light, whether to a nursing home or a neighborhood, a group gathering, small or large – others will see our "good works and glorify our Father who is in Heaven." Unbelievers are drawn to a Christian presence whether they realize it or not, because God shines through us. Nurses and doctors, neighbors and friends are impressed by a Christian's attitude and actions and will then come to our aid or ask about our behavior, want to be with us – or not!

Isaiah describes our being in this way – God says, "I will appoint Peace as your overseer and Righteousness as your taskmaster. There will be no violence, devastation or destruction. You shall call your walls Salvation and your gates Praise" (Isaiah 60:17,18). Beyond the city walls and gates, God guards each individual. No real harm can come upon those who trust in you. It might not look like it, but we are secure in him. Psalm 16:8,9 says, "I have set the Lord always before me. Because he is at my right hand, I will not be shaken. Therefore my heart is glad and my soul rejoices; my body rests secure." Others see that in us, the light that shines in the darkness, and they are glad!

Anger and Meekness

Meekness teaches me when to be angry, how to be angry and how far I must or must not go to be angry. The meek are generally peaceful, like Jesus, but at the right time are able to be angry (Be angry and sin not) and to appropriately express their anger. That's not weakness, but like Jesus, humility, a proper sense of who I am and who God is. The earth that the meek inherit will be peaceful, no longer needing anger. But for now, anger is occasionally appropriate, taught by meekness. Maybe another word for meekness would be helpful – like humility, that right sense of who I am and who God is.

Anger -   You drove the money changers out of the temple.

Meekness - You called little children to your side.

Anger -   You told the Pharisees and scribes just what you thought of them.

Meekness - You loved the woman caught in adultery.

Can you teach me how to be angry with meekness?

Can you teach me the right time and place to express anger?

Can you teach me when it is appropriate to be angry so that I do not sin?

Meekness, humility – Help me get it right!

CHRISTIAN GROUPS

In our church we have many "small groups," groups who gather with a specific aim in mind, like archery class or Holy Yoga or Bible Study groups or to build strong families, or groups that gather for fellowship or bike riding or 4 wheeling. Each of them has an agenda to build up one another, to encourage Christian growth and relationships, to be a witness to those who might come who are not believers.

However, not all "Christian groups" act like we think Christian groups should act. There is sometimes a sense of competition, of who can belong and who can't, of childishness. Those attitudes kind of defeat the name "Christian" as well as defeating the purpose of having the group in the first place.

Dallas Willard, in one of his books gives some guidelines something like this for how Christian groups could and can act.

1. See myself as a whole, blessed no matter what happens.

2. Abandon defensiveness!

3. Have genuine love for one another.

4. Do my part, including giving up my part to let another.

If each member of any group will adopt these guidelines, each person can extend himself in blessing each life he or she touches, devoting our lives in service to others with genuine warmth and welcome.

Romans 12:3-8, 9-21

GOD'S REQUIREMENTS

Isaiah 56:1-8 – "Maintain justice and do what is right." Those commands include right actions towards "eunuchs and foreigners." Could it be that we could turn those words toward homosexuals and immigrants. All that is required of them is keeping the Sabbath and keeping the covenant – not membership or other "churchy" requirements. God says he will give them a monument and an everlasting name. They, with us, can be joyful in God's house of prayer, a house of prayer for all people. The outcasts will be gathered with his people.

However, in verses 9-12 God raises a warning for the outcasts. They will not all be received and welcomed by the leaders, the sentinels and the shepherds. This group is failing in their jobs to protect and guide. They've gone their own way, seeking their own comfort. But the outcasts are to be gathered – don't be afraid. We must all grapple with our feelings about various groups of people and realize that our watchword is love!

NO RUSH

I understand Jesus' need to get away from the people – 5,000 of them (or 50 or 20 or even 10). Jesus needed time alone with his Father, and so do you and I! Since it was evening before the storm came up, it must have been noon or mid-afternoon when he took time to feed the 5,000, which would have taken time, and then he directed the cleanup, and he had been teaching all day. He sent the disciples into the boat and went off by himself to pray.

Now it is evening and a storm came up. He saw the disciples straining at the oars, trying to keep the boat on course, too strong a wind to keep the sail up. But he didn't go to them until at least 3:00 a.m.

He never rushed; he spent this valuable time with his Father; he had his priorities straight. And he knew that all would be well. As we are with him, in him, and he in us, there is no need to rush. He comes with us, to us, walking on whatever is around us, to where we are. We know he comes and we are not afraid, and he speaks peace to our inward soul. "Take courage," whatever the circumstances; "don't be afraid." Be amazed! We need to learn to reflect on those instances. We won't learn if we don't reflect! We'll be like the disciples who hadn't understood, hadn't learned, had "hard hearts" about some things Jesus had shown them, the bread, the storm. Remember! Think; reflect; trust; believe; don't let your heart be troubled.

Jesus got them across the lake and he returned to the familiar scenes of healing which by now were okay with the disciples. They could be calm in that scenario – and it didn't affect them or their lives. "All who touched him were healed!" And the disciples were safe. How did they process that storm and Jesus' walking on the water? Did the experience soften their hearts? It happened; Jesus saved them!

TRAPPED

Jesus associated with religious people and with sinners. We ought to be doing the same – saints and sinners alike. We enjoy and need the time with fellow believers but our task, our mission, is to call the sinners, not the righteous to repentance. Of course we also can be aware of the self-righteous as Jesus often was. They usually do not put themselves in the category of sinners so it is best if I do not put them there as I talk with them.

There are often three categories of people with Jesus – the disciples (Jesus' followers, the learners or apprentices), the sinners (who were eager to hear Jesus), and the Pharisees and scribes (who saw themselves as "righteous" because they obeyed the laws to what they saw as the nth degree). Jesus saw the sinners as closer to the Kingdom than the "righteous" because they were honest and at least some of them were seeking God's kind of life.

Do I have the tendency to label some people as "Pharisees" and others as "sinners"? Is that label a result of discernment from the Holy Spirit or is it judgment based on legalism? What I do know is that what I need to do is love the person or persons and let the Spirit guide my relationship with him or her. I have to avoid falling into the trap that I might be accusing others of being in.

POEMS OF DISCIPLESHIP

THE CROWD

They are poor in spirit, mourners;
They are wimps,
They are hungry and thirsty.
But wait – they are kind and pure;
They work for peace;
They are persecuted for that;
They are the "sat upon, spat upon, ratted on."
They are just the crowd.

But look again; see what Jesus saw –
They are not spiritually arrogant.
Theirs is already the kingdom of heaven.
They may be mourning – loss of husband or wife or child,
a job and security, friends, health, some body part.
It may take time but they will be comforted!
They are meek, gentle, humble towards everything and
everyone. They are the ones who will inherit the earth
because they have taken good care of it.
They hunger and thirst for righteousness, for rightness.
It's never complete, never completely satisfied;
there's always more, a desire to go further up and further
in. And yet there's a moment by moment satisfaction.
They are the ones who are merciful, kind,
compassionate, helpful,
without thought of recompense or reward.
Others will respond and show them mercy,

and so will God on a daily basis.
They have pure hearts, clear motives, good attitudes,
pleasing God because they want to.
People like that see God all around them.
The purer they become the more they can see Him.
They are peacemakers, like Jesus, the Prince of Peace,
sort of all the others wrapped up in this one,
an inner experience that they share
when others are "out of peace."

Do you speak today?

Your words and God the Father's are in the Bible and they speak quite clearly – if we have ears to hear and minds and hearts that will take in what we hear. We can listen to the Spirit as he gives understanding and then we can respond with obedience. The question may not be, "Do you speak?" but, "Do I hear?"

For Moses, the 40 year old, for Samuel, the 12 year old, you broke through using their names. Do you still speak my name to get my attention? The song says,

> "Speak to me by name, my Master.
> Let me know it is to me.
> Speak that I may follow faster,
> With a step more firm and free.
> I am listening, Lord, for thee.
> Master, speak, oh speak to me."
> Salvation Army Song Book #775, vs. 2

At 40 Moses responded, "Here I am!" But when he heard what you wanted him to do, he had a dozen excuses – "Who am I? Who do I say you are? Can I have a sign? How about another one? I'm not eloquent! Send someone else!" God had an answer for every one of them.

At 12 Samuel responded, "Here I am. Speak, Lord, for your servant is listening." The message God had for Samuel was as intense, as frightening as the one he had for Moses. But Scripture records that 12 year old Samuel made no excuses. He simply went back to bed until morning and then opened the doors of the house of the Lord and when Eli asked him about what God said, he willingly told it all.

I think when I was 12, I would have gone anywhere, done anything, said any word God wanted. When I was 40 I made excuses why I couldn't go there, do that or say what he wanted me to say.

Now when I hear my name, I respond, "Here I am, your servant is listening." But I'm still learning to obey.

I'M GOING TO TRY, LORD

I was going to say, "I'm going to try."
But then I realize, I've tried before,
Even over and over again!
Let me say instead,
"I will keep your precepts diligently – with your help!
"My way will be established – in your strength!
"I will be faithful – as I remember!
"I will be obedient - as I rely on your Spirit!
"I will praise you without ceasing –
as I know your presence."

I will do more than try.

HOSPITALITY

Welcome to my home
That's what the sign on the door says.
But do I mean it? What do I mean?
What does it mean to show hospitality?
Saint Benedict and his interpreters say it is form of worship.
What does that mean?

When I worship I should be very aware of the presence of
God.
When others are in my home I should be
very aware of their presence –
Very focused on them, undistracted by my own stuff.

When I worship I should pay attention to God and what he
is saying to me.
When others are in my home I should be
very aware of what they are saying -
Very focused on what they are saying, and not saying.

When I worship I should listen carefully for what God
is needing from me.
When others are in my home I should be very aware of
what they are needing from me.
Very aware of what they may not be asking.

When I worship I should be very respectful of who God is!
When others are in my home I should be very respectful
of who they are.
Very aware of them as children of God, whether they know
it or not.

AN ATTITUDE OF HUMILITY

An attitude of humility
Empty of anything that made Jesus God (except love)
A human slave to all –
Including his willing death for all,
Of all places – on a cross!
The mind of Christ –
Think about what it cost Him.
Study the process;
Look where it led Him;
Can I go that way?
Should I go that way?
Do I want to go that way?

Take a deep breath –
Rest in him, in his plan, his plan for me.
I know that as I do the Father's will,
All will be well!!
Trust Him!!

HEAVEN'S PLAN

Heaven had a plan,
A plan for man's redemption.
God gave every person a free will,
Even knowing we would flaunt it!
An historic plan –
A nation that would fail!
A remnant that would not succumb to temptation!
A plan to replace all other plans –
A man to become the necessary blood sacrifice
A man to take away the sins of the world.
A man to die for all.
A plan to endure the cross
Despising the shame,
And then sit down at the right hand of the Father
Highly exalted,
And every knee shall bow
And every tongue confess that Jesus is Lord.
What a plan!!

KNOWN

Lord, you want to know me,
Fully, intimately
Because you love me
Deeply, completely.
Fact is, you already know me
Better than I know me
But I'm not sure I want to admit that I'm like I am.
Or that I even know that I am like I am.
Lord of love, in love you can help me see me
And I will not be afraid of what you reveal to me
In love.

A seed needs soil, light, warmth, moisture
and time to unlock its vitality.
What do I still lack?

THE MIND OF CHRIST

Paul says we have it, Lord! (I Corinthians 2:16)
How can that be?
"Let this same mind be in you which was in Christ Jesus."
Ah ha – we have to LET it be in us.
What then? If I have the mind of Christ –
I will have his kind of attitude.
I will rest in him.
I will let him do his work in me.
I will do his work in his way.
He let the Father lead him –
No "I should" or "I ought to" about it.
Simply and completely trusting in the Father's plan,
Wanting to do his will.
An attitude of humility,
Empty of anything godlike (except love),
A human slave to all –
Including his willing death for all,
Of all places – on a cross!
The mind of Christ –
Study the process.
Look where it led Him.
Can I go that way?
Should I go that way?
Do I want to go that way?

Take a deep breath!
Rest in him, in his plan, his plan for me!
As I do the Father's will,
All will be well!

THOUGHTS FOR THE SABBATH

A day of Rest:

"And on the seventh day God rested
from all the work he had done."
God had a plan, a pattern he established,
not just for himself but for us.
"He blessed the 7th day and hallowed it
because on it God rested from all the work
that he had done in creation."
Rest for everyone according to his words to Moses -
For me, my children, my servants and animals
and the strangers among us.
Remember the creation story;
Remember the Exodus from Egypt;
Observe the day by keeping it holy;
It's good for you!!

After Jesus came there is a shift -
To a daily relationship with God through the Holy Spirit,
A more personal, one-on-one time with Him,
In remembrance of creation and Christ,
Of deliverance from sin and sinning.
Observing the Lord's Day –
A celebration of Jesus' resurrection,
Though not necessarily a specific day.
Time for soul rest –
"Take my yoke…
Learn from me…
And you will find rest for your soul."

It's a bigger perspective,
a personal perspective.
A personal relationship,
A way of life,
A rhythm for living,
A sacramental life,
A life of caring, worshipping and fellowship.

The Sabbath, a day of rest.

THOUGHTS ON DISCIPLESHIP

WHAT CAN I DO? WHAT I CAN DO.

Jesus, you had the power to raise the dead – the widow's son at Nain, the centurion's daughter, Lazarus. I don't even have the power to relieve a headache – or do I? I think I have some power to relieve, but maybe not to cure. Henri Nouwen says that when he was confronted with a death, he realized that his ministry lay more in powerlessness than in power. "I could give her only my tears." What do people really need in times of need? They might want a cure, a healing, but maybe all I can give is my tears, my compassion, my reach to understand, a touch of my hand. Lord, help me see what I can do, make me aware, alert to the need. I may be "powerless" to cure, but have the ability from you to care, to be there.

MISSING GOD

During the exile and at many points in Scripture, both Old and New Testaments, we see people who, because of circumstances into which they have gotten themselves, either blame God or see him as weak. "Why was no one there when I came?" God asks. How often do we miss God when he comes to help, to rescue, to be with us? "Is my arm shortened that it cannot redeem?" you ask. No, we know it is never too short to reach us, to redeem us. The Lord can do anything and it is always for our good, even the discipline we need. It all reveals who he is and why we must, should, even enjoy following him. The consequences of not heeding the discipline or not responding to who he is are not pleasant. May we be well disciplined, obedient children, not just to please him but to help us become what we can be, what he made us to be.

GOD'S FORGIVENESS

I worked in the hospital gift shop, a novice with the cash register and prone to mistakes, even after 10 years of bi-weekly working there. If I am away for awhile, usually on a trip somewhere, I make more mistakes than usual, sometimes really messing up, but the nice thing to know is that the gal in charge can fix anything I might do wrong!! And she always forgives me!!

I don't think I even know how much God forgives; he just does!! I'm in his hands – what a great place to be!!

GETTING MY WAY

I wonder if I am doing better at accepting when I do not get my way, at not pouting when it doesn't happen, at being content, even rejoicing in compromise or better yet working towards concensus? "Not getting their way doesn't disturb them" – that's a definition of someone who is unselfish, but how do we arrive at such a place? A first step is to realize that I do not have to get my way! I can explain my thoughts calmly and logically and then listen to the other, looking for points of agreement and places where we can come together.

When it comes to what God wants I can do the same, realizing that he knows best from the get-go. I can try to understand his will but sometimes I just don't. If I don't understand it, I can learn to do his will anyway and I can rest in him. I can be flexible with others and let everyone, including God, do their job.

Which question do I ask myself when making choices, "What good can I bring about?" or "How can I get my way?" Like Mary, helping in the kitchen or listening to the discussion, or like me, cleaning the kitchen (my Saturday morning chore), or having breakfast with someone – I can get both done! Do I escape to the kitchen? Sometimes I think I do, but is it always the wrong thing to do? The right thing?

LIVE NORMALLY

I find it is important to me to live life "normally," to have routines, maybe even rituals. God has given us routines to help order our lives – sunrise, sunset, seasons, time in hours and minutes, Sundays or another day for Sabbath which should be different from other days. I thoroughly enjoy rising in the morning, doing some stretching exercises, making coffee, going to my quiet place for an hour with Scripture and prayer beginning with a Psalm for meditation, some study of God's Word and time to reflect and praise and pray. Routines like this are good for me, but I do need to change my order, sometimes my process so that I do not become too routine, bored even, doing it without thought. It is amazing to me that God's word is always fresh and new. It is I who might become stale.

MOTIVATION

St. Benedict says, "God is more concerned with our motives than our failures." Now that's a great thing to remember! I am in charge of leading a Bible Study that seems to be a flop, but I have prayed and studied, prepared and wanted nothing more than to glorify Him, but I feel like a failure so why am I doing this? I go to visit a friend in the hospital and I can't think of the words that will help or comfort or do anything positive for him, but I love him and want health and wellbeing for him, but I feel like a failure so why am I doing this? I am leading worship in the power of the Spirit but no one is enthusiastic in the worship group or in the congregation and I feel like a failure so why am I doing this? What is my motive? God sees my motive, not what I perceive as my failure. It is good to know that.

Nobody's Perfect

Now there's an excuse if I ever heard one! What can we say instead when we know we have failed in some way? "I believe in God's power to transform me into a radical person who does what is right in this circumstance." (i.e. – who pays loving attention to those who annoy me.) There are so many promises to us about living a holy life, a Christlike life!! I know it can be done, without excuses!!

LOVELESSNESS

Assault and withdrawal are two forms of lovelessness which must be broken and disarmed, eliminated! In their place will come constant mutual blessing, make way for the other. "Try to grin in blessing at memories instead of attacking." We do not need to assault or withdraw, but we can bless, grin, enjoy.

WEAKNESSES

God says, "It's all right to be human!" But I must admit that I don't like to be weak, to have a less than clean house, to know there is a closet full of ironing that I promised to do, that there are a string of emails that I "should" write but don't have the energy for. I'm finding it hard to accept those simple weaknesses, those things I can't get my mind around or put out of my mind.

I read that God can use my weaknesses for his glory, but I need to know how to handle them. I want to be adorned with a gentle and quiet spirit that speaks of Jesus in whatever way he wants me to speak. I know I am a "clay jar" that can be used to "show that this all-surpassing power is from God and not from us" (II Corinthians 4:7). I know that "my grace is sufficient for you" and that "whenever I am weak, then I am strong" (II Corinthians 12:8, 10). I know it, but help me to believe it and live it.

TONGUE

Control it and remain silent. Speaking is a sure sign of arrogance so listen and learn humbly. We learn to take ourselves more lightly in the presence of good humor. The humble person cultivates a soul in which everyone is safe. Speak gently, briefly, seriously without raising your voice. We stand in the face of others without taking up all the space. You are God and I am not – what a relief. No exaggerated approval or guilt.

The body needs to be retrained. Doing what Jesus said and did increasingly becomes a part of who we are. I must "subject my tongue (and every other body part) to the grace of God as an instrument reserved to do his will." Then grace comes literally to inhabit and govern it. (D. Willard)

THE MIRACLE OF RELIEF

Life happens! A daughter gets a blow from her advisor and she has to start all over on her doctoral paper. A grandson does a drug overdose. A son is caught dealing drugs. A friend has a horrendous accident. I get sick. The world is in chaos. Life seems to come crashing in. But then, but then with an unexpected suddenness I see a light; I feel the gentle breeze of peace. I can breathe again. It may be a word in a conversation, the memory of beauty, or a wild flower-covered hillside, or just the right word from the Word, or even from a friend – "the miracle of relief." How we need the quiet ministry of the living Spirit of the living God.

AN INNER QUIET

An inner quiet allows me to discern the voice of the Spirit more distinctly. And I think that's a fact, whether alone or in a crowd – an inner quiet. That inner quiet helps me know whether I am "hearing" myself, the evil one, or truly the Holy Spirit. I am certain that God, the Spirit helps me know what to say, what to send, how to respond, what to do.

THE WORLD

The world is a needy place and it cannot meet our needs. It can give us information, but I must learn what to do with that information. It can give us challenges, ministry opportunities, a chance to let our lights shine. The fruit of the Spirit can grow and flourish in the world's environment. The Holy Spirit can prove his power through our weaknesses. Even in the world we have a chance to express our love, to fulfill our purpose which is to meet the world's needs, both physical and spiritual – that's what we are called to do. But it can't meet our needs. Only God can do that!

The Message of Jesus

"The time has come....The time of your salvation....The Kingdom of God is near....Repent and believe the good news." In other words, change your mind after you hear this. It's true!!

WHO TOUCHED ME?

Did you really have to embarrass this woman, Lord? She was embarrassed enough by all she had been through, ostracized by the community, driven to poverty by doctors who couldn't cure her. But then you knew what she really needed and it wasn't just healing! She needed to know more of what you could and would do. If you hadn't called out to her – "Who touched me?" – she might have thought that she could reach out and touch you any time she had a problem, an illness, a need. She might have brought along a pair of scissors to cut off a piece of your garment that she could touch any time. You needed to make it clear that it was her faith that had healed her. She needed to come to you to acknowledge you as her healer. There is no mention of sin, just healing, freedom, peace, and rest.

The Vineyard

In Isaiah 27 God declares, "I, the Lord, am its keeper," referring to how he cares for Israel as for a vineyard. In John 14 Jesus refers to himself as the vine and implies that God is still the keeper of the vineyard. God does say that he will destroy the vineyard if it yields thorns and briars, but if it is restored, Israel will "fill the world with fruit." Jesus says that we as his people can bear much fruit as his disciples, as we abide in the vine. Jesus describes us as branches attached to him though geographically spread throughout the world, unlike the vineyard which was Israel in Isaiah's day. We, as branches however, are each attached to the vine through the Holy Spirit, loving each other, hated by the world, full of joy and peace in Christ, bearing fruit (John 15:1-8).

OIL and WATER

The soil in which things grow best is not a pleasant thing to think about – dead stuff, manure (fertilizer, they call it), mulched by insects and earthworms and bacteria – humus, humility – "to be brought low." "I want the Cliff Notes to faith, not the whole book." (Gire) I want humility, but am I willing to be humiliated to get it? Jesus is our example!

Ken Gire likens the Holy Spirit to the needed ingredient for growth – water! "What water is to the seed, the Spirit of God is to the Word of God." While anyone can read Scripture and understand something of what it says, it takes the work of the Spirit to make it personal, an application to the human heart – the warm, intimate truth God wants to send. Sometimes the seed falls just to lie dormant for a time, waiting for the rain to fall, and it does!

REIGNING WITH HIM

Surrender...abandonment...contentment...participation! Romans 5:17 – we are reigning (yes, even now) in life through Jesus Christ." (That's a verse I have not seen/ noticed before.) D. Willard says we are looking forward to an eternity of reigning with God – but we can practice now. "The strongest human will is always the one surrendered to God's will and participating with it."

PEACE

Peace does "settle over me" in this place and time. It enfolds me in God. I can receive it abundantly and peacefully, with a smile, with joy, in hope. The disciples had denied Jesus, run off when he was in trouble, and three days later he showed up in the room where they were hiding, and what was the first thing he said to them? "Peace be with you." In spite of anything I might do, like denying him or running from him, he comes to me and says, "Peace be with you" and you are still going to use me, send me. WOW! (John 20:21) Of all the things he gives us, he mentions peace often, peace that comes through the Holy Spirit, peace, sent to guard our hearts and minds in Christ (Philippians 4:7).

First, Peace

The first thing you gave the disciples after your resurrection was peace, the thing they needed most in the midst of their confusion and frustration. "You were called to peace; let the peace of Christ rule in your heart" (Colossians. 3:15). Sometimes peace is interrupted by selfishness and the only thing that can drive that out is his peace within. "Great peace have they who love your law," who hide it in their hearts.

JUDGING MYSELF

Luke 6:37 – "Do not judge (either yourself or others) and you will not be judged. Do not condemn (yourself or others)....Forgive (self and others)...." Judging and evaluating yourself is not your role. We tend to always see this verse as referring to our evaluation of others, and while that may be the main thrust, it could also be self judging, self condemning, self unforgiving that we might be guilty of, rightly or wrongly. I think we need to do some self-evaluation – under the direction of the Spirit. But to judge, condemn and not forgive ourselves is not right.

BECOMING CHRISTLIKE

The focus of spiritual formation is the internal change that shows itself in external ways – not the other way around. "The letter of the law kills; the Spirit give life." We go beyond the righteousness of anyone. "They" are not my example. Righteousness is the easy yoke (Matthew 11:29), being clean on the inside (Matthew 23:25), a good tree bringing forth good fruit (John 15:1-4), not heavy or burdensome, living by the rules (I John 5:3). In other words, it is an inside out job that reveals itself in kindness, goodness, meekness, strength – not by trying but by being. "Christ in you!"

That is who we can be, but we sometimes feel inadequate and when we do it helps to remember that God is our "very present help." We don't need to "just hope that someday I'll be Christlike," but letting God do his work day by day in us. It is Christ in me that does the work even as "I work out my own salvation with fear and trembling." Paul reminds us we can "be joyful in hope; patient in affliction, faithful at all times in prayer" (Romans 12:12). Another translation says, "enduring triumphantly." We can be joyful; we can abound in hope. Such truths are not just feelings and reactions but are based on fact and call us to respond to the Spirit at work in us.

David reminds us in Psalm 16:9 - "I bless the Lord who gives me counsel; in the night; also my heart instructs me. I keep the Lord always before me; because he is at my right hand, I shall not be moved. Therefore my heart is glad and my soul rejoices; my body rests secure." He brings the pieces of our lives together in praise. Dallas Willard calls it "becoming the same person all the time." That can happen when the "soul is in order under the direction of a well-kept heart which is under the direction of God. We can learn to build up an equity of trust that keeps us together at all times, no matter what."

WHAT KIND OF HEART WOULD YOU LIKE?

What a question! Let's see – I'd like a I Corinthian 13 heart, a "heart like thine" a song says, a heart that loves without thinking about loving, just does it, a listening heart that controls my mind so that my responses are not reactions but caring, thoughtful, and words or actions that are like Jesus would be in every situation. I want to be a thoroughly good, godly person, without arrogance, or insensitivity and selfishness or a sense of self-sufficiency. The only way that can happen is if I am changed from the inside out and that requires a heart like the heart of Jesus.

GOD'S WILL

"Be joyful always; pray continually; give thanks in all circumstances, for this is God's will for you in Christ Jesus." I have read these verses dozens of times but always as commands rather than as being "God's will for me." God's will is never grievous, but is filled with joy, with possibility, with positivity, with hope. The whole of I Thessalonians 5 is full of these positive encouragements to live in love for one another.

YOU CREATED ME!

One of the Puritan Fathers said, "The whole wisdom of the Trinity was exercised in the making of man." The Psalmist said, "We are fearfully and wonderfully made." A National Geographic article pursued the idea of "genius" in men like Einstein and Picasso. Those words, "the wisdom of the Trinity was exercised in the making of man," "We are fearfully and wonderfully made," are echoed in the fact that man is the epitome of God's creation, his genius! We are made in his image!! Can you believe it? We have a body with which to live in this world, on this earth, an earth God made and so we are fitted for life here and now, and even here our lives can be glorious. God spoke and the sun, the moon and the stars and everything else came into being. But we humans are the work of his HANDS. God "formed man from the dust of the earth and breathed into him the breath of life and man became a living soul." (Genesis 2:7) "Let us make man in our image, after our likeness," (Genesis 1:36) And then he took a rib from that man and with his hands he created a woman, an help meet for him. What a miracle!! How precious it is to think we were made by God, to be like God. (And yet, what will we be like in the new heaven and the new earth?)

DISCIPLINE

We read a lot about the punishment that God metes out in the Old Testament against the nations that attack Israel, about what God does to people, about individuals he wants to rescue but who refuse his ways. But I wonder, is it punishment or is it discipline? I think that's what the "remnant" he always saved realized. They knew they had sinned, or it could be that the individuals of the remnant had not sinned, but stayed true to God or repented, and God saw to their return, their salvation. We can thank God for his kindly discipline! We can be aware of it, listen carefully, repent and return to a full relationship with God.

THOUGHTS ON GOD'S WORD

Benedictine monks memorized most, if not all the Psalms. That was partly because many of them could not read. They would repeat them over and over until they were firmly in their minds. Benedict chose Psalms that we need to hear over and over, things that remind us of the things of God that will challenge us, sustain us, remind us to praise. God delivers; God is our refuge; God saves; God brings us home. We can move from hard times to joy, from feeling like a captive (which sometimes the Psalm writers were) to liberation, from depression and despair to trust as we read those words.

WAIT

How often you tell me to wait!! It is such a hard lesson to learn, but when I do it, especially with patience, I am able to understand why I needed to wait, and sometimes I learn to trust that you have something better in mind, a blessing I didn't see or comprehend; and so, I am learning that every moment should be a moment of praise for blessings seen and unseen.

In Isaiah 26:20, the promise is that as these people waited, even in hiding until the "wrath is past," they will be saved. It reminds me of the death angel of Exodus. God shows us when to hide and when to confront, when to lay low and when to fight. We need God's wisdom in such situations, in large things and small.

THE GOOD OLD DAYS

"I am the Lord, your Redeemer...the Lord, your Holy One, the creator...your King." (Isaiah 43:14) God says that to us, and we have to respond every day with a yes or a no. He has done that for us, been that for us, and keep moving on. Sometimes it is important to remember past things, but sometimes we pine for the "good old days," the days when things appeared to be easy, but we must keep moving on, we must see the "new thing" that God wants to do. He says, "You can perceive it." Whatever it is, it is so that we might "declare his praise." All the good that happens, all the things from which we have been rescued, all the joy that permeates our lives, all the promises that he gives me (and keeps!), all the new things that come into our lives, all the even less pleasant times and events and people – these all deserve praise and honor to him. The great things that have made up our lives are not to be dwelt on because God has promised even greater things. He is always doing new things! There is always a new lesson to learn. Much lies ahead – "Do you perceive it?" There are new friendships to develop, new avenues of service to explore, new ways and attitudes to deal with and maybe just accept, new difficult issues. We need wisdom and courage to see, to perceive those new things, remembering the old, but not living there. Moving on!

STAND FIRM

Isaiah 7:1-9 – Ahaz and the people of Judah are scared when they are attacked. But God said through Isaiah, "Be careful, keep calm and don't be afraid!....It will not take place.... if you do not stand firm in your faith, you will not stand at all.!" Great words of challenge, comfort and instruction! Keep calm but be careful! Stand firm or you won't stand at all. When fear takes over it's hard to be calm or careful, and I sure can't stand firm! Be careful implies to think about how to do what needs to be done – whether an attack by an enemy of any kind (or a hurricane), and plan carefully. Keep calm – that is the aid to thinking carefully. Don't be afraid, which can happen if I am careful and calm! Whatever the attack, it is only with "smoldering stubs of firewood" if I am standing firm in the faith.

WHO IS JESUS?

Isaiah 9 – "…a child is born…a son is given" – son of God, son of Mary – human through and through and yet able to redeem us as God through and through. The government, the authority rests on his shoulders – he is Lord God, King of kings and Lord of lords. My "wonderful counselor" – knowing me so well, expressing himself to me, helping me, guiding moment by moment, yet letting me make decisions, right and wrong and leading me in truth, accepting me as I am while making me what he intends me to be. "Mighty God" – God of all, who can do and does whatever he pleases which is always right, overcoming anything and everything that man might try. "Everlasting Father" – I latch on to that Father image and rejoice that you are eternally so, never leaving or forsaking me. "Prince of peace" – a commodity that is scarce in this world, and yet he bathes me in it every day and in every situation; a peace the world cannot know, but is freely bestowed on those who love him, for he is my prince, my beloved.

These verses are prophecy, and yet they are being fulfilled every day as individuals, me included, yield our lives to God's authority and discover his peace as he becomes our Lord. Isaiah says God rules with justice and righteousness, and he does in our lives as we allow him to be our Lord. "Your kingdom come, your will be done" today in my life!

WARNING!!

Isaiah 29 – A chapter full of warnings! So many foes, enemies are going to come against Jerusalem so that it will be like dust or chaff; there will be thunder, earthquakes, no relief. They won't be able to figure it out. It is because the people honor God with their lips and not their hearts, by rote not real worship. So God promises that he will do things that will "shock and amaze" them. They think they can hide their deeds, their thoughts from God, claiming he had not made them; he has no understanding of them.

Lord, I know that you made me; I know you understand me! And I am glad!! Thank you for making and understanding me, because you made me. Even my weaknesses have a reason. The way I look is by your design. Your design has given me a wonderful life and you continue to teach me how blessed I am, to remind me how rich my life is, has been, will be as I continue to walk with you, as Jesus walked.

The Solution - Isaiah 30:15

After the description of what is going to happen, Isaiah gives the solution. What the rebellious need is to return and rest and they will be saved; in quietness and confidence in God they will find strength. How often have I fussed, fumed with impatience, with not getting my way, talking louder and becoming anxious instead of resting, turning to God, being quiet and simply recognizing that God is in control. I move on through the passage and find these words, "But you would not." And here I am with my excuses and your warning – OK, go do it your way, but be aware you won't succeed. On the other hand, verse 18 says, "Therefore, the Lord waits to be gracious to you; he will rise up to show mercy to you, for you are a God of justice; blessed are all those who WAIT for him." Salvation and strength come in returning and rest and quiet confidence, but sometimes I have let stuff take God's place and thought I knew best. I have found that defeat comes until 1 have recognized that God was waiting to be gracious, to show mercy. My task now is to yield my waywardness to him, the God of justice and thankfully, mercy.

RIGHT COUNSEL

Sometimes it's really hard to know to whom we should listen! Should we play it safe or take a risk? One person says don't be a fool and another says go for it. What do we need to do in such circumstances? We have a great example in Hezekiah in Isaiah 37. The enemy is at their gate threatening to destroy Israel as he has all the other nations they have attacked. But Hezekiah began by repenting of any sins he might have committed. He went into the house of the Lord and he sent for Isaiah. But Isaiah said, "Don't be afraid! [Now that sounds familiar] The king will hear a rumor and return to his own land and fall by the sword."

So here are some steps we can take when we have that kind of choice to make – First, repent; second, go to God; third, seek the wisdom of one who is in communication with God. We don't always even know what's going on, but we can be sure that God does and that he is in control. He always has a plan beginning with "Don't be afraid! Trust God; put your faith in him."

IDOLS, ICONS, AND OBSESSIONS – Isaiah 44:9

It seems so stupid to worship idols, especially wooden ones. "Half of the tree I burned, baked bread on the coals, roasted meat. Now shall I make the rest an idol, fall down before a block of wood?" It would seem that one could see that the thing is a fraud. Icons can become that for some people. That is not what they are intended to be. They are made to help us focus our minds on God, not to worship the icon.

So what are our idols today? Are they things, ideas, power, money, our obsessions that leave out God, the "I'd rather haves" than God. These idols may be harder to define than a block of wood or hammered metal. We can see those, but they are useless. We can even be aware of our obsessions but they are just as useless. God, and only God, is what we need. "Keep yourselves from idols" the New Testament says. I'm not sure that the word idols means anything in our world today, but "obsession" seems to fit what an idol meant to the people of Isaiah's day.

Obsessions are those things that are "fun," that appear to be satisfying, that are the desires of our hearts, that we really "want" or "need," that we give our time and energy to, as the old song says "pleasures of sin for a season," that don't bring satisfaction, that are selfish, that take up the time and energy that we could give to God but are not what God wants us to do. It may be that we don't realize when we are obsessing. We are selfish people who easily give in to our selfish wants. God does want us to have fun, to be satisfied, to experience fulfillment and joy and peace. We can have it all when we worship the only One who is worthy of our worship.

A DISCIPLE'S EAR

"The Sovereign Lord has given me the tongue of a disciple, to know the word that sustains the weary" (Isaiah 50:3). And how did I get such a tongue? "He wakens me morning by morning, wakens my ear to listen like one being taught. He has opened my ears, and I have not been rebellious" (Isaiah 50:4). There are just some people who always know what to say, or not say, who seem to have the right word to encourage or to challenge in just the right way. They are those who have been with Jesus every day, listening to him moment by moment so they can live in contact with him, with his Spirit as they move through each moment of each day.

Each of the first three paragraphs of Isaiah 51 begin with "Listen to me!" God has messages to be heeded. He addresses "those who pursue righteousness...my people, my nation.... You who know righteousness..." He says look to the examples of the past, like Abraham and Sarah. Look to me and remember your salvation. Do not fear others for they will not last. Only his salvation is certain. Listen!!

GOD'S DWELLING PLACE

God says he dwells in a high and lofty place, but also with the contrite and humble. He does not continually accuse nor is he always angry. Yes, he can become angry and rightly so, but he will still heal and bring peace. How gracious, how awesome is God! Isaiah 57 ends on this note – "There is no peace for the wicked but there is peace for all who would be healed." He is with us where we are, every moment of every day. "He became flesh and dwelt among us, moved into the neighborhood" to bring peace and healing to the individual heart.

FOR ALL THE WRONG REASONS

Isaiah 58 – The people of Isaiah's day rebelled and sinned but kept the pretense of doing all the right things including fasting. They were only serving their own interests by fasting. It was certainly not for reasons God chose, which was to become humble enough to practice justice, release prisoners, share bread, clothe the naked and in the process not escape into some spiritual discipline like fasting. When we do the right thing for the right reason we can be sure that healing and light, vindication and glory, answered prayer and God's presence will happen. God's light will arise, guidance will come and satisfaction will be real. There are some things we can do to bring that about – celebrate the Sabbath with delight and honor, enjoy God and serve him with joy.

There is a contrast between doing any spiritual discipline as a ritual and drawing near to God through the disciplines. We can do the right things in his name and be well blessed.

DISCIPLESHIP
Call to follow Jesus – Matthew

As Jesus walked along the road in Capernaum he saw, gave attention to, Levi, also called Matthew, sitting, of all places, at the tax collector's booth. He saw in him something that made him invite him to follow him – and he did, right then and there! Maybe he had heard Jesus preach or watched him heal, and maybe more than once. He probably wasn't in the synagogue because as a tax collector for the Romans, he was an outcast, but Jesus had been there for a time and was back again. The ground work had been laid and Matthew responded – ready to be made a collector of souls!

Being a tax collector, as was Zaccheus, he had money and invited Jesus and his disciples, by this time not just a few, as well as his fellow tax collectors and other sinners to dinner. Did some of the rest of them realize who Jesus was? Did others follow him from this time on? However, Jesus was committing a no-no in the eyes of the Pharisees. He said, in essence, that he went where sinners are, where outcasts are, where people who need are – to call those with whom the self-righteous people would not associate. Jesus set the example for all of us to follow, one that is not always easy to follow. Matthew was not an ordinary outcast, though. He had money, position, but he was needy in Jesus' eyes. He was invited to join with four fishermen. I wonder how they felt about that, how Matthew felt about that, how they felt about each other.

DISCOURAGED?

God has a plan! He answers prayer, sometimes when and how you least expect it! So he can boldly say over and over again in many kinds of circumstances, "Do not fear....Do not be discouraged" (Isaiah 54:1-8). Why? Because God is our Maker, the very Lord of Hosts, the Holy One, your Redeemer, God of the whole earth! God admits that he has abandoned Israel at times when they needed a wake-up call. He does the same with us, not abandoning us exactly, but seemingly removing himself from us, when the question really is, "Who moved?" He says to us, "But with great compassion I will gather you....I hide my face from you, but with everlasting love I will have compassion on you." There really is no need for fear or discouragement because even in the midst of discipline he is still our Redeemer who loves us with great compassion. Walk in his way there will not even be any need for severe discipline. Should we choose to walk a different way, we can choose to return and experience again his great compassion.

KNOWING YOU – GRACE AND TRUTH

How is it that God in the form of Jesus was in the world in physical form – teaching, healing, loving, doing all the miracles he did – and yet the world did not know him? He even came to his own people and they did not know him – not foreigners but Jews who did not accept him. The prophets had told them he was coming and the "religious" leaders refused to believe that he was who he said he was. Fortunately, there were those who "received" and "believed in your name." How thankful we can be for them because it is through them that we have the privilege of believing and receiving. Those two acts, believing and receiving, give everyone the power, the right to become children of God, born again by your will, in a sense, just as Jesus was born of your will.

You, very God, the "us" who said, "Let us make man in our image," became flesh like us and lived like the people of his day And yet there was a glory about him that revealed you as the only Son of the Father, "full of grace and truth." I wonder if we would have seen that grace and truth had we been alive. Grace is such a big word.

One night we were playing a game with our grandson, Dylan who was 10 at the time. I was most anxious for him to see the difference between the 6 and the 9 on the Phase 10 cards. However, I did not use much grace in showing him. In fact, it wasn't my responsibility to instruct him at all. He is one smart kid who learned to play very quickly and doesn't mind others moving ahead of him in the game. He quickly understood what he needed to do and sorted his cards correctly, figuring out on his own the way to sort them that worked for him. I learned that I need to be gracious with the truth and not try to cram truth into his or anyone else's mind. Was I harsh? I shouldn't have been. Was I gracious? I should have been. Maybe I should have said nothing. Grace and truth apply to my speaking as a mother, a grandmother, a wife!

John went on to say in 1:16, "From his fullness we have all received grace upon grace." John the Baptist insisted that Jesus ranked ahead of him – a gracious acceptance of his position as Jesus' forerunner, not the One. The law is good for truth, for learning but without grace it becomes legalism, often without love. Grace enables us to live according to the intention of the law which Jesus summed up as loving him and our neighbor, and living as if we really do love them. When we look to Jesus we see how to do that; we see Jesus' example of loving God and loving others from family to people far away who are all our neighbors. It also includes loving ourselves and sometimes that is the hardest. Without being gracious to ourselves, it is almost impossible – grace to forgive ourselves, grace to love one another, grace to learn from the experience and move on, grace to be patient!

Authority

Authority comes from being given or appointed to a position. Leadership comes from vision and charisma in concert. (Benedict). Both may not reside in the same person! If we can be united in the "tenuous" search for the will of God, realizing that there is more than one way to do something, we can learn from each other. "Together" has something to teach us all.

The function of leadership is to call us beyond ourselves.

Mysterious Lives

Wow! Listen to this: "Those who have abandoned themselves to God always lead mysterious lives and receive from him exceptional and miraculous gifts by means of the most ordinary, natural and chance experiences in which there appears to be nothing unusual." (Jean-Pierre Cardin)

The challenge for me is to slow down, look, gaze upon the ordinary, see! Did I see the sacred in the ordinary, in every event today? Conversations, the beauty the earth, the beauty of the people, the wonder of God's presence – did I recognize it?

IT WILL HAPPEN

Many years ago I saw a movie in which the triumphant King Arthur is passing through a desolate land with his knights of the round table. As he passed, all the flowers began to bloom, the fruit appeared on the trees, the crops in the fields ripened, joy was abundant, peace flourished, all was well!! Chapter 35 of Isaiah brought that scene to mind. The desert bloomed, the people were strengthened, the frightened were encouraged. "Here is your God...to save you." The blind, the deaf, the lame, the mute were released from their handicaps. Streams flowed in the desert; springs of water came from the earth; a highway on which only God's redeemed people will travel, with no fearsome animals or unclean people, will be available. The ransomed will come into Jerusalem on that Holy Way, but there will be no weariness, just singing and great joy.

Much of this sounds like the second coming rather than the return from Babylon, or it may be a somewhat fanciful description of that great day. However, it might well describe the Second Coming as John describes it in Revelation. It will be a greater day than even the return from Babylon! What a day that will be!!

REST – IT'S GOOD FOR YOU!

"Six days you shall labor and do all your work.
On the 7th day you shall rest."

Evil doesn't take a day off! –
No Sabbath break for Satan.
So work against evil – disease, hunger -
From those we cannot take a break either.

But rest is important – it's good for you.
Then again "rest" should be part of every day –
Soul rest, daily time to rest in the Lord.
"Take my yoke upon you…
Learn from me…
And find rest for your soul."

It can be a way of living, of sacramental living.
It's good for you!

MEDITATING ON SCRIPTURE

For me this book began when I began doing just that – meditating on Scripture. My daily journals are full of daily thoughts – I sometimes wonder where they come from. Now I am sharing some of those with you. Here's how it happens for me.

These days I begin my day with my Quiet Time in the alcove off our bedroom where I am surrounding by books, a photo of my boys, inspirational art, two windows that allow me to watch the birds, the deer, and the squirrels. I've always had a special place, sometimes a corner of the couch in the living room, sometimes a chair in the bedroom, always somewhere that my family knows is my place in the morning, not to be disturbed. (We are a small family of quiet people.) But that time has had to be adjusted to accommodate young children, demands of ministry, and other scheduling, like vacations.

I always begin with one section from Psalm 119 and another Psalm. Most of the time I am reading a book of the Bible, like a Gospel or a letter from the New Testament or a book of history from the Old Testament or one of the prophets. Sometimes I will use a devotional book. My favorite, which I go back to time and time again, is Disciplines for the Inner Life *by Benson and Benson, a father/son team. It is now out of print but usually available through Amazon.*

I record my thoughts, my responses, my sense of what is important in the passage of Scripture I am reading, my reactions which can be praise or awe or prayer or confession or amazement or challenge, in my journal.

I have chosen some pretty random thoughts here except in "Musing from Mark" – that section is a pretty complete look into my heart. Listen to my ponderings and maybe you'll hear the voice that I heard and maybe you'll do some pondering of your own.

That's my way of meditating on Scripture, the way in which God comes to me every day, even when we are on vacation, in a motel or our camper, when we visit friends. I rarely miss that morning hour when I meet with God in His word and in prayer. He always has something to say to me and he always listens to me.

PSALMS BY ME

OBSERVATIONS ON PSALM 119

Psalm 119, the longest of the Psalms, is in fact the longest chapter in the Bible. The Psalmist uses 8 different terms for God's Word. The chapter is divided into 22 stanzas, with 8 verses per stanza, each stanza beginning with a letter of the Hebrew alphabet.

"Teach me thy statutes" is a common prayer the Psalmist includes in vs. 12, 26,33,64,63,66,68,108,124,125,135.

The Psalmist declares that God's Word gives us a lot of things -

Light	Understanding
Redemption	Teaching
Hope	Truth
Deliverance	Compassion
Salvation	Restoration
Strength	Grace
A Song	Discernment
Good Judgment	Knowledge
Comfort	Stability
Victory	Answers for others
Wisdom	Insight and Direction
Restraint	

It's a good Psalm for daily reading and memorizing, for appreciation of God's whole Word.

An Acrostic Psalm

Awesome God, I come to you in humility because that's the only way I can come, full of gratitude for who you are, yet caring about me as I am.

Bountiful Creator of all that is beautiful, the way you intended it to be, give me wisdom to handle that bountiful beauty with a steward's heart.

Compassionate Friend, I praise you for understanding me when I am weak and reminding me of the many times you have shown your compassion in my distress.

Defending Helper, I am attacked by Satan's imps who tell me I am weak, incapable, a failure; yet when I turn to you, you remind me that you are my sure defense.

Everlasting Father, it is to you that I come, to whom my father and mother came, and to whom Abraham, the Father of faith came, knowing you then, knowing you now, and knowing you into the future.

Forgiving Father, keeping your promises and always ready to forgive, I dare to remind you that if I confess my sins, you will forgive and cleanse me of all my sins.

Gracious Guide, I am always in need of guidance in my everyday, sometimes exciting, sometimes mundane life and encounters because I want to do your will.

Holy Lord, with the cherubim and seraphim, with the saints of old and the saints of today, I acclaim you, my holy Lord who has made me in your image, with a goal to be like Jesus, holy.

Incomparable Judge, I am thankful that I can trust myself and all I love, in fact all people, to your judgment and need not make any judgments myself.

Jealous God, I desire to please you, to honor you, to lift you up, to defend your honor, to give you praise for all things, giving you credit for who I am becoming.

Knowing God, all-knowing Father who sees all I do, hears all I say, I want to honor you in all things and bring delight to your heart.

Listening Lord, I thank you for hearing all kinds of people, all kinds of prayers, all the time – I can't comprehend it, Lord, especially when one of them is me.

Merciful Father, you put up with so much from me – failures of obedience to your gracious commands, words of unkindness to my family, so much and you just give mercy.

Nearest Friend when human friends are far away or nearby friends don't know me well enough to understand me, I praise you that I can be honest and vulnerable with you.

Opener of my ears so that I hear your voice, and the cries of all those in need, I praise you for the direction you give me as I hear your Spirit giving me guidance.

Present God, I think of all your attributes this is the one for which I am most grateful, to know that you are with me morning, noon, and night, everywhere I go – you are always present.

Quiet Voice, I praise you for speaking gently to me, because you know me and what I best respond to, whether I am alone or in a crowd so that I can hear and respond.

Rock-solid Master, I know I can trust you through any storm – you are a sure foundation even when I am on sand. You are a safe place to abide in the face of any enemy.

Saving Lord, sins are ugly and lead me in to wrong direction, into selfishness and pride, but you don't let me stay there. You offer your saving hand and I am pulled back to you.

Trustworthy Guide, I know what to do and what not to do and I know I need not go astray from even the narrow way, even when other paths look good, for you know the way that leads to Life.

Understanding Teacher, sometimes I am like your first disciples, not a good learner. Please don't give up on me; tell me again until I remember what I am to do and to be.

Valiant Deliverer, I praise you for every memory of times you have brought me through situations that would have defeated me, and I know you can do it again.

Watcher God, I praise you that your eye is on the sparrow and I know you watch over me; so I have confidence to be where I am, to be who I am.

Xray Healer, I praise you for your ability to see deeply into me, even though I would rather you didn't sometimes, because you want me to be whole.

Yearning Father, you long for me to follow your leading, to be in step with you all along the way, calling me back to your side when I wander off in the wrong direction.

Zealous Guard, thank you for keeping me as a Shepherd watching his flock, keeping me from going astray, protecting me from danger, guarding my soul.

AWESOME GOD

Our God is an awesome God, not just an Awesome God, but THE Awesome God. There is none like him. How can we describe him – Creator, Preserver, Governor of all things, Ruler, Majestic in Power, Invisible and yet always present with us through the Holy Spirit, Head of the Church through Jesus Christ, Giver of Life abundant; Awesome in works and deeds and wonders, Awesome in glory, Awesome in majesty.

He is more awesome than all who surround him. His work is awesome on behalf of us, his people. He inspires awe in us – look at all he has made!! We stand in awe of all he has made and of all he has done.

"...let us be thankful and worship God acceptably with reverence and awe, for our 'God is a consuming fire' (Deuteronomy 4:24)." (Hebrews 12:28-29)

BOUNTIFUL CREATOR

Bountiful Creator of all that is, I am in awe of your creativity. I think of the variety in shapes and sizes and colors and density and fluidity. There is round and square, triangular and trapezoidal, oblong and circular, jagged-edged and pointed. There is large and larger and largest, small and smaller and smallest, tall and taller and tallest, short and shorter and shortest, wide and wider and widest, thin and thinner and thinnest. There is yellow, red, and blue and such a variety of mixtures of those besides black and white (I can't begin to imagine a world without color – one of your finest creations, as far as I'm concerned). There is solid rock and porous rock, hard word and soft wood, soft fur and coarse hair, smooth skin and tough hide.

There are people of every kind, color, and shape. There are animals large and small. There are plants, too many to name, of every genus and species, many yet to be discovered and named. There are mountains and hills, rivers and streams, meadows and deserts, forests and orchards, canyons and crevices, oceans and lakes, grasslands and moors, wheat fields and hedgerow, salt water and waterfall. There are pine trees and fruit trees, deciduous trees and evergreens, flowering bushes and needled cactuses, each perpetuating its own kind. And yet every living thing is evolving, intermingling within its species, and I see that you are not done creating yet. This is your world and you aren't finished!!

"The world is so full of a number of things; I'm sure we should all be as happy as kings." And we are stewards of it all!!

And then there is the sun, the moon, the stars, the planets, the clouds, ever changing, coming and going, bearing rain and snow, bringing shade and moisture. What else is "up there," Lord, that we don't know about yet? There is so much yet to learn.

There is the wind – gentle breezes and fierce hurricanes, tornadoes, "stormy winds fulfilling your word...."

COMPASSIONATE HEALER

Compassionate healer who knows and understands me better, so much better, than I know and understand myself, I praise you! You made me, as David said, "knit me together in my mother's womb." You know every cell of my being every molecule and sinew. You are aware of every breath I take, every move I make, every blink of my eye, every letter I write – not to control or to punish, but you do concern yourself with me, with my life. I am "fearfully wonderfully made!" "Body and soul, I am marvelously made" (Psalm 139:14 NIV, MSG)! What a creation!

But it is a creation, while intended to be perfect when you made it, is subject to this imperfect world which man has harmed, and a body which is, therefore, subject to all this imperfection. And Life happens! What I know for sure is that you can, that you will heal compassionately. That means that you always heal one way or another, though you don't always cure. As Matthew puts it, quoting Isaiah, "I would heal them" (Matthew 13:15), if they would let you, if they would believe, if it were best for them, if they would hear and understand.

Healing comes in many forms, and that's where your compassion comes in! The best healing may be to die and go to live with you. But then sometimes healing does not come, at least not the way or in the time frame that we had in mind. Sometimes healing comes but leaves the consequences. Sometimes healing is complete and there is no residue of pain or incapacity. Sometimes there is a steady weakening in the body, but for some reason you aren't done with me yet. That doesn't mean giving up or giving in but seeking help, continuing to do what I can, exercising as able, working and resting, understanding myself, possibly researching the options. In your wisdom and with your compassion you know what is best because you love me unreservedly, unconditionally, totally, lovingly, yes, compassionately. There are lessons to be learned, spiritual growth to be developed, maybe some other direction you want me to go. Sometimes, I think, the only way to get my attention is through my body or through the body of a loved one or a friend. Help me, I pray, to reach an understanding so that healing, the kind you want to do, can happen.

DEFENDING HELPER

I am attacked by Satan's minions who tell me I am weak, incapable, a failure; and they can be very persuasive! Yet, when I turn to you, you remind me that you are my sure defense, a very present help in trouble, that you even call me your beloved – WOW! I am loved by the God of all the universe, Father of Jesus, the awesome, Almighty One, the Creator of all that is beautiful. You tell me that you are with me to keep me from falling, to forgive me if I do fail – although you tell me that I do not need to fail. You tell me that you are patient with me even if you have to remind me of your love, your grace, your presence over and over again. You never give up on me.

But I do feel weak sometimes, Lord; a weakness that makes me feel afraid. I do feel incapable and that also makes me feel afraid. What am I afraid of? I suppose I am afraid of failure, of disappointing someone, especially a family member, of not being able to do something required or expected of me, of losing something or someone valuable to me because I fail to do something right, of suffering and pain.

Peter says, quoting Isaiah, "Do not fear what they fear" (I Peter 3:14). When Isaiah spoke those words, he was warning the Israelites not to worry about what their enemies would do because God, Immanuel, was with them. There was a conspiracy against them, but they did not need to be afraid; he, God, would be their sanctuary. Isaiah declares, "I will wait for the Lord...I will put my trust in him" (8:17). Peter puts a slightly different spin on it when he prefaces the quote in this way – "But even if you should suffer for what is right, you are blessed." He knew, as we should, that we have a defending helper at our side.

Jesus said, "So don't be afraid; you are worth more than many sparrows" whom he says will be noticed if one should fall (Matthew 10:29). "Don't be afraid, just believe" (Mark 5:36). Don't let your heart be troubled and do not be afraid" (John 14:27). God has promised, "'Never will I leave you; never will I forsake you." So we have confidence. "The Lord is my helper; I will not be afraid. What can man do to me?" (Hebrews 13:5b-6).

So, Lord, I can see that I need to know the truth of your many promises and I need to memorize them. You are my fortress, my cornerstone, my victor, my deliverer, my dwelling place, my hiding place, my rock, my savior, my protector, my shield, my stronghold. Whom should I fear? I am blessed with enough strength, enough gifts, enough wisdom, enough of everything I need with your help to fight off the worst that Satan can send my way and in the power of the Spirit.

EVERLASTING FATHER

It is to you I come, that one to whom my father and mother came, the one to whom Abraham came, knowing you then, knowing you now, knowing you in the future. This name was part of Isaiah's prophecy regarding Jesus (Isaiah 9:6). When Jesus was being questioned by Philip regarding seeing the Father, Jesus responded, "Don't you know me, Philip, even after I have been among you such a long time? Anyone who has seen me has seen the Father. How can you say, 'Show us the Father?' Don't you believe that I am in the Father, and that the Father is in me? The words I say to you are not just my own. Rather, it is the Father, living in me, who is doing his work" (John 14:9-10). We believe that God, Father, Son, and Holy Spirit, is outside of time as Creator of time and of all that is and as everlasting beyond time – a concept we cannot grasp, just as we find it hard to think of "everlasting" in terms of a future eternity.

In Isaiah, however, we have a name that has great appeal and carries wonderful meaning for us. Let's consider first the word "Father." For many, including me, that has a depth of wonderful meaning and emotional response because we had the kind of earthly father who was, as my husband says, "good for nothing" – good, not for what it got him, but just because "good" was the right thing to be and to do. So the image of father carries with it love, kindness, caring, meeting needs and often wants, understanding, helpfulness, listening, consideration. And such is my image of God.

However, as JB Phillips, in his book <u>Your God is too Small,</u> reminds me, that is not the image that is brought to the minds of many people by the word "father." Some fathers are cruel or mean; others are disinterested or even out of the picture. If this is how we see "father," even God as father, we may need to refine the image because it is a favorite Scripture image and a sacred relationship to be cherished by believers.

Jesus taught us to address God as "Our Father in heaven...." (Matthew 6:9), one who feeds the sparrows (Matthew 6:26). He reminds us that he is in the Father and the Father in him (John 14:10), implying that they are one. And Paul in Romans 8:14-17 declares, "...those who are led by the Spirit of God are sons of God. For you did not receive a spirit that makes you a slave again to fear, but you received the Spirit of sonship. And by him we cry, "Abba, Father." The Spirit himself testifies with our spirit that we are God's children. Now if we are children, then we are heirs – heirs of God and co-heirs with Christ." "Those who are led by the Spirit of God are SONS of God." He is our Father!

Yes, the word "everlasting" is hard to grasp, but it is a concept that is very Scriptural, actually more in the Old Testament than in the New. "Stand up and praise the Lord your God, who is from everlasting to everlasting" (Nehemiah 9:5b). "Before the mountains were born or you brought forth the earth and the world, from everlasting to everlasting you are God" (Psalm 90:2). "The Lord is the everlasting God, the Creator of the ends of the earth" (Isaiah 40:28). The more common New Testament word is eternal or "ever and ever" often referring to eternal life or eternal damnation. Two key verses, however, refer to Jesus, the everlasting Father, alive forever and ever – Hebrews 1:8: "Your throne, O God, will last forever and ever." Revelation 1:18: "I am the living One; I was dead and behold I am alive forever and ever!"

Trying to grasp the idea of "everlasting" is challenging. It's another concept we have by faith. But he is Everlasting and he is our Father! Praise Him!!

FORGIVING FATHER

You who keep your promise and are always ready to forgive, I dare to remind you that, if I confess my sins, you will forgive them and cleanse me of all unrighteousness.

I have called you "awesome and almighty!" And I think one of the ways in which you are most awesome is in your ability, your desire, your willingness to forgive. If I, in my humanity, were invited to forgive me for my neglect of you or anyone else, for my lack of obedience to your wise and judicious commands, for my demands and my rudeness towards you, I don't think I could do it. But you are utterly, completely gracious and merciful, not just forgiving but forgetting – "As far as the east is from the west, so far has he removed our transgressions from us" (Psalm 103:12). And that's a very long way! And there seems to be no end to the number of times you will forgive for the same thing. You suggest that we should forgive 70x7, but you don't even seem to count! You just do it, removing it from me as far as the east is from the west.

I realize that you require me to acknowledge my guilt before forgiveness will be granted which seems obvious, and I think that also requires that I ask for forgiveness. Sometimes it's not hard to admit that I have not been as faithful to you as I should have been, have neglected you and not been obedient, but sometimes I don't notice those things nearly enough, and I pray that you will show me, remind me, give me a swift kick – whatever it takes to let me know I've failed.

Then there's the whole issue of my forgiving others. You taught us to pray, "Forgive us...as we forgive others." Sometimes that is so much easier said than done. I can think of times when I've taken that to heart and readily forgiven others. But, sadly, other times when their offense has gone deep, forgiving has been really hard to do. But, Lord, I want to be like you so, I pray, help me to be forgiving of all the offenses that come my way. May I remember how often and how much you have forgiven me and make me like you who said, "Father, forgive them for they don't know what they are doing."

GRACIOUS GUIDE

I am always in need of guidance in my every day, sometimes exciting, sometimes mundane life and encounters because I want to do your will.

Dallas Willard wrote a book some years back (1984) called *In Search of Guidance* which he updated and changed the name to *Hearing God* (1999). I wonder why the name change. Is there a subtle shift in emphasis? Is there a relationship between searching for guidance and hearing God? Maybe it's more about hearing you as we search for guidance. Can we find guidance outside of hearing you? As Christians I think guidance does come mainly from you whether you speak through your Word, through others who speak or write, or directly through the Holy Spirit. Maybe you don't tell a man which T-shirt to wear, or a shopper which oranges to buy, or a group which restaurant to have dinner. Sometimes we may feel strongly about the more common decisions because you have a reason for us to do certain things or be in a certain place. But usually you want to guide us in the areas of life that really matter, in the big decisions we have to make. Yet even there you do not dictate; you guide; you give options; you are gracious.

At my age and station in life one of my frequent requests for guidance is what to use for my devotions or study time. Sometimes it's a matter of convenience – we're going on vacation and I need something compact, easy to carry in and out of a motel room, etc. Sometimes a book of the Bible will seem to be just right or the Bible along with another book. You give options and yet you seem to make it clear, and if I choose wrongly you graciously redirect me in my spirit with your Spirit.

I also deal with the issue of the wise use of resources – money, time, talents. Do I give and how much? Do I volunteer here or there? How do you want me to use my gifts? But as I pray, there comes a sense of what the options are and then you guide me to a yes or no as I weigh the implications of each option. One of the lessons I have learned is that if I follow your guidance through the process, there is always enough of whatever I have. Gracious guidance from my gracious guide!

And so, Lord, be my gracious guide today, whatever my choices may be.

HOLY LORD

With the cherubim and seraphim, with the saints of old and the saints of today, I acclaim you my holy Lord who has made me in your image with a goal to be like your Son, Jesus, who is Lord of all. Actually, I'm having a hard time distinguishing between you as Lord and Jesus as Lord, but then since you are God - Father, Son and Spirit - I probably don't have to distinguish between you at all. What I know and what I don't have a hard time saying is that you are holy and that you are Lord, Lord of all.

I am remembering Mary Miller's poem in which she said that it was easy to let you be my Savior because I know I need a Savior, need your pardoning grace, your perfecting love. It's not so hard "to admit that I lose my cool..., do things my way..., do what comes naturally." But it is hard to say that I need a "lord," someone to tell me what to do, to tell me when I am wrong, to correct me, to give up myself. And yet you have made me and planned for me and you want to help me live this life to the fullest. You will do that with holiness, with grace, with rightness because you have made me and you know me so well that you will only do the very best for me. Why, then, is it so hard to call you Lord, to make sure that you are LORD? All who have done it, the saints of old and the saints of today, recommend it highly. I know it's a good idea to have you as Lord of my life! O may it be so!!

Yet you are holy, perfect, without fault or blemish. You've never made a mistake; you've always been morally and ethically right, righteous. It is your nature, a unique quality of your character. The seraphs gathered around the altar in the Holy of Holies when Isaiah was there cried out, "Holy, holy, holy is the Lord Almighty." In Revelation 4:8 the "living creatures" cry, "Holy, holy, holy is the Lord God Almighty." I suppose that nature, that characteristic of yours could be frightening. How can I approach someone so perfect, so holy? But if I am called to be like you, the only way to learn is to be with you, learning from you like the disciples did when you were here on earth. Being in your presence, listening to your Word, to your Spirit, reminds me of the things I have done, or not done, the things I have said, or not said, the attitudes I have expressed or carried in my heart that have made me less than holy. Peter reminds me in I Peter 1:15, "As He who has called you is holy, you also be holy in all your conduct." And the writer of Hebrews says, "Make every effort to live in peace with all men and to be holy; without holiness no one will see the Lord" (Hebrews 12:14). It can be done! I know it can, especially if I fix my eyes on you, make you the focus of my attention, determine in the power of the Spirit to be like Jesus. I can't do it without your presence; but with you all things are possible. You are Lord!! You are my Holy Lord!!

INCOMPARABLE JUDGE

I am thankful that I can totally trust myself and all whom I love, in fact all people, to your judgment and need not make any judgments myself, and particularly not the eternal one on anyone. One of your attributes is justice, and that's because you know every one of us inside and out; you know our motives, our most inner thoughts, our sometimes convoluted plans and ideas. And that's one of the reasons I can trust you to judge rightly. "Can not the judge of all the earth do right?" (Genesis 18:25c).

Court judges don't know nearly as much you do. They may hear the evidence of many people, but those people, including policemen, family members, friends, witnesses, can't read the minds of others. They don't know the heart of those about whom they are talking. They can be swayed by lawyers and their kinds of questions. They are called judges, but will they do what is right if they don't really know the facts or the heart?

I can't even judge my best friend, or my husband sometimes. I know them fairly well, maybe better than anyone else knows them, but so often I make a wrong assumption, but you never do. They make wrong assumptions about me also, and we may both judge based on what we think we know. Now I know that there are certain things, certain actions, even words about which I can make a judgment and sometimes that judgment needs to be spoken, hard as that may be. But I certainly need to weigh my words, pray about my feelings, check to see if what I am feeling is a reaction or if it is a proper response, the one that is my "right" to make, if it is in keeping with your Word, if the thing he or she did is sinful, inappropriate or in some way not in keeping with the Word. I need to be very conscious of the Holy Spirit speaking to my heart! And I need to listen to what may appear to be a judgment coming my way, again listen to the Holy Spirit and know whether that judgment is from you through the other person. I cannot be offended or defensive; I cannot argue; I must listen and hear from you.

"I do not judge even myself," Paul says (I Corinthians 4:3), but he says that when he knows his conscience is absolutely clear, and then he adds, "But that does not make me innocent. It is the Lord who judges me." What a blessing it is to have you as my judge. You help me to see my faults, my shortcomings. You gently remind me of what I should be, should do, should say and let me know if I am not what I should be or have not done what I should do or say. You don't appear as judge; more like the loving Father who wants only what's best for me. In that I can rest assured of love, of honest judgment, of caring direction, of forgiveness!! Thank you, incomparable Judge of all the earth who does what is right!!

JEALOUS GOD

I desire to please you, to honor you, to lift you up, to defend your honor, to give you praise for all things, giving you credit for who you are and for who I am becoming. You have every "right" to become jealous when I do not do those things. You made me, created a plan for my life, did everything to make it possible, even to giving up your heavenly throne to become human in Jesus, to dying on the cross to save me from myself and my sins. However, I "have sinned and come short of the glory of God." (Romans 3:23). You declared as long ago as the Ten Commandments, "I, the Lord your God, am a jealous God…" (Exodus 20:5). You want your children to realize who you are, what you have done for us, and want to do in and through us. But we have all sinned; I have sinned.

Jealousy doesn't seem to be an attribute that you would have. We are so often warned against being jealous that it doesn't seem as if you would have that "emotion" in you. The dictionary defines jealous as "intolerant of rivalry or unfaithfulness; suspicious that a person one loves is not faithful; hostile toward a rival." The third definition is "careful in guarding a right or possession." That comes closer to a definition I can live with that would apply to you. I am quite amazed at how many times in the Bible you are called, or even call yourself, "jealous." In fact, the quote from Exodus 20:5 appears again in Deuteronomy 4:24, 5:9, 6:15, and Joshua 24:19. "The Lord, whose name is Jealous, is a jealous God" (Exodus 34:14). You said, "I will be jealous for my holy name" (Ezekiel 34:14). The prophets declare, "…they provoked the Lord to jealousy" (Ezekiel 8:3).

You do love the people you created so much that you are "careful in guarding" us. Paul in writing to the Corinthians asks, "Are we trying to arouse the Lord's jealousy" by being disobedient to his Word? Whenever we arouse your jealousy we can plan on knowing it, either by your Spirit telling us or by feeling your wrath. It is not a pleasant thing to fall into the hands of an angry God aroused by jealousy.

However, it is not your desire to make us feel your wrath. It is rather your desire to pour out blessings – grace, forgiveness, love, peace, joy, hope. When things I do indicate that I have put other gods before you, when I am following after the things of this world rather than the things you have planned for me, when I have lost the peace, the joy, the hope and become aware through your Spirit's work in me that I am about to incur your wrath, I can repent, turn, change my mind after hearing that news, the news that you love me and want only the best for me.

Yes, you have every "right" to become jealous, and I'm really glad that you love me enough to be called "jealous!"

KNOWING GOD

All-knowing Father who sees everything about everything including everything about me, all I do, all I say, I want to honor you in all things and bring delight to your heart. There is nothing about me that is hidden from you, including my thoughts. The Psalmist describes it this way – "Before a word is on my tongue you know it completely, O Lord" (Psalm 139:4). And if you know my thoughts it must be that you know everything! Now that could be scary! But because I belong to you, I am very glad to know that, because it reminds me that you can stop me from saying things, doing things I ought not to do. In fact, you can stop a thought that is in my head from remaining there. Your Holy Spirit tells me that I should not be thinking those things and with my permission removes them from my mind.

But not only do you know all about me, you know all about everything!! Do you know how to operate a computer? Well, yeah, you created the mind that "created" the computer! You not only know how to operate one, you could make one. You don't even need to make one; you can answer any question we might have about anything without using "Siri" or Echo or any other device. But you let us learn how to make those things, operate those things. You help us learn the answers and put them into a machine.

Do you know about the universe? Well, yeah, you created the universe, put it into motion, put the stars in place, hung the moon and the sun and you keep them all in your care. You know what planets are out there, long before we "discover" them. You created the sun and the moon so that every hundred years or so the moon eclipses the sun!!

Do you how a butterfly flies? Or how many times a hummingbird moves its wings? Or how a fawn gets rid of its spots as it grows? Or how a goldfinch changes from dull brown to gold every spring? Lots of these kinds of things have been studied and can be scientifically described, at least to some degree, but we have a long way to go before we know what you know, and I doubt if we ever will know it all. We don't even know much about ourselves as human beings. A Puritan Father once said that we will never know ourselves until we know you, and it's a certainty that we will never really know you until we get to Heaven. It is good to know you now. You said through the Psalmist, "Be still, and know that I am God" (Psalm 46:10). And that may be the best way to know you, and really all we can know about you – that you are God and we are not. In fact, we do not know what a day may bring (Proverbs 27:2) Or James 4:14, "Why, you do not even know what will happen tomorrow." But you do!! And it is enough for me to commit my way to you, trust in you and let you bring it to pass. It will be what is best – I am in your hands!! And I'm really glad!!

LISTENING LORD

I thank you for hearing all kinds of people, all kinds of prayers, all the time – I can't comprehend it, Lord, especially since one of them is me, talking about all the stuff that is important to me. The Psalmist said, "The eyes of the Lord are on the righteous and his ears are attentive to their cry" (Psalm 34:15). I know that you are a Spirit and don't really have eyes or ears. In fact, they would be quite limiting if you had them. Instead in your form, however the simplest of people might describe you or the greatest theologian might write of you, you do listen to us, not only to our prayers, but to all we say, all we think as described in Psalm 139. I am sure that you also listen to the cries of the animals who are hungry or injured, and you hear their songs of joy, their bellows of excitement, their murmurs of contentment.

The most amazing part of that for me is that you hear it all at the same time, understand it all, take action about it all, receive it all. I am so limited when I listen that sometimes I don't even hear all that one person is saying to me when I am listening and wanting to hear. My mind can't take it all in or I am distracted by something outside of the conversation, or even by one thing, even one word that they say. But you hear all of us, all of creation, all of the time, and you comprehend it all, you begin to answer our prayers even before we speak them. Yeah, there's also that! You know what we are going to say, even before we say it – your "ears" are that attuned to each one of us!! You are "attentive to our cry," even before we cry!

Why do you do that, Lord? It can only be because you love

your creation; you want to come to our aid; you know our needs and our wants; you are available; you are present. You really do hear prayer! In your Word you said, "My eyes will be open and my ears attentive; (II Corinthians 7:15); my eyes and heart will always be there" (I Kings 9:3). You hear the prayers of the righteous (Proverbs 15:29); and the prayers of the needy (Psalm 69:33) and you hear when I call (Psalm 4:3). Yes, you are present when I pray - how can that be? It's because of who you are – God!! How I praise you for being present, knowing my fears, my weaknesses, my needs, and understanding how I feel and why I feel the way I do. "This poor woman cried and the Lord heard her" (Psalm 34:6). You who made the ears and eyes hears and sees (Psalm 94:9).

Thanks for listening, Lord, to my feeble attempt to write about such huge ideas.

MERCIFUL FATHER

You put up with so much from me – failures of obedience to your gracious commands, words of unkindness to my family, neglect of duties that could be a joy, actions that are less than gracious towards others. And you just give mercy. "Your mercies are new every morning; great is your faithfulness" (Lamentations 3:23). It's as if you let me start each day with a clean slate, as if I hadn't made any mistakes the whole day before. "Your mercies are new every morning."

This idea keeps coming up again and again, in different guises, using different words, but "your compassions, they fail not; as Thou hast been Thou forever shalt be." This compassion, these mercies do not negate your justice or mean you are not a "jealous God." But it's as if you have taken my punishment, which I so justly deserved, and it's "just-as-if-I'd never sinned." Yep, that's exactly what happened! You are so merciful, so full of love, so "jealous" for me, your child, that you just keep on forgiving, loving, pouring out grace, drawing me back to you, every morning.

There is an element of my responsibility here, I know. When I become aware of my shortcomings, or whatever I call them, I must own them and admit my, ok, I'll say it, sin. If I am sincere, if I mean I am sorry then I can say that to you, and then your mercy flows over me, through me, and I am forgiven!! What an incredible blessing!!

NEAREST FRIEND

When human friends are far away or nearby friends don't know me well enough to understand me, I praise you that I can be honest and vulnerable with you. "There is a friend that sticks closer than a brother" (Proverbs18:24), an unseen friend, a never-failing friend, a friend who always understands, who can wound me to help me and can always be trusted to do and say the right things.

When I was younger I had quite an assortment of friends, buddies with whom to play; as a teen there were fewer friends with whom to be close, but friends who I could trust; as a young adult who moved quite often for work, the friends I valued most were those from childhood whom I saw occasionally, or a few who I learned to trust; as an adult friends have become special treasures, especially my spouse who was and is closer than a brother, who at least tries to understand, and who can wound me and still be trusted.

But only one friends fits the thought of being the perfect, the always near, the never-failing friend and that's you, my God as seen in Jesus Christ and known through the Holy Spirit. With you I can be completely vulnerable and totally honest and you will never laugh at me or reject me. I can get angry (and you listen). I can cry (and you collect my tears in a bottle). I can joke (and you get it and may even laugh). I can just sit (and you sit with me). I can talk (and you hear). I can sing (and you harmonize). I can be anywhere (and you are with me; we never have to say good-bye). My nearest Friend loves me – Amazing!

OPENER OF MY EARS

Opener of my ears so that I hear your voice as well as the cries of those in need, I praise you for the direction you give me because I hear your voice guiding me into "paths of righteousness for your name's sake" as well as for my own sake and for the sake of others.

I want to be like Samuel, who said, "Speak, Lord, for your servant is listening." I want to be like Ananias, who when you sent him to Saul, his enemy, just went. I want to be like the sheep who hears only their master's voice. I want to be quick to listen and listen attentively to you and to your Word. I even want to listen to the heavens declaring your glory and proclaiming the work of your hands. I want to hear the voice behind me saying, "This is the way; walk in it." I want to hear your voice and open the door so that you may come in.

I don't want to hear your voice and harden my heart, close my ears. I don't want to be like those who have ears to hear, but do not hear. I don't want to be always hearing but never understanding.

You have called me to be a disciple, to be a saint, to be holy, to live according to your purpose. You have called me to live in peace and with hope, to be free, to live in the light. And you have called me to your eternal glory. Open my ears, Lord, so that I hear your voice, and I will obey.

PRESENT GOD

I think of all your attributes this is the one for which I am most grateful, to know that you are with me morning, noon, and night, everywhere I am – you are always present. You are, after all, Emmanuel – God with us! There are two pieces of literature which help me to realize how wonderful, how important, that presence is.

Psalm 139 which declares, "You know me!" You know when I sit or stand; you know what I am thinking – you're that close; you know if I am running away – there's nowhere to go to get away; you see me in the darkness as well as in the light; you knew me before I was born and had a plan for me." That can be scary! But it goes on to say, "How precious to me are your thoughts, O God! How vast is the sum of them" – so far beyond what I know about myself. And you love me anyway!

And there is a song we have sung in church, "There was Jesus." It reminds me that in the waiting or the searching or the healing or the hurting, every minute, every moment, where I've been and where I'm going, even when I couldn't see it, like a blessing buried in the broken pieces – there is Jesus. You take all those things that I have experienced and make them great, blessing even the broken pieces.

"I will never leave you or forsake you," God said to Joshua (Joshua 1:5). As Jesus was leaving, he said to the disciples, and to us through them, "I am with you always, to the very end of the age" (Matthew 28:20). Those promises are sure and "Amen." He is our Present God.

QUIET VOICE

I praise you for speaking to me gently because you know me and you know the voice to which I am most likely to respond, and that's whether I am alone or in a crowd. It's the voice that will open my ears. Isaiah reminds me that it is in "quietness and confidence" that my strength will be and that the effect of righteousness will be quietness. (Isaiah 30:15, 32:17).

Sometimes our world gets very loud – arguments, discussions, noises of all kinds, inside our heads and all around us. It can be very confusing, until we turn it all off and listen for that quiet voice. Elijah discovered that. Even when God promised to reveal himself, he did not come in the earthquake or the wind or the fire. He came in a still, small voice, a gentle whisper (I Kings 19:11-12).

You went to lots of quiet places, feeling the need to communicate with your Father, a place where you could really hear his quiet voice. We also need those quiet places – sometimes for hours, sometimes for five minutes. We can find them in lots of places: in the bathroom or with an apron thrown over our heads – that's how John Wesley's mom found quiet in the midst of her 12 children – in a designated prayer or War Room, under a tree in the yard, or walking around the park. But we need to remember that you speak in a quiet voice most of the time. So we will hear best when we are in a quiet place, like you did! Thank you!!

ROCK-SOLID MASTER

I know I can trust you through any storm – you are a sure foundation even when I am on "sand;" you are a safe place to be in the face of any enemy, even myself. The illustration you gave us at the end of the Sermon on the Mount shows us what that means. The wise man built his house on the rock; the foolish man built his on the sand. And that makes what you are saying meaningful and visual – whether we live on a bluff in California or on a sand dune overlooking Lake Michigan.

Of course you were talking about our lives being built on you, and only you are Rock-Solid! Even in Genesis the people knew you as the "Rock of Israel." The Psalmist referred to you as the Rock and Redeemer. You said you would build your church on a rock, one which the powers of hell could not overcome. We need a solid foundation and you are it – the church and each of us as individuals. Then the powers of hell will not be able to prevail against us. "On Christ, the solid rock, I stand; all other ground is sinking sand."

SAVING LORD

Sins are ugly and lead me in the wrong direction, selfishness and pride, but you don't let me stay there. You offer me your saving right hand and I am pulled back to you.

The first step you took for me was to save me from my sins. You did that by dying for me and you showed me my sins and said you were willing to forgive me, no matter what I had done. And you did it. As I learned more of you, you continued to show me what you wanted for me. You said that the blood of Jesus could and would keep me clean. It's as if the blood of Jesus is coursing through my veins, like my physical blood in keeping me continually clean on the inside (I John 1:9). You keep the blood flowing within so that I am aware of my thoughts, my words, my actions and can allow you to keep me clean in body, mind and spirit.

Sin in the form of Satan still comes along to tempt me to selfishness, to pride, to anger, but you are with me to remind me of your love for me, to offer me your strong right hand, to keep me from giving in, or to pull me back to repentance and grace, to you. Oh, Saving Lord, I am grateful!

TRUSTWORTHY GUIDE

I am sure I will not go astray from even the narrow way, even when other paths look good, for you know the way that leads to Life and I will walk with you. The old King James version of the Bible puts it this way, "I will instruct thee and teach thee in the way which thou shalt go: I will guide thee with mine eye" (Psalm 32:8). I always like to think of God's guidance that way – that all he would have to do is give me "the look" and I'd know which way to go. A more modern version says "with my eye upon you" and the NIV says, "I will instruct you and teach you in the way you should go; I will counsel you and watch over you."

You have been a trustworthy guide ever since you took Abram out of Ur of the Chaldees and showed him which way to go to find his new home. You guided the Israelites out of Egypt to the Promised Land with a pillar of cloud by day and pillar of fire by night. You guided David from the sheepfold to the throne. When the children of Israel would not be guided by you, you allowed them to be taken captive by Assyria and Babylon, but when the right time came you guided them back to their land. You used prophets and priests and kings to guide them, and when they just didn't listen you sent Jesus to show the way, to be the Way.

Now we have the Holy Spirit whose task is to "guide us into all truth" (John 16:13), and what a guide he is!! You never lead us astray or down the wrong path. Even when the way is rough, you provide all we need, maybe not all we want, but always all we need. The Shepherd Psalm, the 23rd, reminds me that "I shall not want. He makes me lie down in green pastures, he leads me beside quiet waters, he restores my soul. He guides me in the paths of righteousness for his names' sake. Even though I walk through the valley of the shadow of death I will fear no evil, for you are with me." What confidence we can have in our Trustworthy Guide.

UNDERSTANDING TEACHER

Sometimes I am like your first disciples, not a good learner, definitely not a fast one. Please don't give up on me; tell me again until I remember what I am to do and to be. You taught in parables so that people, including the disciples, would remember what you had said. You taught the disciples how to interpret the parables so they would catch the deeper meaning, but sometimes they just didn't get it. You healed and restored and walked on water and fed thousands, but every time it was as if they didn't remember and you would have to say, "Don't you get it yet?"

Lord, I have several thousand years of examples and sometimes I don't get it. It makes me very grateful that you are an understanding Teacher, patient, willing to explain again, sometimes disciplining me when I really don't remember. I'm so glad that the purpose of discipline is to help me understand, to refine my character into your likeness, to encourage me to go on, try again, become like Jesus. Use whatever method will finally make me realize what it is I am to learn and to do in order to become the person you have in mind for me to be.

VALIANT DELIVERER

I praise you for every memory of times you have brought me through situations that would have defeated me, and I know you can do it again. You are "my rock, my fortress and my deliverer" (Psalm 18:2). Jesus taught us to pray, "And deliver us from the evil one" (Matthew 6:13). I look back and remember what you have done. I look at recent events and experiences and I know that you are able today. I look ahead and with confidence I pray, "Deliver us from the evil one."

Memories are good things, even though I'm not sure how we store them away, but in times of distress and stress, when things aren't going the way I would like them to go, I am glad to be able to remember how God has brought me through in the long ago past and in the recent past. I need to remember the wonders you have done. Isaiah said to the Israelites, "Though one cries out to an idol, it does not answer; it cannot save him from his troubles. Remember this, fix it in your mind. To remember the former things, those of long ago; I am God and there is no other; I am God and there is none like me." Especially remember this – "I make known the end from the beginning, from ancient time, what is still to come. I say: My purpose will stand, and I will do all that I please…Listen…I am bringing righteousness near and my salvation will not be delayed."

In the New Testament Jesus himself said, "I am with you always" (Matthew 28:20). The work of the Holy Spirit is to remind us of Jesus and His victories in us and for us and to assure us of his presence in the midst of temptation. The secret is to pray with confidence; to believe that we can have the victory; to trust in his power; to know that he can do it again. He is God and there is no other. His purpose will stand, as long as we are in him.

WATCHER GOD

I praise you that your eye is on the sparrow, and I know you watch over me; so I have confidence to be where I am, to be who I am. When I think about "Present God" and how frightening it could be to have you always watching me, I realize how blessed I am, instead of frightened, that you are watching, watching for things that could harm me, watching for things that would tempt me, and always providing a way of escape. Sometimes you take me around things that could endanger me physically. Sometimes you make ways of escape from things that could ensnare me spiritually. Sometimes I see those things and I am amazed at how you have rescued me. Sometimes I don't even see them, but I know you provided the way out.

I know I have to watch out as well. You warned the disciples, "Watch and pray so that you will not fall into temptation" (Matthew 26:41). You knew it was coming, fast and furious, and you warned them, but they fell asleep. Paul warned Timothy to "Watch your life and doctrine closely" (I Timothy 4:16), because he knew how easily we can fall into temptation. You are there to watch over us, to prepare us for what is coming. Your promises are sure – "He who watches over you neither slumbers nor sleeps" (Psalm121:3); "The Lord watches over you – the Lord is your shade at your right hand…he will watch over your life; the Lord will watch over your coming and going both now and forevermore" (Psalm 121:3,5,7,8). He wants none of us to perish. He wants us to be victorious, to find those ways of escape. O Lord, watch over me!!

XRAY HEALER

It was hard to find a word beginning with X, and I'm not sure I found one that is really a word, but it is one that expresses who you are, the one with the ability to see deeply into me, even though I would sometimes wish you didn't. The reason you see so deeply is to reveal to me those things that are keeping me from being whole, holy, like Jesus. You not only see them, but you are the healer who can make me whole.

Sometimes I know the parts of my life that need your cleansing and when I am ready, when I repent, confess, admit to my failing in some area, you do, indeed cleanse me. But sometimes I am not even aware of a fault, a sin, some piece of myself that you haven't yet dealt with, that I haven't noticed. Then I need you to look deep, whether I want you to or not. It took two touches for you to completely heal the blind man. After the first one he could only see "trees walking." But when you touched him again he could see clearly. Make me see clearly, Lord! When you healed the woman with the issue of blood as she touched the hem of your garment, you called her out so that she could be completely clean, not just of her disease but even of her sins.

Whatever may still be hidden within, deep within, Lord, I pray that you will show me as you shine that xray light on my inmost self and cleanse me so that I will be whole, holy, like Jesus.

YEARNING FATHER

You long for me to follow your leading, to be in step with you all along the way, calling me back to your side when I wander off, keeping me on the narrow road that leads to life. You long that none of your Creation should perish.

You are like the Shepherd who goes looking for one lost sheep, like the woman looking for her one lost silver coin. You are like the father of the Prodigal Son, yearning that all your children would come home, watching for the lost one day and night, but forcing none of us to come. You have a banquet, a ring, new shoes waiting for us; you long to throw your arms around any of your wandering ones who return. You'd like to have a party!!

I'm not sure I can comprehend how great is your love for your children. "For God so loved the world," each person in your world, "that he gave his only son so that whoever believes in him would not perish but have everlasting life" (John 3:16). It doesn't matter what we've done, where we've been, how we've lived our lives, the lives you have given us. You just yearn for us to come home, to follow your leading, to bring us back from wandering, to keep us on the road that leads to life, to throw a party. Why would you want to do that? And yet, and yet, you do want to; you will throw a party. And what a day of rejoicing that will be!!

ZEALOUS GUARD

Thank you for keeping me as a Shepherd watching his flock, keeping me from going astray, protecting me from danger, guarding my soul. Paul tells us that we should "rejoice in the Lord always. I will say it again: Rejoice....Do not be anxious about anything, but in everything by prayer and petition, with thanksgiving present your requests to God. And the peace of God, which transcends all understanding will GUARD your hearts and minds in Christ Jesus" (Philippians 4:4-7).

Your desire is for us to be safe in Christ Jesus where nothing and no one can harm us or even cause us to fear. He gave this plan for those of us who love and serve him – "I know the plans I have for you, plans to prosper you and not to harm you, plans to give you hope and a future" (Jeremiah 29:11). That sounds like a guard who will give us the best protection, who will not fail us as long as we are in His will. "His way is best, you see. I'm in his hands."

MEDITATIONS ON DANIEL

~

ANCIENT OF DAYS

I wonder where that name came from. It makes sense to call God Ancient of Days. He was before time began. He is now in the present; and he will be when time ceases to be – Ancient, in fact, eternal, everlasting. Daniel alone calls him that and in his vision he describes God as we would describe a venerable old man, but one who has not lost his vigor – "advanced of days," "pure white hair and dressed in shining white robes. That person took his place on a throne blazing with fire, a river of fire flowing from before him" surrounded by an enormous crowd waiting to hear the judgment that was to be meted out to the evil one (Daniel 7:9-10).

He alone, this Ancient of Days, greets the Son of Man awarding him with the crown of universal dominion won through his sinless life, his redeeming death and his victorious resurrection. Yes, Jesus, the Son of Man, our Savior will come before his Father God, the Ancient of Days, and be given "authority, glory, and sovereign power over all peoples, nations, men of every language" and they will all worship him.

John describes the Son of Man in terms that Daniel used to describe the Ancient of Days, uniting Father and Son – "I saw…someone like a son of man, dressed in a robe reaching down to his feet….His head and hair were white like wool, as white as snow and his eyes were like blazing fire. His feet were like bronze glowing in a furnace and his voice was like the sound of rushing waters" (Revelation 1:13-15).

Our Ancient of Days and Jesus, the Son of Man, Messiah, Savior will conquer, "Lift up the strain. Evil will perish and righteousness shall reign."

> O worship the King, all glorious above,
> And gratefully sing his power and his love;
> Our shield and defender, the ANCIENT OF DAYS,
> Pavilioned in splendor and girded with praise.
>
> O tell of his might, O sing of his grace,
> Whose robe in the light, whose canopy space;
> His chariots of wrath the deep thunderclouds form,
> And dark is his wrath on the wings of the storm.
> (Salvation Army Songbook #16)

#1 Daniel 1:1-2

"In the third year of the reign of King Jehoiakim of Judah, King Nebuchadnezzar of Babylon came to Jerusalem and besieged it. The Lord let King Jeohiakim of Judah fall into his power, as well as some of the vessels of the house of God. These he brought to the land of Shinar, and placed the vessels in the treasury of his gods."

Sometimes God "lets" the strangest things happen, like this-

"The Lord let King Jehoiakim of Judah fall into his

power...," to be taken captive to Babylon along with vessels from the temple and other members of the royal family and the nobility. It occurs to me that over the years the Israelites had become very insular, keeping to themselves, enjoying their peculiar status as God's people, unwilling to share the treasure they possessed in their relationship with God and the Law. They had not ventured to other lands, other peoples to talk about their God.

I think of Jonah, who was reluctant to go to Nineveh. Even when the Ninevites repented Jonah became angry with God for being so good. He did not want the Ninevites to worship his God. Becoming so separated from the rest of the world had not increased the Israelites faith or developed their love for God. Was God again saying, "It's time to get out of your cocoon and help others discover me?" I had only thought of this exile as punishment for the many sins the people had committed including getting further and further away from real worship. I'm sure that was part of it, but Godly wisdom is so far beyond my thinking and so much bigger than my thoughts. I am sure that God had a lot more in mind than just punishment.

I need to think about the things that sometimes seem like punishment in my life. What is God saying to me? Maybe I need to be reminded of who God is, reminded that he is in charge. Could he be making me get out of my cocoon and do something extraordinary for him right where I am?

Help me to see what you are up to and get in on it, Lord!

#2 – Daniel 1:3-6

"Then the king commanded his palace master Ashpenaz to bring some of the Israelites of the royal family and of the nobility, young men without physical defect and handsome, versed in every branch of wisdom, endowed with knowledge and insight, and competent to serve in the king's palace; they were to be taught the literature and language of the Chaldeans. The king assigned them a daily portion of the royal rations of food and wine. They were to be educated for three years, so that at the end of that time they could be stationed in the king's court. Among them were Daniel, Hananiah, Mishael, and Azariah, from the tribe of Judah."

Chosen because they were of the royal family and nobility, chosen because they were handsome, perfect specimens, chosen because they were already "versed in every branch of wisdom, endowed with knowledge and insight and competent to serve in the king's palace," they were the best of the best. But they did not know the literature or language of, at that time, the greatest kingdom on earth, the Chaldeans. Chosen, but they had a lot to learn about their new home. Had the Israelites forgotten there was a world out there needing God? Evidently there was nothing "wrong" in the Jewish tradition with learning the language and literature of this foreign land, but they would not break their dietary vows as Hebrews and consume what was offered them, even if, they were assured, they would become stronger and wiser by doing so.

How is it that these four Hebrew boys/young men, with all

the sin and corruption going on around them back in Israel, managed to maintain the standards of the Jewish faith? The nation as a whole, including those in power, had wandered far from their God, but somehow these boys, individuals in that nation, had learned the essentials of their faith and kept it strong. Who had taught them? Who were their mentors? Did they have godly parents, teachers, faithful rabbis? Why were they totally committed, at the risk of their lives, to the God of Abraham, Isaac, and Jacob?

#3 – Daniel 1:3-6 (see above) and Daniel 1:17-20

"To these four young men God gave knowledge and skill in every aspect of literature and wisdom; Daniel also had insight into all visions and dreams. At the end of the time that the king had set for them to be brought in, the palace master brought them into the presence of the king who spoke with them. And among them all, not one was found to compare with Daniel, Hananiah, Mishael and Azariah; therefore they were stationed in the king's court. In every matter of wisdom and understanding concerning which the king inquired of them, he found them ten times better than all the magicians and enchanters in his whole kingdom."

These young men had been treated like other promising young men of the Chaldeans – taught the language and literature, offered the richest of food and forced by these things to become Chaldeans. King Nebuchanezzar had not realized that being a Jew, an Israelite, was much more than a matter of birth or even choice. It was a mindset, a way of life, a commitment to the God of gods, the Lord of Lords, the Ruler of the universe and the King above all gods. They would learn the language and the literature, but what God had written God had written and they would not break his law. New names would not make any difference either. So they ate vegetables and drank water for three years, in obedience to God. In the end, they looked better, were wiser, and knew more than any of the others. In fact, they were "ten times better than all the magicians and enchanters in his whole kingdom!" And in addition, God gave Daniel the gift of insight into dreams and visions. Diet? – I'm sure that helped; good living? – that helped also; the Spirit of God at work in their lives? – beyond a doubt!!

And he still does those wonders! He makes us wise, reminds us of what we have learned, gives us the insights we need, walks with us as we are obedient because the Spirit of God is at work in our lives.

#4 – Daniel 2:1-23

One thing that magicians and enchanters were able to do, or at least could fake doing, was interpret dreams. When Nebuchadnezzar had a very troubling dream he called them in, only this time, to test them, he demanded that they not only interpret the dream but also tell him what the dream was, definitely something they could not do. They told the king, "No one can reveal it to the king except the gods, whose dwelling is not with mortals." Hmm! Interesting statement. So what does Nebuchadnezzar do but order them all killed.

Evidently our four Hebrew friends were not there, but they were included in the execution order.

By now Daniel had gained enough of a reputation to convince the Commander of the king's guard to give him some time to find the explanation the king was demanding. He and the other three began to pray earnestly and, lo and behold, the mystery was revealed to Daniel in a vision that night. And what does Daniel do? He blessed the God of heaven with a prayer given to us in verses 20-23, a wonderful prayer!! - one I would do well to memorize and pray when God answers prayer for me. Instead, I am prone to go running off to tell the dream and the interpretation, to celebrate a victory, to rejoice with friends in a healing, to go on my merry way, glad for whatever it was that has happened, but neglecting to take time to thank the God who made it happen.

God, you do so much more than I can ask or think, and when you do sometimes I neglect to give you the praise that is due your name. I want to remember to be like Daniel and thank you first, first above all else.

#5 – Daniel 2:24-49

"There is a God who reveals mysteries," Daniel said to King Nebuchadnezzar, when no wise man, or enchanter, magician or diviner can do so. And so Daniel told the king not just the interpretation of the dream but the dream itself. "You were looking, O king, and lo! There was a great statue....Its appearance was frightening." He described the statue and then proceeded to tell the king what each part of the statue represented. This giant figure of gold, silver, bronze, iron mixed with clay looks into the distant future where the world rulers would each be defeated until finally they would all be destroyed by a stone, not cut by human hands that struck the feet of iron and clay and broke them to pieces. Every piece of the statue became like "chaff in the wind and not a trace could be found." But the God of heaven "will set up a kingdom that will never be destroyed, or left to another people." And then Daniel added, "The dream is certain and its interpretation trustworthy." And we can trace its accuracy in the annals of history.

When God gives an answer we can be sure of its authenticity, as prophecy of things yet to come or the best way to live right now or what to expect when we do what is right or what is wrong. He is, after all, the sovereign Lord of all, Creator, Preserver and Governor of all things. And he knows the outcomes and the consequences. As Nebuchadnezzar acknowledged, "He is the God of gods and the Lord of kings and the revealer of mysteries."

#6 – Daniel 2:24-49

One of the things I notice about Daniel is that he was a highly disciplined man, and we'll see more of that as we continue his story. As I read, it occurs to me that discipline of any kind is a choice I make. It is not something required by law, or that failure to do would lead to punishment. It is something that will make me better, whether it's physical activity, meditation, service, prayer, study, keeping to a schedule, being on time, practicing music, whatever it is. I can choose to do it or not. I think I am a fairly disciplined person, but I don't have a regular physical exercise routine. I have no doubt that I would be better physically if I did. It is so easy to make excuses. I can find a way to get it done, if I really want to, if I am disciplined, if I choose to be healthier.

Daniel was able to interpret Nebuchadnezzar's dream because he was disciplined, spending time with God in prayer regularly and not just when he needed something. It appears that he meditated on the Torah which he had learned as a child. He had studied not only the Hebrew Scriptures but now was a Babylonian scholar, and he benefitted from both. What discipline do I need to further develop in order to become all God wants me to be? Discipline is the lifestyle of discipleship, and I want to be above all a disciple of Jesus Christ.

#7 – Daniel 3:1-12

The story in chapter three is a lesson in worship. Nebuchadnezzar had a statue made of himself and ordered the people to worship the statue or die. How easy it would have been to go through the "acts of worship" without meaning them, to bow down in mock obedience whenever the trumpets blew in order to save his life. But Daniel and friends were disciplined for and committed to the worship of God and God alone. "Hear, O Israel, the Lord our God is one and thou shalt worship the Lord thy God and him only shalt thou serve." So they did not bow in mock obedience! So what is worship? Is it possible to pretend to worship? Can we do acts of worship that are not real worship?

As I consider those questions, it seems to me that worship is an attitude of the heart, a concentration of the mind, a connection of the soul/spirit with God's Spirit, a recognition and honoring of who God is, giving him thanks and praise. I can't judge if someone else is really worshipping, but I can create an atmosphere in which I can worship, the kind of place and time where I can think of God. For some that atmosphere is centered in formality, ritual, procession, repetition. For others it is spontaneous, even disorganized and informal. For others it is somewhere in between. But however we "do" it, worship is an attitude of the heart, in humble adoration of God, our Maker and Friend. It is a time and actions that lead me to realize the presence of God, to help me see, and the Spirit of God to help me hear the voice that speaks to me through the Holy Spirit and Scripture. It's seeking, knowing, confirming that God will be with me, guiding me through another day, another week. It's letting God love me and me loving God back. I never know what's going to happen as I worship or as a result of worship!

#8 – Daniel 3: 1-12

What a statement these three young men made when they said to Nebuchadnezzar, "We will only worship our God, not you. We will not save our lives with a falsehood, with betrayal of our God. We trust only Him and what he will do with and for us." I can imagine Nebuchadnezzar coming back at them with a list of all he had done for them, the new life with all the luxuries he had provided for them, what they "owed" him. Then he also may have regretted causing them to make such a statement because it meant they had to die and they had already proven to be of great value to him. However, this was the law and it had to be followed through!

But these three and countless others have come through such fiery trials, some unharmed and accompanied (visibly or not) by the Spirit of God. Sometimes, however, martyrdom is the result and God uses both means to accomplish good for his kingdom. I am thinking of Jesus as well as those apostles who died a cruel death because they refused to give up worshipping the one true God.

I think of Detrich Bonhoeffer who stood firm in Nazi times, determined to worship God even when the church failed to hold firm and who was eventually killed because of his beliefs. I am remembering Nina Davidovich, a lovely, hard working Russian Salvationist, who was placed in a pit for three months because she was teaching children about Jesus. She did not become a martyr, but like the three Hebrew young men was released and continues to serve the God she loves and worships. Fiery trials may come, but "it has no power over our bodies" (Daniel 3:27). Our faith may accomplish what the faith of Shadrach, Meshach, and Abednego accomplished. The king declares after they are released from the furnace, "Blessed be the God of [these three men]….There is no other god who is able to deliver in this way" (Daniel 3:28-29).

Who will I influence by my stand for God today? God is able!!

#9 – Daniel 4:1-36

Another amazing dream, interpretation and fulfillment, beginning and ending with praise by King Nebuchadnezzar who has been so affected by the faith of Daniel as well as Shadrach, Meshach, and Abednego and the work God did for them and through them. This chapter begins with a statement the king made after the experiences of the rest of chapter 4. He learns a lesson in this chapter about who God is. I may acknowledge with some understanding that God is sovereign, but I don't think anyone has had that sovereignty demonstrated more forcibly or dramatically than Nebuchadnezzar.

Daniel told Nebuchadnezzer that if he would atone for his sins, mainly the sin of pride, by "showing mercy to the oppressed," whom he probably didn't even know existed, and "with righteousness," then his "prosperity would be prolonged." However, he chose to ignore the warning and had to endure the humbling experience of being stripped even of his sanity before he would do the acts that God required of him. When his sanity was restored he blessed the most high (Daniel 4:34-35) and ended his praise with "for all his works are truth, and his ways are justice and he is able to bring low those who walk in pride." Now that is an amazing statement from the mightiest king on earth at the time. Would that all rulers, all people for that matter, would know, acknowledge, live in that truth. God can and will "bring low those who walk in pride." He is sovereign and he will prove it, now or later!

Lord, help me to show mercy to all people and to act righteously in all I do so that I will not need to be humbled by you.

#10 – Daniel 4:34

In the midst of Nebuchadnezzar's recognition of God as God, he says, "…his sovereignty is an everlasting sovereignty." That statement helps me understand that word, "sovereignty," and allows me to grasp free will at the same time – a paradox for many of us. What I see here is that God's sovereignty is huge but is evident much of the time only in the big picture. God has given us lots of freedom to make choices, not wanting us to be puppets. He wants obedience to be an act of love, but in the long run, in the big picture, he is everlastingly sovereign. He does what pleases him. In the end, we make the choice and realize the consequences. That may not be seen day by day. God ultimately does what he "wills with the host of heaven and the inhabitants of earth" (Daniel 4:34). We cannot stop him except in rare instances (as Moses did once and the king who begged to be healed). We cannot say to him, "What do you think you're doing?" in such a way as to show contempt for him, questioning his wisdom and knowledge. God in the book of Job, chapters 38-41, challenges Job who had been through experiences similar to

King Nebuchadnezzar, wondering what God was trying to do. The tough statements God gave to Job make us realize that he is sovereign no matter how things look to us in the present moment. Or maybe we should read those chapters before we ask such a question!!

Lord, give me a vision of you, an experience with you, continued realization, deeper and deeper that will cause me to worship more completely, know you as fully as possible, and thus become able to know and do your will most acceptably - to remember, you are able and you are sovereign – the big picture!!

#11 – Daniel 5:1-30

Suddenly in chapter 5, we are introduced to a new king, Belshazzar, who was the son of Nebuchadnezzar according to verses 18 and 22. He doesn't follow in his father's footsteps or learn from the lessons his father was taught. I love the word "remember" because I have discovered its value as an action word. I have learned that if I don't learn from what has happened in my own past or from the past of others, both the positive and the negative, I will suffer the consequences. Belshazzar knew what had happened to his father but he refused to humble himself before God and in fact exalted himself to the point of showing contempt for the true and living God. He praised false gods using vessels from God's temple in Jerusalem that had been carried to Babylon with the captives. Therefore, God said through Daniel, "God has numbered the days of your kingdom and brought it to an end; you have been measured (as we all have been) and found wanting....Your kingdom is divided and given to the Medes and Persians." And that very night Belshazzar was killed!

If he had only remembered what his father had learned; he could have been king for a long time, but he chose not to remember and so he died.

Remember! God is always able to do what needs to be done whenever and wherever, and he will do it in his way and in his time, every time. My faith is strengthened every time I remember who he is, and put today in perspective of his everlasting sovereignty.

#12 – Daniel 6:1-9

When jealousy rears its ugly head, even the best people, people like Daniel against whom his enemies could find no fault, will find they have enemies. Others who were vying for position with the new king, Darius – yes, another new king, this time a Mede – began to look for ways to eliminate their chief rival whom Darius wanted to appoint over the whole kingdom. Only one possibility could be found to trap him and that was somehow through his connection with the law of his God. Daniel did not live a righteous life in order to gain position and power but because he knew it was the right thing to do. His only purpose was to honor God and when honoring God turned out to be the thing his enemies would use against him, he still honored God.

Being blameless is no guarantee of safety today either. There are bullies looking for someone to pick on; employees who are jealous of the good work we do because we want to please God; people who want what we have gained because we have integrity; those who will accuse us of wrongdoing just to see us squirm when we really have nothing to squirm about. The only way we can be trapped is in connection with the law of God, demanding from us something that would be against our faith in God, our worship of God, our walk with God.

Lord, help me to stand firm, no matter what others may say against me in any arena of my life.

#13 – Daniel 6:10, 11

If I prayed three times a day as Daniel did, how, when, where would I do that? Did he have set prayers like the Psalms? I know that monks and nuns do that as well as praying for specific needs each time they pray during the day and night. Daniel prayed towards Jerusalem each time, but I know that God doesn't live in a specific place; however, I have a place of prayer to which I go to be alone with him and to meditate, ponder, contemplate, and experience his presence. Do I need to add a time or two of prayer each day, a specific time that will bring me closer to God, make me stronger in times of temptation? Can I learn to "practice the presence of God" and be always living on two levels, one in the world and the other in the presence of Him who will lead me each step of the way?

Which is best for me where I live and in the times in which I live? This practice of spiritual formation certainly made Daniel strong in faith, able to face certain death with calm and confidence! Somehow I know I should follow his example!

Should I follow his example also about things like diet? Oh no, not that, Lord!! But I do want to be healthy, and I want my family to be healthy. Help me to find the people who will hold me accountable to spiritual disciplines that will make me like you. Give me courage to practice the disciplines that will make me like Jesus. Lead me, Lord!!

"They found Daniel praying and seeking mercy before his God." Of course they found Daniel praying; it was his habit, his holy habit. They knew exactly when and where he would be doing that very thing because the law of the Medes and Persians was not the ultimate law in Daniel's life. He knew what was coming but he did not break his habit; he sought the mercy and grace he would need when he suffered the punishment for doing God's will, even a lion's den, which isn't likely for me today.

Whatever circumstances and situations I face today, I can worship, pray and seek "mercy and strength to help in time of need" or worship and praise and seek God's guidance, be in his presence, enjoy the outpouring of grace, love, peace, and joy – whatever I need to prepare me for the tasks at hand.

#14 – Daniel 6:20

One thing Darius realized is that our God is the living God! He makes that declaration quite clear when he comes near the lion's den after Daniel had spent the night there. Darius cried out, "Daniel, servant of the living God, has your God, whom you serve continually, been able to rescue you from the lions?"

In his subsequent edict he says, "He is the living God, and he endures forever; his kingdom will not be destroyed, his dominion will never end." He lists the characteristics of our living God, some of which I sometimes forget - He endures forever, is indestructible, the deliverer, rescuer, worker of signs and wonders in heaven and earth. It helps me to spend time each day considering who God is, the God I love and try to serve. The Psalmists are a great help; they seemed to have an understanding and an ability to express who God is.

My God knows what is best for every situation – even a fiery furnace or a lion's den even though people sometimes die there – his omniscience always knows what is best and right so I can trust him!

#15 - Daniel 7

Chapter 7 is Daniel's vision of four terrifying beasts, the last one being the worst, until the Ancient of Days comes to sit in judgment, destroy the beast and the "little horn" and set up the new kingdom of the "Holy Ones of the Most High" – an everlasting kingdom. It is easy to see how people have speculated and continue to speculate about who or what each of these beasts represents. Has it happened? Is it happening?

When Hitler, a man of small stature, seemed to be taking over the world, some thought he was the "little horn," but then he was defeated and the "Holy Ones" did not take over. And so on we go. Judgment is yet to come. In many places you, O Lord, appear to be "on the back burner," not eliminated since you can't be and you still have many who are faithful to you in all places, but many places are ripe for someone to "save it," to rescue it, to rescue us. Reading the biography of Bonhoeffer and the book of Daniel at the same time helped me to see how history and prophecy, the times of all sorts, come about. I cannot attempt to put labels on people or on events, but I see you at work. I am not terrified like Daniel, maybe because I've never seen anything like what he saw. I know You, the Ancient of Days, and I am confident that you will come again at the right time and you are Life Eternal.

#16 – Daniel 8

A ram, a goat, horns that grow, are broken off, change into many horns – all symbolic of world powers that come in force and are defeated in weakness, none lasting nearly as long as their initial power and conquering might would indicate they could. Kings and kingdoms will all pass away, but your kingdom, O Lord, is from everlasting to everlasting. Their transgressions may reach full measure (verse 33) and another may come up who will succeed with even worse destruction, but he, too, "shall be broken and not by human hands." Daniel understood it was not something soon to happen. But it was terribly frightening, not something to be figured out, but a warning – this exile and cruelty he was facing would be repeated – but it was also a promise; in the end, all that evil would be broken by God. Hold on!! Whatever the world and Satan may plan in order to overthrow the very Kingdom of God would not in the end succeed!! Hallelujah!

#17 Daniel 9:1-19

Daniel's expression of praise, confession, and petition in this powerful prayer is all he can do. How often we face situations where we feel helpless, and here is the answer – all we can do is pray for mercy as Daniel did, and not so much for our own sake as for God's (verses 18 and 19 sum it all up). Is there anything I have done to bring disgrace to God's name? Did I fail your church? Did I fail to show an example, to pray, to disciple? Help me, O God, to know what to do to redeem the situation for your sake, O Lord.

Another lesson to be learned here, I think, is that we must be careful how we interpret your word, and we must read it for understanding from the Holy Spirit. These people had been in captivity for 490 years. Where had God's Word been in that time? Had they let the Word through Jeremiah remain unread and now as Daniel reads that word how does he interpret it correctly? Lord, help us to read and understand all of your word in the light of Jesus and the work of the Holy Spirit. May we not jump to conclusions, but continually search for understanding.

#17 – Daniel 10-12

These three chapters are one story – a vision of what is to come, whether it has happened or is still to come I don't know. My interest in finding out that sort of thing is limited, but I do understand why it is so fascinating to some people. It is Daniel's encounter with the "one in human form," maybe Gabriel, and the "one who touched" him that speak to my heart today. Daniel was obviously overwhelmed by this encounter, but the vision was not just vision, but reality as he felt the touch and heard the voice. "Greatly beloved, pay attention to the words I am going to say to you." Listen! "Do not be fear, greatly beloved; you are safe." Daniel admits that he was strengthened by these words – and surely we can be strengthened because God through the Spirit continues to say these things – Listen to what God is saying and do not fear.

The world would see kings rise and fall, great kings, strong kings, but always there would be people who were loyal to God and the covenant who would stand firm and take action (Daniel 11:33)!! There would be purifying of the saints through suffering and the righteous who would lead others to righteousness shining like the stars. (Daniel 12:3).

But Daniel was told to seal this vision, this prophecy. It is to remain secret. Is it too much for those in captivity to bear to know it's only going to go on even after their release? Is there no hope, no end to this cycle? Or is it because so many will try to figure it out and cause themselves and others much distress? I'm with Daniel. I've read it; I know in the end God will triumph and the faithful will share in the triumph, but I will go my way and rest secure in him. "You shall rise for your reward at the end of the days." It doesn't mean "rest" as in do nothing, but as in "rest in the Lord," "take my yoke," wait on him," "let him direct your paths," "do not worry, little flock, for the Lord has promised you the kingdom." Seal the book – not everything is to be shared, but so much is.

Lord, guide and guard your word that is in me and my sharing of that word. Use me as your spokesperson, when and where and how you can best use me. I feel "dearly beloved!" Thank you!!

THOUGHTS FROM MATTHEW

AUTHORITY in the Storms of Life

I've never been in a storm at sea, but I have been on an airplane in the middle of turbulence – scary! "Without warning a furious storm came up on the lake" – scary! Without warning the plane began to buck and shake; dishes fell out of cupboards in the galley; the pilot told us to be sure our seatbelts were fastened; the stewards sat down quickly and buckled themselves in – scary! "But Jesus was sleeping!" The disciples woke him saying, "Lord, save us. We're going to Drown." I think I prayed, "Lord, save us; we're going to crash." Jesus simply rebuked the wind and waves and it was completely calm. The pilot guided that plane through the turbulence and it was completely calm.

We've known all kinds of storms in our lives and we have been afraid, but when we know our Father is with us, we can trust ourselves to him, even as we cry out, "Lord, save us." An old chorus says, "He knows; He knows the storms that would my way oppose. He knows; He knows, and tempers every wind that blows." I ask myself, "Do I really believe that he has authority over everything?" I don't have to waken Jesus when the "storms of life come rolling over me." He is present and ready to go with me through any storm, or he can calm the storm as he sees is best for me. He knows.

AUTHORITY over sin

Here is a story (Matthew 9:1-8) I wish I knew more about! Some friends brought a paralyzed man to Jesus. We have no information as to why he was paralyzed, but it seems obvious that his friends, at least we assume they were friends, wanted him to be healed, and they believed Jesus could do it. In fact, Jesus saw their faith and said to the man, "Take heart, son; your sins are forgiven." What?!?! Now that, I'm sure is not what the friends or the paralyzed man had in mind when they came to Jesus. The bystanders, some of whom were teachers of the law, couldn't believe it. "You can't do that; only God can forgive sin; it's blasphemy."

Jesus' reply first says that those teachers of the law were thinking evil thoughts. Then he says, "Which is easier to say, 'Your sins are forgiven,' or to say 'Get up and walk.'" Jesus knew that anyone could SAY, "Your sins are forgiven," and you'd never really know if they were or not, but only he could say with authority, "Your sins are forgiven," and they would be, but the teachers of the law didn't believe in Jesus' authority so they didn't believe it could be true. Maybe to show that he had to release the man from some bondage that held him in paralysis, Jesus said to him, "Get us, take your mat and go home," which he did to the amazement of the crowd.

Most of us are not paralyzed by our fears, our sins, our lack of belief, our doubts, but there may be things that keep us from being our best self, and Jesus can free us from those things. We will then be able to get up and do and be whatever is our best self. "When sin is dealt with, resurrection can't be far behind," says Tom Wright.

AUTHORITY over the evil one

One thing I noticed about Jesus as I read the stories of his encounters with people who were demon possessed – he did not shy away from confronting them and the evil within them. He knew, and so should we, that Jesus' authority and power are greater than Satan's – why, even the demons recognized it. They knew who he was and were afraid, and they certainly didn't want to be sent to hell. Their choice was to enter pigs (Mathew 8:28-34).

Satan seems to be using different tactics today, more subtle, more "civilized;" possession acted out differently, but needing to be confronted - the urge to molest children or women, to kill, to cause chaos and fear. Is Satan using addictions? All can be healed, as this man was, by the power of Jesus let loose in his life. "Deliver us from the evil one" in whatever form he may appear or whatever he may throw our way.

AUTHORITY with compassion and grace

For three chapters in Matthew (5-7) Jesus has been teaching with authority, and "not as their teachers of the law." But beginning with chapter 8 he shows his authority in physical, practical ways by healing a leper, restoring a centurion's servant, relieving Peter's mother-in-law of her fever, casting out demons from those who showed up at the door and in fact healing all the sick, fulfilling prophecy from Isaiah. "He took up our infirmities and carried our diseases" (Isaiah 53:4).

Jesus is still doing that, though not always making them go away. He has other purposes to fulfill in many incidences, but he does work with us through them, sometimes carrying our load or helping us bear it with grace as he pours his compassion on us.

Authority and sacrifice

A teacher of the law (Matthew 8:18-22), maybe one who had heard Jesus teaching on the Mount and then witnessed the miracles, decided, maybe impulsively, that he wanted to follow Jesus "wherever you go" – a pretty impulsive decision. Considering what he had heard and seen over several days, he may have wanted Jesus' kind of power and authority, but Jesus told him another side of the story – the life he lived was a sacrificial life which meant giving up some physical securities. Jesus said he had "nowhere to lay his head." Was that a bit much to think about for this man?

Another man in the crowd said he'd like to go with Jesus also, but only after he had buried his father. That seems like a legitimate reason to delay. Matthew said that these two were Jesus' disciples, and maybe had even made a tentative commitment but weren't so sure that now was the right time.

We have the record of Jesus choosing the 12 to be with him, and these two were not among them. Jesus did not call either one of them, the one to give up everything and the other to come now and leave his father. Jesus did not call or choose either one of them and it really did have to be Jesus' choice. There are many ways in which to be his disciple, many places in which we can witness for him, many ways to show compassion and kindness. We each need to find His choice for us.

MUSINGS IN MARK

Before we begin –

The Gospel of Mark is easy, quick to read, and we are continually pushed forward by his many uses of "at once," "immediately," "as soon as," "one day and then another day." But then again Mark calls us to pay attention to details and there is so much to see and ponder. The Gospel can be a quick read or a long meditative read.

Take a moment to just read the first three chapters. Look at all that goes on, the variety of things that happen, that Jesus took care of – his temptation, the calling of the disciples, driving out evil spirits, healing a man with leprosy, the stretcherbearers, answering questions. There are miracles and teachings and confrontations

Chapters 4-6 have many wonderful parables along with an explanation of why Jesus used parables so much in his teaching. Then there are healings and challenges and the miracle of feeding 5,000. And we ask the question, "Can I do that?"

Mark was not an apostle, one of the chosen 12, but he was a believer, whose source of information when he chose to write his Gospel was probably Peter. We catch some of Peter's impetuousness and excitement in the style with which Mark writes. It is not chronologically accurate but the attention to detail in many of the incidents is amazing. He is probably the John Mark we read of in the books of Acts, whose mother's home was a gathering place of the believers (Acts 12:12) and who traveled with Paul and Barnabas on their first missionary journey, though he left them part way through (Acts 15:37) and is mentioned later by Peter as being "his son" (I Peter 5:13).

But that's enough background and introduction. Let's get into the book, the Gospel, and do some meditating, some pondering, some looking at detail and at the big picture.

WHO IS THIS ABOUT?
Mark 1:11

Mark calls him, "Jesus Christ, the Son of God." We could take a long time just to think about that!

Jesus – human name, born, raised in a loving home as an ordinary/extraordinary child, teen, young man who left home at the right time. He was about 30, not too early or too late, mature and ready to do the will of his Heavenly Father, eventually completing his work by dying – the end of his human life.

Christ – the Messiah, the One who would do the impossible, who as the human Jesus died but as the Christ rose again.

Son of God – the expression of God, the Word of God come in the flesh, a designation that we humans give him that is so far beyond our comprehension to understand or verbalize. This person, Jesus, is God come to earth as human, as our pastor used to say, "crammed into flesh," but now alive, living in Heaven – I can't explain it!!

The amazing thing is that I can have that same familial relationship with God – I too am human. It's a father/daughter/son relationship. God called Jesus, "My son, whom I love" at his baptism (Mark 1:13) and later at the Transfiguration (Mark 9:7). And according to Matthew, invites us to talk to our God as "Our Father...." (Matthew 5:9). Not everyone is comfortable with calling God "father." Often that is because of a difficult relationship with their earthly father, but if we can imagine God calling us his son or daughter, and he does, then the designation "father" can become a loving one.

For the Jews, for whom Mark would be writing this Gospel, the connection to Isaiah in verse 2 is very important. The "beginning of the Gospel" actually goes all the way back to Isaiah, not simply the coming of Jesus but the fulfillment of prophecy from ancient times. And then Mark links the prophecy to John the Baptist, the one sent ahead of Jesus to "prepare the way." Don't we all have that task – to prepare the way for Jesus to become real in the lives of those around us?

And suddenly "the whole countryside" came out to hear what John was saying, to see this phenomenon, this man dressed like the Old Testament prophets, who ate strange things from nature, whose message was, "Repent for the forgiveness of sins." We may not get the "whole countryside" to come to us to hear the Gospel, and I'm sure God will not ask us to wear strange clothes or eat weird food, but he does ask us to prepare the way.

Who showed up but Jesus – and he will "show up" when we tell our friends and family about him - and John baptized him, and the heavens were "torn open and the Spirit descended like a dove on him and a voice said, 'You are my Son, whom I love; with you I am well pleased.'" The whole Trinity is present – Father, Son, and Holy Spirit! They are present when we are preparing the way.

That's who this is all about – Jesus Christ, the Son of God. Just think about it!!

GOOD NEWS
Mark 1:1-8

The Gospel, the Good News, began long before what we call the Gospels. It began in Genesis 3:15 and Mark says it is prominent in Isaiah mentioning God's messenger who would precede Jesus, preparing the way, crying in the wilderness, "Prepare the way for the Lord." There were signs from the beginning of time, and on through Isaiah and Malachi that Jesus was coming.

"So John came," the preparer of the way. Repentance, forgiveness, confession, water baptism! John was a simple, but complex man who drew a crowd, many of whom believed. However, he always pointed to the One who was on the way, who would soon arrive. He was just preparing the way. I can be a preparer of the way today!

John's message was that someone greater, more powerful than he was coming, someone whose sandals he was not worthy to untie. A slave would quickly untie sandals, but John says Jesus is so worthy that he, John, would be less worthy than a slave. He baptized with/in water for repentance, but when Jesus came he would baptize with the Holy Spirit. There was no question but that he would come, and come with power, with fire according to Luke. This is a new power, a new resolve to walk in the Spirit, moment by moment.

SOMEONE ELSE IS COMING!
Mark 1:7-8

John proclaimed the need for a baptism of repentance and people flocked to him and were baptized in the river. But that was not his whole message. He immediately told them that someone else was coming after him who was more powerful than he. In fact, he said, "I am not worthy to untie the thongs of his sandals. I baptize you with water, but he will baptize you with the Holy Spirit." What John was doing was a symbolic cleansing in water, but the one who was coming would do a deep, thorough cleansing by the Holy Spirit. He was saying that those who receive that "baptism" will be completely different people, inside and out.

Symbolism is often good and for many people and in some circumstances, it is very helpful. However, the deep meaning can be lost or misinterpreted. It can become the excuse for not living the life the symbol is intended to bring about. We need the baptism of the Holy Spirit to break our tendency to wander, to drift, to lose the motivation, to be caught in the emotion but not in the commitment we may have made at the moment. Water baptism is symbol. Spirit baptism is not. Water baptism is done by man on the outside. Spirit baptism is accomplished by God on the inside by the Holy Spirit. Water baptism is a first step for many people, but it is incomplete until we allow the Holy Spirit to take over our lives completely, become our Lord, and thoroughly cleanse us from all sin.

Jesus' baptism was a move from his home to his ministry. The Spirit came and settled on him, indicating the beginning of a new era, a Holy Spirit era, a beginning that would not be completed until after the Resurrection and Pentecost, when the Spirit came in power (Acts 2:1-12). We, who live in this era after Pentecost, can have the same experience Jesus had - the Spirit can speak his affirmation to our hearts, confirming his constant, unchangeable love for us all the time.

But beware, the first thing that happened to Jesus after that baptism was to be led or sent by the Spirit into the wilderness to be tempted by Satan, be with wild animals and, thank God, be attended by angels. And that's all Mark says. You can check out more detail in Matthew or Luke.

"Follow me!"
Mark 1:14-20

What drew Simon and Andrew, James and John to leave their nets without hesitation and follow Jesus? Luke and John give us a little background, but Mark simply says that Peter and Andrew were casting their net and James and John were preparing theirs when Jesus came by and invited them to go with him. James and John "left their father, Zebedee, in the boat with the hired men." Did Peter and Andrew have their own business? Had all four of them heard him prior to this encounter and begun to believe that the "time had come?" Had they recognized that "the Kingdom was near?" "Had they repented?" Jesus knew they were ready and they responded! Their hearts were ready and their bodies responded!

For us, we may need to have a daily response as well as a lifetime commitment. "What do you want me to do today with all you have entrusted to me?" We have made a lifetime commitment, maybe a call to a particular work, or a ministry that is full time, but it still needs to be a daily commitment as well, one step at a time.

CALLED

Not everyone was or is called out of what they are doing to do something totally different. Many, if not most are called to continue doing what they are doing but to do it differently, or God's way, with all their might and integrity and in the name of Jesus.

Some throughout history and today are called to something else. As I prepared to teach high school English, I heard, "Come, follow me as a Salvation Army officer and I will make you a teacher of my Word." I left my classroom and followed him; I left my mom and dad in Decatur, Illinois and followed him. I am still learning how to teach and I am still teaching, still following him where he is leading. It has taken me from The Salvation Army college, through Michigan, Illinois, Indiana, Russia (and Finland), to Army headquarters in Chicago and now to Colorado, to serve and worship him at The Army in Fountain and now the WLC/ Nazarene Church in Woodland Park. I may not move house again but I will go where opportunity in the Spirit leads. I will be "obedient to the heavenly vision." It may be a process of teaching that will change – from "classroom" to writing, always knowing that God's leading is always right. I don't want to waste the gifts God has given me. God, help me see what you want from me now in my life, to know where you are leading me. I will follow, whatever that might mean.

HERE I COME, READY OR NOT!
Mark 1:14-39

"The time has come. The kingdom of God is near, is at hand. Repent and believe the good news!" According to Mark, these are the first words out of the mouth of Jesus. I wonder if the crowds that heard him understood what that meant or was it something they would remember and ponder? Time's up! Here comes God! Everything is ready and prepared! Here I come; ready or not!

And you know it's going to happen again, without warning next time if we read your word correctly. The facts are the same – "repent and believe the good news!" The Kingdom of God is near, at hand! Life, real Life, is available now! Life abundant!

Two sets of brothers from two families, all fishermen who were dependent on their profession of fishing, one set of brothers are casting their nets into the Sea of Galilee and the other set cleaning their nets, when Jesus passed by and simply said, "Come, follow me, and I will make you fishers of men." And they did! How amazing is that – maybe not the whole story (See John's Gospel 1:40), but amazing! Sometimes God's challenge to us can disrupt life, the life we had planned. In the Bible, he called only 12 to actually follow him, but he calls many to live for him every day – in fact, that's a call to all people. Many, maybe even most, are called to continue doing what they are doing, but do it differently, with integrity and in the name of Jesus. These four, however, were called to learn a new vocation and they went with Jesus immediately. "Here I come, ready or not!"

They, these four and Jesus, went into the nearby town of Capernaum, entered the synagogue and Jesus began to teach, with amazing authority, and in the middle of service a demon possessed man interrupted him, yelling out, calling him, "the Holy One of God." Jesus said "sternly, 'Be quiet! Come out of him!'" And it did! "Here I come, ready or not!"

A bit less dramatically, he moved on, into a home and healed Peter's mother-in-law and in the evening, he healed all the sick and demon-possessed who came to the door. "Here I come, ready or not!"

What a day!! The next morning, after what we hope was a good night's sleep, he needed some time alone. But those four found him and told him there were people looking for him again. But now he knows it's time to move on, to visit other villages and preach, and off they went, traveling throughout Galilee, preaching and casting out demons. "Here I come, ready or not!"

And that's what happened in chapter 1:1-39 and we aren't even to the end of chapter 1 yet – I'm already exhausted.

Solitude
Mark 1:30

"Very early in the morning...a solitary place." That's when and where Jesus went. I wonder if he did this every day. He didn't have a "Bible" or scrolls to take with him, and we never read of his writing anything (except in the sand once). What a treasure his journal would be!! But it seems to me that the early morning in a solitary place (maybe not so much "early" in the morning) is a wonderful idea.

I have had such places everywhere I've lived, even if it was in the living room in small houses, but now in a lovely spot in our present home. My only distractions are the beauty of the scene outside the window whether of snow or birds or deer or squirrels, darkness in winter giving way to light over Rampart Range. In the room are books, items that evoke memories, pictures of our boys, a tryptic of the Tetons. Sometimes it's enough to remember that "the whole earth is filled with his glory." Jesus met with his Father on this morning. Thank You for meeting with me in the morning!

Actions and words
Mark 1:35

"In the morning, while it was still very dark, he got up and went out to a deserted place, and there he prayed."

The disciples found Jesus in the "solitary place." They wanted him to know that everyone was looking for him. He responded by saying, "It's time to move on to other villages so that I can preach to them." He had been listening to his instructions from his heavenly Father and he does not mention healing or casting out demons. In fact, he says, "Preaching is why I have come," even though the next verse says he did drive out demons. All the miracles would have been senseless without his spoken word. People needed to hear the truth as well as see his power. His mission was to say, "The time has come; the kingdom is near; repent and believe."

Mark is probably using Simon Peter's reflections on Jesus' life, and knowing what we know about Peter as a man of action, he probably mentioned healings and casting out demons more than Jesus' words; those were more easily remembered by a man like Peter. But Jesus put the emphasis here on being with his Father, sticking with his mission.

WHAT DOES GOD HEAL?
Mark 2:1-12

When Jesus returned to Capernaum and crowds gathered, he preached to them first and then healed those who were in need. Mark, and maybe his source Peter, seem to remember the miracles or the confrontations and less the preaching, which I can understand. (John, in his Gospel, has more of the teaching/preaching words.)

In Mark 2:1 we have the incident of the paralytic brought to Jesus by four friends who let him down through a hole in the roof because there was no room to come in through the door. Jesus' healing was first for the man's sins. To the Jewish leaders, this was blasphemy – no one, not even the Messiah, could forgive sins, only God Himself. They did not recognize that Jesus was God and so they could not accept his words. Jesus' response – "Which is easier to say? Your sin is forgiven or get up and walk?" One could not be seen and therefore could not be verified, and the other could. I guess they needed to see the miracle, so Jesus proved his point by telling the man to get up, take up his mat and go home. And he did!! The healing miracle may have been done to prove that Jesus was the Son of God, the Messiah, but the real proof was that the man's sins were forgiven, the real miracle which wasn't confined to physical healing.

The people, including the teachers, had never seen anything like this! The focus was really on those teachers. Jesus knew what they were thinking and confronted that thinking. Would the man have been able to walk once his sins were forgiven or did he need Jesus to say, "Take up your bed and walk?" Did the man realize the completeness of the miracle before Jesus went on to address him again? I think he knew, but maybe wondered in wonder! He stopped to listen and then did what Jesus told him to do. I can imagine Jesus smiling at him and him smiling back in astonishment and then gratitude, leaving the place and saying to his friends, "Did you hear that; did you see the look on their faces? And look at me!!"

Compassion and confrontation! Forgiveness and healing! Jesus went to the heart of the man's need and met it. Amazement, joy, thanksgiving, praise!

DOING THE RIGHT THING
Mark 2:18-22

"Everybody is fasting" – everybody, that is, but Jesus' disciples. Why is that? Everyone is doing it – it's even the "religious" to do it! We've always done it and done it this way. But does that mean it's always the "right thing to do?" It's easy to be religious without being a Christian. And we need to be careful of that, of being a traditionalist or a legalist and losing our way, or loosening our relationship with Jesus and becoming critical of those who don't do as I do or as I say.

Jesus used the illustration of wineskins and of old and new cloth to show the difference between doing things because they are tradition and doing things because they are right. Sometimes, though not always, the traditional, the old wineskins, the old cloth, will tear or the wineskin explode if used improperly. Jesus had a fresh, new approach, bringing to us a newness that can't be confined to the old forms. However, he doesn't just throw out the old forms. Everything has its place as long as none of them become "legal" or "illegal." When they do they can ruin both the Word and the bearers of the Word for people who are seeking the Truth.

SABBATH KEEPING
Mark 2:23-28

And boy, did the teachers of the law, the Pharisees, have a lot of laws about Sabbath Keeping. Here they jump on Jesus and his disciples for plucking some heads from the grain as they passed through a field on the Sabbath – law breaking!! Jesus said that none of the accusations were true. In this case, he referred to David, the honored king who could do no wrong, the Pharisees' hero. When David and his friends were hungry they ate the consecrated temple bread that David got for them.

God made the Sabbath for us, so that we would have one day a week for rest and refreshment. God did not make the Sabbath for man to punish us if we did something "wrong" on this day. He is Lord of the Sabbath, as he is of every day of the week. The restrictions had been imposed by the rabbis, enforced by the Pharisees, but they were not God-given or even godly. One day a week for rest, just like God. Legalism sure gets in the way of being Godly!!

WHAT'S RIGHT?

There are times when fasting is appropriate,
But it can't be legislated, done by the rules.
There are times when feasting is appropriate,
But it can't be legislated, done by the rules.

Both of them are ways in which to express
our relationship with Jesus.
Someone has said that fasting (i.e. – dieting) has been
taken out of the sacred realm
And made it a wholly secular thing,
and it shouldn't be.
Someone has said that feasting (i.e. – overeating)
has been taken out of the sacred realm
And made it a wholly secular thing,
And it shouldn't be.

Have we taken fasting,
which God said was a good idea, for a good reason,
And made it something God did not intend it to be?
Have we made it ineffective, difficult, secular
Rather than part of holiness, sacredness?

Have we taken feasting,
Which God said was a good idea, for a good reason,
And made it something God did not intend it to be?
Have we made it ineffective, difficult, secular
Rather than a celebration of him?

Why fast? Why feast?
Do it all to bring God glory!!

HEALED!
Mark 3:1-5

He left the synagogue with a completely restored hand –
  Right in front of their eyes
  The crippled, withered fingers could move again;
        He could shake his neighbor's hand as they
        left the synagogue;
        He could hold his child's hand as they
        walked home;
        He could grasp his utensils and tools;
        He could play baseball;
        He could brush his teeth.
  What had been useless was made useful once again!
  Delicate surgery done in an instant, with a word.
  Fully restored!

MISUNDERSTOOD
Mark 3:20-22

Jesus was the most misunderstood person in history, I think. His own family greatly misunderstood him – "He's out of his mind!" they declared. And yet great crowds came to hear him, so much so that his disciples couldn't find time to eat. I wonder if, at this time, his family included Mary, his mother. I'm sure she was concerned about him. The stories she may have been hearing had caused others in the family to think he might be out of his mind and in need protection. Possibly his half brothers were jealous of all his attention, or were they concerned at this point.

The teachers of the law also misunderstood Jesus! They certainly were not trying to protect him but to accuse him. "He is possessed by Beelzebub!" was their analysis. This was more a reaction to protect themselves from those above them, the religious rulers, who were looking for faults in Jesus and his ministry.

Do we ever do that – misunderstand others, reach out to protect them from themselves, or react as we expect others to react without knowing the situation? Maybe what is happening is not at all what we expected. We think we see misguidance or "putting the cart before the horse," poor planning, not thinking ahead. We need to take the time to see the person or the situation from a different perspective. We can find ways to help, to provide what is needed (maybe just a listening ear), to encourage, to lift, but never to tear down!

A short time later Jesus' brothers came again to see him, bringing his mother with them (Mark 3:31). They may have thought that she could influence him to get off this dangerous course he was on and come home to Nazareth. I think, however, that she knew him and his intention and came along to humor her other sons. Jesus' answer to the news that they had come may seem strange to us, and probably did to them at first, but I don't think we have the whole story. Jesus could have gone out to see them or maybe they came in after he was finished teaching, after he had said that those with him, those who do God's will, are his mother and his brothers.

That's how we describe the church today. We have lots of brothers and sisters, and our biological family may know that or not. We have lots of moms and dads who nurture us spiritually along the way, and our parents know that. Mary may have come along this time to help her other sons understand him. It is important for us to have a supportive family around us and if not our biological family then our church family. We have each others' backs, support and lift each other, care deeply as we would biological siblings. Thank you for giving us family, Lord! Help us to take time to understand each other!

ON SOWING

The important thing is to scatter the seed wherever I might go, wherever it may land. Kindness can take root eventually; interest in the other can do miracles; even a smile can accomplish great things. My job is to scatter. God sends the "sunshine and the rain" to nurture the growth, or to soften the hard places. Speaking to Isaiah God said to keep on telling, sowing, until ruin comes and only a tenth remains because out of that tenth will come a harvest. Sometimes we don't understand, and when the disciples said that to Jesus, he explained it so that they would be able to apply the principles to other parables and other people. Mainly he said, Listen! Hear! Learn! "Only those who have faith understand." People who are ready to do that are the good soil.

So the farmer sows the seed, the Word. We can live out and tell the story in many ways, and it will fall on all kinds of hearts and minds. Some of them are in the world where it is a new thought, never heard before. It is unbelievable, and quickly rejected. Some are in the church, but troubles at home or on the job or in the news bring doubts and the cares of everyday life or the desire for more squeezes out the good news. The deception of ads or keeping up with friends or neighbors can overwhelm the truths of the Gospel. But praise the Lord some have been well prepared to hear and believe the possibilities of godly-living in the everyday life they have to live.

Each of these kinds of hearers may hear the same message and react to it differently because of the preparation, or lack of it, in their hearts. We are not responsible for their reactions, but we are responsible to put God's word into action through our actions and our words. We are sowers of the Word; God will do the rest.

MORE ON SOWING: Mark 4:26-29

A man scatters seed, again. I wonder if the disciples' ears picked up as Jesus said these words. Would they get it this time? The seed lies in the ground waiting to do its thing whether the farmer sleeps or spends all his time in the field watching for it to spring up. Rain and sunshine come and go and all by itself the seed produces whatever it was meant to produce. Man can improve, manipulate, but the seed, once it's in the ground comes up as what it was intended to be.

The seed is the Word. Get it into a person who is ready to receive it and it will become, will develop a Christlike person. There is a process. The person needs to be prepared, cultivated, have a desire to know Christ and to discover what this Christian walk is about. The gospel message has power in itself to become what it is meant to be in the life of a person. Our task is to sow the seed with thought, using love as our only real tool. We can enjoy the harvest!

The farmer may plant a mustard seed – Plant, not scatter. I think this means a more deliberate act, taking one individual and pouring ourselves into them. Billy Graham had a Sunday school teacher who did that with him, and look at the results. One on one ministry becomes effective in the life of the other so that they become a place of refuge where others can find Jesus. This method may take longer. These plants keep growing for years before they become mature, but on the way to maturity they become valuable to the Kingdom. It takes both kinds of plantings to extend God's Kingdom.

Sometimes I scatter; sometimes I plant; sometimes I nurture what others have planted; sometime I take part in the harvest; sometimes I plant for the now; sometimes I plant for the future.

RESPONDING TO THE STORM

When a storm hits, how do I respond?
> Jesus slept in peace and confidence.
> The others feared for their lives and awoke him.
> He simply said, "Peace, be still."
> And there was a dead calm.

I wonder what the disciples expected him to do.
> Help them row?
> Fix the sails?
> I don't think they understood how he could sleep.
> They hadn't experienced him in this setting before.

I know these stories;
> I know what you can do!
> I can be at peace in the storm.
>> Do I want you to help me row?
>> I may experience fear,
>> Or I can remember what you can do.
>> I can take precautions,
>> Or I can panic.
>> I can protect others who may be in the
>> storm with me.
>> And I can trust you.
>> No matter what kind of storm I may face.
> Your word to me in the storm –
>> "Peace, be still."
>> You will take care of us.

THE RIGHT APPROACH: Mark 5:21-43

Jesus always had the right approach to people when he met them or when they came to him. It might have been a demon possessed man in the tombs or a distressed woman among the crowd on the street or a blind man sitting by the side of the road, or a distraught father finding him in the middle of a crowd. In the case of the father Jesus went with the man, and even though he was interrupted by a woman who needed him and he stopped to help her, he stayed on mission even when others came to tell the man that his daughter had died.

If Jesus had come earlier, the father, Jairus, thought, the child would not have died. If you hadn't stopped to help that woman, my daughter would still be alive. But Jesus turned to Jairus before he could express those thoughts – "Don't be afraid" – of the storm or the demons or of death itself, "Only believe."

Now there's a statement for every scary, horrible experience. "Don't be afraid! Only believe." Our thoughts so often go to the worst that could happen, and it could, but we don't have to be afraid; just keep walking with Jesus and see what he will do.

Was the child, by now, dead or asleep? She could have slipped into a deep coma from which Jesus could and would awaken her. Jesus reached out, took her hand and helped her up. Mom and Dad were completely astonished. But Jesus' practical side told them to "give her something to eat." That might forego any rumors that she had died. An ordinary thing like eating would not immediately follow resurrection. Jesus always did exactly the right thing for exactly the right reason.

JOLTED INTO WONDER
(Mark 6:1-6)

Too busy to see
Too critical to notice
A crumb, a hem, a mustard seed,
That's all it takes to start;
Then Jesus takes that little bit
And works his wondrous art.

TWO BY TWO

When you sent the disciples out two by two,
    I have a few questions, Lord.
        Were they nervous?
        How prepared did they feel?
        Who partnered with whom?
Did they get to choose or did you choose for them?
How soon did they encounter the first demon
possessed person?
        Did they have an early morning prayer time
        each day?
        Was there a dominant member of each pair?
        Did they have success teaching, healing?
    Besides that, what did you do while they were
away?

What a celebration when they got back!

GETTING THROUGH THE STORM
Mark 6:47-52

Do I want God to help me row
Or does he want me to believe he will calm the storm
(or calm me)?
How do I limit Him?
Do I want Jesus to fix the problem
Or am I just expressing myself
And maybe seeking his guidance?
Jesus knows what I really need and He will provide it.
Intervention to still the storm
Or peace in its midst.

RITUAL OR REALITY
Mark 7:1-23

For the Pharisees it was all about ritual – not just the ceremonial handwashing, but also the dishwashing – cleaning the cups, and pitchers, and kettles. I don't know how clean the disciples' hands were, but the Pharisees jumped on them and on their leader, Jesus. Some of the Pharisees had observed that they were eating without the ceremonial washing. They insisted that they all "Live according to the tradition of the elders." But then they had to admit that it was not God's law, but tradition. Jesus answered from the book of Isaiah, "This people honors me with their lips, But their heart is far away from me. In vain do they worship me, teaching as doctrines the precepts of men" (Isaiah 29:13). Then he adds, "Neglecting the commandment of God, you hold to the tradition of men." Tradition for them was more important than the commands of God.

Can we, do we do the same? Can we, do we set aside the commands of God in order to observe our own traditions? Can we, do we in some way use our own excuses not to help our parents, our neighbors? The commandments are really only two – Love God and love your neighbor – no excuses.

It could be that, as the crowd was listening to Jesus reprimand the Pharisees, they could have been gloating over their condemnation, but now he turns to the whole crowd; everyone is included. "There is nothing outside of a person that can make you unclean, unless, that is, you let it in. Then what comes out of your mouth proves you are unclean." Could Jesus have been referring to what he was aware they were saying or even thinking against the Pharisees? Were they led to pray for them or make accusations against them? What thoughts do we harbor in our minds about the people we condemn as doing wrong? Do we pray for them or just think bad thoughts against them?

IS HE TALKING ABOUT FOOD? – Mark 7:17-18

When he had left the crowd and entered the house, his disciples asked him about the parable. He said to them, "then do you also fail to understand? Do you not see that whatever goes into a person from outside cannot defile."

The disciples have a dilemma. They have to admit that some of what Jesus says is beyond their understanding. Unfortunately, Jesus asks, "Are you so dull?" Yes, Lord, and so am I! Were you talking about food? Well, that was the last thing they had been talking about so they would naturally think he was continuing that discussion. No, he told them. Literally nothing that enters the body from the outside can make us "unclean" in the ritual sense. "It doesn't go into the heart/soul but into the stomach, then out of the body" (clearly food). But what comes out – and then he gives a long list from evil thoughts to murder, to envy, arrogance, sloth, and malice, ugly things that come from within to show an unclean heart.

What comes out of my heart – expectedly and unexpectedly? How do I respond or do I react? What do I try to hide? I need to look carefully at myself – hopefully before I react – to things each day. Do I have anything in my heart that would be contrary to your plan for me? Do I have a clean heart that will respond appropriately to whatever may come my way?

Moving on to chapter 8, we find the disciples have the same dilemma again – Is he talking about food? They have traveled from Tyre to Decapolis and back to Capernaum, have fed another large crowd of 4,000 and as he talks to them he says, "Watch out for the yeast of the Pharisees." Again they were sure he was talking about food because they have forgotten to bring enough bread for the journey. But what he said had nothing to do with bread! Yes, Jesus was upset with them, but not about bread. It had to do with ideas that can so easily permeate our thinking. Having physical bread was the least of their concerns – just remember feeding 5,000 with five rolls and 2 fish and feeding 4,000 with 7 loaves and a few fish and having leftovers both times!? In the middle of what's going on we don't get it, and if we don't ponder it later we still may not get it! It's important to ponder, to get the complete message Jesus has for us through the Holy Spirit. It may not be what we thought it was at all. It may not be about bread at all.

I CAN SEE CLEARLY NOW!
Mark 8:22-26

The blind man knew what trees could and could not do. He knew what people could and could not do; so when Jesus partially healed him, he could see fuzzy things, but they looked like trees, except that they were walking and trees can't do that; so Jesus took a second step and completed the healing. He wants to do that for us, to give us full spiritual vision, not blurry or fuzzy, "not the half, but the whole."

So Jesus touched the man again and he was "fully restored and he saw everything clearly," just like God wants us to see Jesus and ourselves and all spiritual things clearly. We don't even have to have clear physical vision for that. We could be blind and see clearly, or we could keep running into "trees" or be limited to seeing "trees walking." "Open my eyes that I may behold wondrous things out of your law" (Psalm 119:18). With the work of the Spirit in us we can see what God wants us to see, in ourselves, in the world and the people around us.

WHO ARE YOU? Mark 8:27

"Who do people say that I am?" a question you asked the disciples. So many people believe in God, but as an impersonal being, not someone with whom they want a relationship; maybe the creator, but one who is disinterested in "me"; maybe someone to call on when there's trouble, but other than that just someone out there who might be able to do something to help.

And what about me? Who do I say that Jesus is? Peter's exclamation, "You are the Christ!" was a particularly powerful statement in his day and to the other disciples, but what does it mean for us as individuals today? Is there something different today about what you are to us, to me? I am not a Jew; I am a Gentile in need of a Savior, not a political or national hero, but a personal one. So how do I answer the question?

You are my Redeemer even though I am not a Jew. I am a Gentile and yet you are still my Redeemer. Mark often described Jesus as going to the Gentiles and including them in the Salvation Story, healing them, their loved ones, casting out demons from them, not neglecting the Jews but including those who were not part of the Jewish culture, preparing the groundwork for the great outpouring of your grace on the whole world which you loved, even though it was unexpected.

So who is Jesus? – the Son of God, God, the Word, His Word made flesh, Savior, the One and Only, our Brother. There are other words – Vine, Light, Bread, Water, Resurrection, Life – each a fragment with which to describe you – allegories, metaphors.

FOLLOWING JESUS
Mark 8:34-38

We usually think of Jesus saying, "Follow me," but here he says, "Come after me." Does it mean the same thing, something else, something more? He gives three conditions – deny yourself (don't be the center of your universe), take up your cross (be willing to do whatever I ask), and come after me, follow me. Follow has a different meaning now than it did then – for many it was literal then – go where I go. To follow now means adhering to God's will, whatever that is for each person. It means living according to God's law of love first and then being obedient to his direction in my life. I cannot completely do that without denying myself and willingly taking up whatever "cross" he's given me. Doing those things means saving my life, my Life. Not doing them may save my physical life but losing my eternal life, my Life.

I think about being ashamed of Jesus and his words, and I wonder if I have been. Are there times I could have spoken his name in praise, or offered to pray with someone right then and there, or said I would pray for someone or even admonished or challenged someone and failed to do so. I am proud to be a Christian, called by his name. May I show it in my everyday life, wherever I am by word and by deed, unashamedly. That's denying self and taking up my cross and following.

CHOSEN
Mark 9:2-8

I often wonder why Jesus chose certain people in Scripture – chose some he would heal, chose some to follow him, chose one or two for special messages, chose three for a special experience. Why? And particularly here? Why Peter, James and John to witness the Transfiguration? What an event that must have been!!

Peter had just recently acclaimed Jesus as the Messiah and then he said to him, "No, Lord, you can't mean that you will die – I'll protect you." And then Jesus called him "Satan." Why was he included to be with Jesus at this great event? I know that in spite of his shortcomings he became the head of the church after Pentecost, preaching that sermon with so much power that 3,000 people were saved that day. James will become the first martyr, the first to die because of his proclamation of the Gospel. John would be the last living apostle, who would write so much about Jesus as the God of Love, a thoughtful Gospel, and three letters that are full of love, yet never a word about this Transfiguration experience. They were an interesting choice. Had they been the better listeners, the most responsive to Jesus' words? Were they the ones who would need this experience the most?

And why does he choose me?

HELP MY UNBELIEF
Mark 9:14-29

Mark tells us, "All the people were overwhelmed with wonder" when Jesus came down the mountain. However, Mark also says that the other disciples who had not been with Jesus on the Mountain, were engaged in an argument with the teachers of the law. Did the disciples and teachers ignore Jesus until he asked them what they were arguing about? Or were they among those who ran to greet you? A man in the crowd explained, "Your disciples could not heal my son." Jesus' response seems strange partly because I don't know whom he was addressing when he said, "O unbelieving generation." Could have been the crowd, could have included the disciples, and probably did include the teachers of the law. As a man, Jesus didn't know how long he would have to put up with them. I sense Jesus weariness with them for not getting it. He must feel that way with this generation also, including me. How often could I have stepped up to do his work and didn't? Could whatever it was have been accomplished by me, even to healing someone?

As soon as the evil spirit in the boy saw Jesus, it brought on a convulsion which Jesus did not stop immediately. Instead he asked a question – "How long has he been like this?" The boy's father answered, "Since childhood, but if you can do anything, have pity and help us." Jesus' response to that is, "If you can? Everything is possible for him who believes." So why hadn't it happened before this moment, through the disciples? Was it the father or the disciples whose belief was limited – or both of them? Could it have been just the disciples who didn't have enough faith to believe that they could heal the boy? Did the disciples believe that they could, but were they limited by the father's lack of belief in them?

Now the father exclaims, "I do believe; help me overcome my unbelief." And Jesus must have answered that cry because as a larger crowd came running, Jesus seemed to quickly call the spirit, a deaf and mute spirit, from the boy. It looked as if he was dead, but Jesus took his hand and lifted him up and he stood up. Jesus moved as he needed to, as he always does, sensitive to the father, to the boy, even to the needs of the disciples and the crowd.

It would seem that the crowd dispersed after the healing and Jesus went indoors with the disciples who were, no doubt, disappointed that they could not heal the boy. "Why couldn't we drive it out?" they asked. "This kind can come out only by prayer," was Jesus reply. I wonder what the disciples had tried. Maybe they just commanded the spirit to come out without referencing God's help.

I need to always remember that in whatever I do I need God's help; I need to know his will, his power to accomplish things, anything for his kingdom and in his name. I remember, though, that "in your name" is not a magic formula and will only accomplish the work I am doing if what I am doing is God's will.

BELIEVE IT OR NOT
Mark 9:30-32

Three times between Mark 8:31 and 9:32, Jesus had told the disciples what was going to happen. The first time, Peter rebuked him; the second time the disciples couldn't understand what "rising from the dead" meant, and the third time none of the twelve could understand and they "were afraid to ask," maybe afraid Jesus would get upset with them or afraid that the truth would be awful.

Hindsight is certainly clearer in this instance! But I can sympathize with the disciples. I wouldn't have wanted Jesus to be betrayed or killed and, while I would want him to rise, I wouldn't have understood how that could happen – even though I believed he was the Messiah. The disciples were in a conflict of belief/unbelief, I think – wanting yet not wanting the truth.

HIS WAY IS BEST: Mark 9:31-33

Jesus said he was going to suffer;
>   Be rejected by the elders, chief priests and teachers
>   of the law;
>   Killed and after three days rise again.

Peter was not expecting that to be the "rest of the story"!
>   "You can't do that, Lord!
>   "You've got the wrong plan.
>   "Let me tell you how to be the Messiah, the Christ."

No, Peter. You aren't listening!
>   Satan is up to his old tricks;
>   Planting wrong ideas in the mind of a friend.
>   Let God do things his way –
>   The Grace-filled way!!

AN EMBARRASSING MOMENT
Mark 9:33-36

How embarrassed the disciples must have been when you asked them what they were arguing about! They knew that arguing about such a thing as who would be the greatest was the wrong thing to argue about – but arguing is what one does when the subject is who's the greatest. Jesus did not argue about such a thing; he simply served by healing, feeding, caring for everyone including them. His answer to their argument was to sit down and call them to himself and say directly to them that the way to live was to be the "servant of all. If you want to be first, you must be the very last." The real test is not to want to be first. Welcome children which in that society would not be the thing to do to get ahead – much like today. And Jesus added to the disciples and to me, "Welcome a child and you welcome me and the one who sent me."

This is an area in which I have to be careful. I am less likely to welcome people in general than others that I know. I don't always "see" people. I may feel awkward, not know what to say, fear being rejected. I don't seek out new people, am sometimes preoccupied with my own needs, my issues, or responsibilities. Lord, help me to see people, especially children, and welcome them! Save me from the sin of inattention.

A CUP OF WATER, A DASH OF SALT
Mark 9:41, 50

Jesus told us that giving a cup of water in his name will bring us a reward. Some will do great miracles and some will just give a cup of water – "just give a cup of water" – but they will all be rewarded. I think of great preachers and I think of the Emergency Disaster servant! What a great promise! When it is done in Jesus' name there will be a reward. I am not the judge. It's in the motive that we can't read and shouldn't even try. I can read outcomes, see signs. It's all about caring for people, whatever their need. What needs will I perceive in people today? What needs can I meet? How can I be the hands and feet of Jesus?

"Everyone will be salted with fire," says Leviticus. "Add salt to your offerings." And then in Colossians 4:6 Paul says, "Let your conversation be always full of grace, seasoned with salt, so that you may know how to answer everyone." Mark 9:50 – "Have salt in yourselves and be at peace with one another."

What good is salt? It is a preservative, a seasoning, but just enough so that things will taste better. With too much salt, there is a bitter taste. So we need to speak with grace as well if we are to be the salt of the earth as Jesus wants us to be. We've got to have the right amount of "salt" and grace.

"ONE THING YOU LACK!"
Mark 10:17-31

"Good teacher," the man called to Jesus as he walked along the road. Was he calling Jesus "good," or was he saying he was a good teacher? "What must I do to inherit eternal life?" Jesus' answer is a question. "Why do you call me good?" Jesus seems to hear the man saying, "You are good." And he says to him, "No one is good except God alone." Then in answer to the man's question he may be implying that no one can "inherit eternal life." To have eternal life you must obey the commandments, all of them – the ones about how to treat others and the ones about loving God so much that you are willing to give anything God asks. For this man it would mean selling everything and giving away the money, in that process storing up treasure in Heaven and then coming to follow Jesus.

I wonder if Jesus saw in this man the qualities he was looking for in his disciples. Was he inviting him to actually come with him? Or maybe it was more a general call to follow him in the sense of doing God's will wherever he might be. "One thing you lack." One thing!! Just one thing would lead to total, full out commitment to Jesus. Eternal life isn't about inheriting or getting – it's about giving and receiving; it's about hearing and obeying.

The man went away sad – he had great wealth! Jesus was also sad – we can hear it in his response. "How hard it is for the rich to enter the kingdom of God." The rich have a hard time giving up their wealth in order to receive what Jesus has to give. They may hear but find it hard to obey, to come under the command of another, even God, trusting wealth more than trusting God, and it doesn't really seem to matter how much "wealth" one has.

I am struck by the sadness of these two – the man and Jesus himself. Jesus loved him! But the man could not bring himself to do what Jesus asked and that made him sad, as if he knew this was the right thing to do, but he loved his wealth or didn't want to disappoint his parents or his wife or.... Jesus watched him go and in sadness said, "How hard it is for a rich man to enter the kingdom." Jesus emphasized that as the disciples expressed their amazement.

We humans find it hard to give things up, even when it keeps us out of the Kingdom. We have to give up pride, relationships, possessions, status – anything that comes before God. I have to ask myself every so often, "Have I given it up? Am I holding on to anything new – time, treasures, talents. Maybe I am holding on to them and could be using them for God. Have I gone further up and further in; am I all in for Jesus sake? Or am I sitting at ease in Zion?"

The disciples couldn't grasp the concept. So "Who can be saved?" they asked. "With man this is impossible," Jesus replied, "But not with God. With God all things are possible!" I may think, as Peter did, that I have left everything to follow Jesus. But when we do leave "everything" it will be restored to us, along with persecutions, but also in the future eternal life. On the other hand, many who are first shall be last, the last first – if I have given up pride and everything else that will be okay. If I realize, recognize God's great love for me, he will be enough. All things are possible with God!!

NO FIGS!
Mark 11:20-24

One day Jesus and the disciples walked past a fig tree that was full of leaves but no figs. He cursed the tree and went on his way. The next day when they passed it, it was withered!! There are questions about that incident that cause us to ponder. Your statements are, "Have faith in God. Truly I say to you, whoever says to this mountain, 'Be taken up and cast into the sea,' and does not doubt in his heart, but believes that what he says is going to happen it will be granted him...believe and you have received them...Forgive...so that your father in heaven will also forgive you."

Is Jesus referring to their ability to curse a fig tree, move a mountain, or the need to forgive. Maybe he had the bigger picture in mind, like the destruction of the temple which is coming later. When we turn anything sacred, buildings, relationships, possessions – into something wrong or evil God will destroy it. A commentary says that the fig tree had leaves that suggested it also had fruit, and when it didn't have what it "said" it had, Jesus cursed it. When the temple, a beautiful place intended for worship and prayer, was used for commerce and chaos, you "cursed" it. At that moment Jesus warned the perpetrators, the chief priests and teachers of the law, to "clean up their act." But the time was coming for their order to be done away with. When we do not "produce the fruit" Jesus is expecting from us, when we do not allow his Spirit to indwell us so that we become a place intended for worship and prayer, will we also be cursed? Think on these things!!

THE LOVE OF GOD

What an amazing thing to think about!
Your two greatest commands –
Love God with all your heart and soul and mind.
Love your neighbor as yourself.
How do I do that?
If I allow God to immerse me in his love,
If I realize how high and deep and wide and complete is
his love,
If I recognize that he wants to engulf me in his love
So that I walk in love,
God himself being that love,
My only response can be to love him.

Now he begins to plant his love in my heart
So that I begin to love as he does –
Not perfectly because I have a lot to learn
about what that means
I have a lot to work through and overcome.
But as I allow his love to rule in my life I will
Love differently,
Love more deeply,
Love unconditionally,
Love those I've rejected,
Love those to whom I've been indifferent,
Love those I have only tolerated.

Lord, I want to be lost in your love
So that I can learn to love like you.

WHAT A QUESTION
Mark 12:18 –27

What a question!! The Sadducees don't even believe in the resurrection, yet here they are, asking you a question that deals with that very subject. "At the resurrection whose wife will she be, since seven brothers all married her?"

Jesus answer to them was, "God is not the God of the dead, but of the living." Does he avoid an answer to their question? No, it seems to me that his emphasis is on the present. We must concentrate on the here and now, on living for God. He is the Father of the living, of all he created, preserves, and governs. We should not worry about silly things or, for that matter, anything else, especially about who's going to be married to whom in Heaven. We are often in error, full of misunderstanding or misinterpretation about some things when there is so much we can know and should obey, and we should do a lot less worrying about things we don't need to know. We can live each day in him.

Lord, help me live today to its fullest, in love, with patience and gentleness, with grace, sometimes "seasoned with salt" as necessary, fully alive.

ON LOVING GOD and YOUR NEIGHBOR
Mark 12:26-34

A teacher of the law asked, "Of all the commandments, which is the most important?"

Jesus answered, "'Love the Lord your God with all your heart and with all your soul and with all your mind and with all your strength.' The second is this: 'Love your neighbor as yourself.'"

The teachers responded, "You are right...To love him with all your heart, with all your understanding and with all your strength, and to love your neighbor as yourself is more important than all burnt offerings and sacrifices."

I notice, if the translation is correct, that the "teacher" said, "...with all your understanding..." instead of mind or soul. I wonder if "understanding" is correct – do I need to understand or do I sometimes need to simply have faith? Why does that teacher leave out soul? Do these words mean the same to me as they would have to this teacher. Maybe the words make no appreciable difference in the meaning but they do make for interesting thinking. The teacher appears to get the idea that love is more important than all the burnt offerings and sacrifices. Jesus indicated that this thought was bringing him close to the kingdom of God.

But did he hear all the implications of love? Had he heard Jesus tell the story of the Good Samaritan and did he understand who his neighbor is? Did he observe Jesus forgiving the woman taken in adultery and agree with his actions? Was he there when Jesus brought Zaccheus, that

Jewish tax collector, into his fellowship? Did he know that Jesus loved little children and said we should be like them?

Love is more important than anything else, but it needs to be lived out through the emotions (heart) and in the soul, and by the body, and in the mind – the whole person. Then we have the answer to all the questions about how to live. Are my motivations love? Are my actions, my thoughts, my words full of love?

"From then on no one dared ask him any more questions." When we understand that answer, we don't need to ask any more questions; we don't dare ask any more, because we know what the answer is!!

DINNERTIME
Mark 14:1-9

Jesus and friends were enjoying a good meal in Simon's home in Bethany when a woman with an alabaster box came in, broke the box and poured the contents over Jesus' head. "What a waste," someone at the table said. "It was the equivalent of a year's wages and could have been sold to care for the poor for a long time."

But Jesus answered, "Why are you bothering her? She has done a beautiful thing for me. You'll always have the poor with you, people you can help, but you won't always have me. She did what she could." She was in a sense preparing Jesus for burial and her story is a beautiful one which will always be told in her memory. "She has done a beautiful thing...She did what she could."

When we do things out of love – simple or extravagant – they are beautiful. When I use my gifts to honor someone, family and friends who mean something special to me, I am doing a beautiful thing. I need to do more of that, more often, more thoughtfully - words, small gifts, a poem, even a touch, a hug and on occasion something more extravagant, a surprise. We have so much; we give so little. Some people have the gift of giving or of making things to give. All it takes is a little thought.

I think there's another point here, as well. When gifts are given to us, we should accept those gifts with grace. Others are honoring us with a gift – a hug, a present, words, whatever it is. They are expressing love or appreciation and, like Jesus, we should accept that gift with grace.

REFLECTIONS ON THE GOSPEL OF JOHN

The Word

Day 1

The Word

John 1:1 – God verbalizing; God expressing Himself; God, heard or read and understood by those who will listen, read, and ponder. He had spoken by the prophets and some listened. That word fell on some receptive ears and reached into some people's hearts. He spoke through kings and judges, and continued to use prophets who wrote volumes and prophets who wrote a paragraph or two, but many who could have heard had hard hearts and itching ears, wanting to hear only what they thought was good for them.

Did God fail? No, God had good communications skills – He knew how to reach them and he knows how to reach us. The question is, "Do I have good listening skills?" Do I really hear the Word? I know you want to be heard. What words will I hear today? Where will they come from? How much attention will I give them? How much time will I spend listening to YOUR WORD?

What are you saying to me in this verse? As I read it again, let me think of it in this way –

He said _____

I heard_____

He said _____

I understood _____

My prayer for today: "Speak, Lord, for your servant is listening."

Day 2

John 1:1-4 – "The Word was in the beginning" – not created, already there.

> "...with God" – together, Oneness
> "...was (is) God" – the "I am," God complete as Father, Son & Spirit
> "...He was in the beginning" – a person
> "...all things were made" – created everything
> "...in him was life" – source of life
> "...that life was the light of men" – source of light, inner light

Read and ponder the relationship between Genesis 1:1 and John 1:1.

What does this say to me?

What do these ideas from John 1:1-4 say to me about God?

About the Word? About creation? About life and light?

John 1:5 – Compare several translations of this verse. Paraphrase it for myself.

John introduces three key words for his Gospel in these verses, words that describe Jesus – Word, Life, and Light.

> Word instead of Silence
> Life instead of Death
> Light instead of Darkness

I want to see these three words as I read the Gospel, remember to mark them and what John does with them.

My prayer for today: "Help to see you in new ways today, Lord Jesus."

Day 3

Doing God's will

John 1:6-9 -John was a man fulfilling the role all God's people are intended to fulfill – bearing witness to the Light, not being the Light. His job and ours is to reveal the Light to the world in which we live. We become the means by which others may comprehend the Light. Some may try to extinguish the Light in us as we reveal it. Remember, "people love darkness rather than Light because their deeds are evil" (John 3:19). Look what happened to John! (Matthew 14:1-2)

John was nevertheless, "a man sent from God...as a witness of the Light, so that through him all men might believe" (verse 7) Write that verse using your own name.

Write your testimony in a way that will specifically "bear witness of the Light" in order that others will believe.

My prayer for today: Lord, help me to see opportunities to witness about you, the Light of the world. May my words today bring light into the darkness.

Day 4

We need the Light

John 1:9 -Because of the way God made us, we need light, both physical and spiritual. Jesus, the Word who created light, also is Light, the illumination by which we can see ourselves and the world in a way we cannot see them without him – THE LIGHT. Try to see things today, through his eyes – yourself as a person loved and gifted by God; your family members as God sees them; the grocery store clerk and the guy next door, the person who works next to you and the boss whom you might encounter. What do you see in each of these people that you might have missed had you not prayed to see them as God sees them?

Look at the world around you, the world he created, the ants and the snowflakes, the birds and the landscape in which you live. "And God saw that it was good" (Genesis

1). Enjoy his creation!!

When you look at yourself you may see some sin/s that need to be taken care of them. Remember that the intention of light is to reveal and it can reveal things we are not proud of, but the intention is not just to reveal but to lead us to cleansing. If what God shows us in ourselves is something that needs to be cleansed, healed, made right with God, this is the time for it to happen. "If we walk in the light as he is in the light...the blood of Jesus, his son, purifies us from all sin" (I John 1:9).

My Prayer for today: Help me to see myself, my world, all things today as you see them. You are the light that will help me see it all in the right way.

Day 5

Part of the Family

John 1:10-13 - The world He had created did not know Him.

His own people whom He had chosen, rescued, guided, loved did not receive him. Was the Light too bright? Did it show them things they did not want to see?

"But as many as received Him to them He gave the right (authority, power) to become children of God...born, not of blood, nor of the will of man, but of the will of God" (New King James Version).

"But whoever did want him
        Who believed he was who he claimed
        And would do what he said,
He made to be their true selves
        Their child-of-God selves.
These are the God-begotten,
        Not blood-begotten,
        Not flesh-begotten,
        Not sex-begotten," (Message)

We are part of the family, the family of God, not by adoption, but by the new birth!! Jesus, himself, explains this more fully to Nicodemus in John 3:3-8. Born of the Spirit, natural children, born through belief, "god-begotten," spiritual children of our heavenly Father. Every child in the family is unique, special, with an inherited ability to be Godly. It's in our spiritual "genes" because the Holy Spirit dwells in us.

Who are you most like – your mom or dad?

What characteristics do you share with brothers and/or sisters?

How are you like your Heavenly Father? Name three ways at least.

Day 5

The Word become flesh

John 1:14 – Read this verse in several translations.

In case you don't have the Message this is how Peterson puts it:

"The Word became flesh and blood and moved into the neighborhood."

The Word became flesh – He didn't take on, over himself, clothe himself, put on – He BECAME, all the way through, HUMAN. He even chose a human fleshly means of "coming into the world," through human, bloody birth, and would leave the world through a human, fleshly means, through human, bloody death. His body had all the parts of a human body. His body needed all the things a human body needs. He became flesh. It seemed as if people couldn't believe if they didn't see; so here he is, in the flesh. Now will you believe?

At one time the mayor of Chicago moved into a rundown high rise apartment building in a ghetto to "live where the people live." Of course she had it remodeled and kept her very exclusive mansion home in a posh neighborhood. Mother Theresa also lived "where the people lived." Her convent room was right there among the poorest of the poor and there she stayed. "He became flesh and dwelt among us."

If Jesus moved into your "neighborhood" today and dropped in for tea this afternoon, what would you do? He will be there today and not just for tea, you know!!

My prayer: Thank you, Lord, for being where I am. May I realize that as I go through this day, aware of your presence, conscious of your guidance. Give me the courage to invite them in for tea, tea with you!

Day 6

Beholding His Glory

John 1:14-18 - "…and we beheld His glory, the glory as of the only begotten of the Father, full of grace and truth."

John is very clear in these verses about his purpose in writing and Jesus' purpose in coming. He wants us to get to know God. We have many images of Him – Father, Friend, Judge, Creator, King, Revealer, Priest, Redeemer, Shepherd.

Which is the one you relate to the easiest?

Which do you think was the most common in the Old Testament?

But now John says, "Here is the only begotten of the Father, full of grace and truth." "The law was given through Moses, but grace and truth came through Jesus Christ." And Jesus, who has seen God, been with God, existed at the very heart of God, has shown Him to us very clearly. If you want to see God, see Jesus. (Watch for this theme often in the teaching of Jesus recorded in this Gospel. You might want to come back to this page and list the references.)

How might this description, grace and truth, differ from

some of the Old Testament images of God? Some of your images of God?

If we take time to discover Jesus, get to know Him, learn about Him, spend time with Him, we will get to know God. Working through John's Gospel, seeing Jesus and learning about Him, can help us do that. "No man has seen God at any time; the only begotten God, who is in the bosom of the Father, He has explained Him" (John 1:18 NASB)

My Prayer: Open my eyes, Lord, I want to see Jesus, full of grace and truth.

Day 7

Who Are You? John 1:19-28 John identified himself by his calling and his message.

> John's calling – "I am the voice of one crying in the wilderness."
> John's message – "Make straight the way of the Lord."

Who am I?
> My calling _____
> My message _____

John again says he is not the Messiah. How does he describe his relationship to Jesus?
> John 1:15 _____
> John 1:27 _____

We have each been called by God to a special task. We each have a special message. What is your relationship to Jesus? Spend some time meditating on your answer to that question.

Interesting things to notice: Compare verse 10 with verse 26. What phrase is common to both?

John does not complete his statement, his answer about baptism in verse 26 until later (see verse 33), but he implies that his task is preparation for what will happen when "he" comes. John's baptism was the pattern of proselyte baptism. There was something else coming. Get ready.

My prayer: Thank you for my calling and the wonderful message that I have to tell. May my relationship with you grow so that I can be effective in sharing that message.

Day 8

HERE HE COMES!

John 1:29-34 - Read this passage in a couple of translations; read it over until you know the sequence of events well. Now close your eyes and use your imagination. Put yourself in the scene. Where are you in the crowd? Imagine the look on John's face, on Jesus' face, on the people in the crowd. Listen to how John says those first words. The Message says it this way – "John saw Jesus coming and yelled...." Is that how you would have done it? Spend several minutes living this passage, being there, experiencing your first view of Jesus.

John says three new things about Jesus –

> He calls him the "Lamb of God."
> He says he is the One who "will baptize with the Holy Spirit." (recall verse 26)
> He says, "…this is the Son of God."
>> Lamb of God – sacrifice for sin
>> The one who baptizes with the Holy Spirit – the fulfillment of the plan.
>> The Son of God – the One who can be the sacrifice and the fulfillment.

What does this mean to you?

My Prayer: I worship you this day, Jesus, the Lamb of God, who, because you are the Son of God, can be the sacrifice for my sin.

Day 9

TWO TONGUE-TIED MEN

John 1:35-42a - Andrew and another disciple of John the Baptist's (Might it have been John, the writer who never identifies himself throughout the Gospel?) – two introverts to whom John the Baptist says, "There's the Lamb of God." How do they approach Jesus? Two tongue-tied men and a gracious Jesus. An invitation to tea and conversation and new life begins. What did they talk about during that "10th hour" conversation? Whatever it was, "the first thing Andrew did was find his brother Peter and tell him, 'We have found the Messiah,' and he brought him to Jesus." I don't know if Peter resisted or not. I'm inclined to believe that Peter was convinced by the enthusiasm of his normally quiet brother. But he needed to see Jesus for himself.

Later Peter would speak for all the disciples when Jesus asked, "Who do YOU say that I am?" (Luke 9:18-20). But he first heard the answer from his brother before he even met Jesus – You are the Messiah, the Christ.

Andrew's story in the Gospel is brief but each time we meet him, he is bringing someone to Jesus – here in John 1:35-42; also in John 6:1-13 and in John 12:20-22. Read these verses and get acquainted with Andrew and with the man I think may have been John, the author's, best friend.

My Prayer: Lord, I thank you for those who brought me to you. (Take time to let them know how much you appreciate their part in bringing you to Jesus.)

Day 10
LOST AND FOUND

John 1:42-51 - Andrew <u>found</u> Peter (vs. 41).
Jesus <u>found</u> Philip (vs. 43).
Philip <u>found</u> Nathaneal (vs. 45).

They each seemed to think of someone to whom they

wanted to give a special message. And they went in search of that person until they <u>found</u> him.

Who "found" you?
Whom have you "found"?
Whom do you know that still needs to be "found?"

There is an interesting list of names Jesus is called in these verses.

Verse 45 _____ and

_____

Verse 49 _____ and

_____

Note which are human names and titles and which are Divine. Note which Jesus uses of Himself. How is each one significant to who Jesus is?

My prayer: Lord, I want to help _____ and _____ find you. Give me opportunities to lead them to you.

Day 11
JUST FOR YOU

John 1:42-51 - Jesus had great insight into people, even at what appears to be their very first meeting.

> Simon – "You are Simon, son of John. You will be called Cephas."

Philip – "Follow me" (And that's all he needed to
say).
Nathaneal – "Here is a true Israelite in whom there
is nothing false."

He knew each of them; he knows us.
    He read their hearts; he read our hearts.
        He understood them; he understands us.
            He may want to give us a new name.
            He may want us to do
            something special.
                He may see in us
                something we don't
                see in ourselves.

Listen for the special message he has for you today.

What does he call you?

What does he tell you about yourself?

My Prayer: Thank you, Lord, for loving me just as I am.
You know me better than I know myself and you see in me
things I do not see in myself. What do you want me to do
for you? I am willing!

Day 12
COME AND SEE

John 1:44-46 - Our feelings can keep us from knowing some
very special people. His prejudice almost kept Nathanel

from meeting Jesus. Let the Holy Spirit show you any prejudices you have.

Philip, fortunately, knew exactly how to answer Nathanel's objection, the only way to win him over – "Come and see." It was the same answer Jesus gave Andrew and his friend in verse 39 – "Come and see." That's how we overcome prejudice in ourselves, get to know the person, seeing him or her through God's eyes. People who reject Jesus don't know him; haven't met him, haven't been with him. We can introduce them to him. The only way to do that is to

> Spend time with them as he would
> Listen to them as he would
> Love them as he would

My prayer: Help me, Lord, to see my prejudices and be willing to get to know those who are different from me. Then I will be able to love them and invite them to meet you.

Day 13
YOU CHOOSE

John 1:1-12 - Listed below are three ways of looking at this passage of Scripture. Each is briefly sketched to give us a beginning. Choose one of them to expand on with your own thinking, ideas, development. Be sure to ponder with each passage what God wants to say to you that may be different from what is shared in this writing.

Thought #1 – Our first glimpse of Jesus in ministry publicly is at a party, a wedding party. The Messiah whom the five disciples have met in serious conversation takes them first to a party. At the party he performed his first miracle making the party even more exciting! He displayed his glory, and as result the disciples believed in him. (verse 11).

When you think about Jesus, what is the first emotion that comes to your mind? _____

Thought #2 – Paul Tournier has an interesting approach to the role of Mary, the mother of Jesus in this story. In his book, *The Gift of Feeling*, he suggests that even though Jesus protested, "My time has not yet come," Mary sensed intuitively that it was time, and she pushed him in the right direction. Tournier suggests that this gift of feeling is one of women's gifts to the church and ought not be taken lightly. Most of us have needed a push to help us get moving in the direction God wants us to go, what he wants us to do. Think back over those moments when someone has given you a word or has done something that has caused you to move ahead when you didn't think you were ready.

Thought #3 – "Do whatever he tells you," Jesus mother said to the servants. And they did! "Fill the jars," Jesus said, and they filled them to the brim. Water is now wine, the best yet served at the party. God does wonderful things whenever we do what he tells us to do.

Develop a prayer topic based on the thought you choose to pursue.

Day 14
PASSION, CONCERN, ZEAL

John 2:13-25 - "Passion for your house burns within me."
"Concern for God's house will be my undoing."
"Zeal for your house will consume me." (verse 17, NIV)

Passion, concern, zeal – what is my burning passion? What causes me to become angry enough to do what needs to be done to make a change? What do I care about so deeply that I will risk the reaction of others?

When Jesus replied to the Jews who demanded a sign, he talked about his body. That reminds me that today our bodies are the temple in which the Spirit dwells. Other questions arise when I realize that – How am I caring for this temple where the Spirit dwells? Diet, exercise, rest? Doing what the doctor says in order to enjoy life? How about the dentist? "Do you not know that your body is a temple of the Holy Spirit who is in you….?" (I Corinthians 6:19)

My Prayer: Lord, I've had to ask myself a lot of questions today. Help me to give myself and you honest answers that will cause me to make the changes and improvements that will make me more effective for you.

Day 15
BORN AGAIN?!?

John 3:1-12 - Born again, born from above, second birth

– different translations to help us understand a concept that was certainly new to Nicodemus but one with which we tend to be too familiar. Yet it may be one we do not understand, one that can cause confusion if we just drop it into a conversation with someone who doesn't have our Christian lingo.

Jesus helps us understand that just as our physical birth brought us into this world, our spiritual birth brings us into the Kingdom of God. Without the second birth, we cannot enter his kingdom any more than without our physical birth we could not have entered this earthly kingdom. Both births are necessary – one for life and the other for Life (verse 6). The first is by water and the second is by the Spirit (verse 5). Jesus himself said that how it happens cannot be explained; it can only be experienced.

Nicodemus was a teacher in Israel and he didn't get it even when Jesus used the wind as an example of things that cannot be explained only experienced. Oh sure, we can explain scientifically what causes the wind, but we can't "tell where it comes from or where it is going" though we can experience it.

Among the first verses most of us have learned is John 3:16. What do you think is the most important word in this verse? Why?

Jesus uses references to light in verses 19-21. Make a list of the contrasts and results of light, one of the key words in John's Gospel.

My prayer: Lord, there are many things that I cannot explain but I can and do believe in Jesus, my source of Light and Life. I want to live my Life in you, in the Light.

Day 16
"HE MUST BECOME GREATER AND I MUST BECOME LESS."

John 3:22-36 - John, the Baptist, gives us a wonderful study in how to react to those who become more "successful" than we are, even if we were before them. In the chart below make a list of who John says he is and who he says Jesus is. Then below think about who you are and how you react to others who may be younger than you, who are less experienced than you, who are wiser than you, who may be in authority over you. Listen to the Holy Spirit and be honest with Him and with yourself.

JOHN THE BAPTIST	JESUS

I am _____

I feel about those who are "over me" in these ways:

_____

My Prayer: I know who I am, and Lord, make me aware of who others are so that I do not presume on their authority.

Day 17
GETTING THE BIG PICTURE

John 4:1-42 - Today just read this passage in order to get the whole story. Visualize the events. Identify yourself with the various characters in the story – the woman, a disciple, a person from the town, Jesus himself. Try thinking of how it might occur today. Where could it happen? Who would compare with this woman today? Where would Jesus find her?

Today live the story. Write the story as you visualize it. If ideas or questions come to mind, record them for further thought in the next few days.

Day 17
WHO IS SHE?

John 4:1-14 - Woman……..Samaritan Woman………
Immoral Samaritan Woman

Not one thing in her favor except that none of it mattered to Jesus. He loved her. He loves you. Think of yourself in three words or phrases.

Which of these words or phrases matter to Jesus; which makes a difference to you?

Think of someone you are working with, or someone who lives near you, someone who attends your church, someone with needs or problems.

Describe them in three words of phrases.

Which word or phrase makes a difference to Jesus, which matter to him? He loves them, and so can you.

Jesus met the woman at the well. He asked her for water from the well, and offered her living water from a spring. Another thought you might want to look at – compare water from a well and water from a spring. How do you get water from each? What is the water like from each? What emotions does each evoke in you?

My Prayer: Thank you for loving us all just as and where we are. Help me to do the same. May I be willing to offer living water to all I meet today.

Day 18
WORSHIP

John 4:15-26 - The Samaritan woman was bound by tradition – "Our fathers worshipped…." (verse 20). They worshipped

God but only according to their ancient ways, based on the Pentateuch. They had refused to accept anything more, except that they had adopted some of the "traditions" of the Assyrians who had moved into their part of Israel at the time of the OT captivity.

Bound by tradition! What traditions do we have in our church? Have we taken on any traditions from the world? Are we bound by traditions that close us off from others, make us exclusive, demonstrate a lack of openness?

Jesus said, "We worship what we know for salvation is from the Jews."(verse 22) Here is the voice of authority. "...a time is coming and has now come when the true worshippers will worship the Father in spirit and truth, for they are the kind of worshipers the Father seeks." (verse 23) Here is truth! Yes, the Messiah is coming and when he does then the place of worship will no longer matter. What will matter is the manner of worship – "in Spirit and in Truth."

Where do you worship?

What does worshipping in Spirit and in truth look like?

How do you define worship?

My Prayer: Lord, may I see those things that may keep me from really worshipping you and see as well those things that will cause me to worship you in Spirit and in Truth.

Day 19
READY FOR THE HARVEST

John 4:27-38 - "The fields are ripe for harvest." How is that possible there in Samaria? These people had not accepted any Scripture past the first five books of the Bible. Could they have been seekers? What does God require for a soul to be ready to receive his truth? It seems to me that there must have been true seekers after God – people who remembered those stories from Genesis and the other books, priests who knew those Scriptures and were really awaiting the Messiah and teaching as much truth as they knew. Some were seekers who were about to be rewarded by an encounter with Jesus!

Today people are looking for the answers to their life dilemmas, looking for someone who will accept them just as they are and love them. Jesus is doing that, but he needs someone to be available to them to say, "Here he is!" We have all been sent into our part of the world with the message of his love, to be his witnesses.

Name some of the people you know who have something in their lives with which they need help, who are looking for a Messiah, who need to know how much they are loved by you and by God.

How can you show the love of God to each of them? How will they know that you and God love them?

My Prayer: Love these people through me, Lord, so that they will see my love and realize that it comes from you through me.

Day 20
LEAVE YOUR WATER JAR

John 4:27-42 - No woman, no matter what would cause her to hurry off, would leave her water jar by the well! Yet our Samaritan woman did so. Why? What caused this woman, this outcast, to hurry into town and call out to all the people in the streets, "Come, see a man...Could this be the Messiah?" (verse 29).

In the meantime, the disciples returned from having gone into town to buy food. Think about Jesus' reaction to their offer. What is his "food?" Have you ever felt that kind of satisfaction, either from some event in your everyday life or in your spiritual life?

"Because of his words, many more became believers." (verse 41) Our testimony is critical to drawing people towards Jesus, but we must also give them his words which are the words of life. What do they need to hear from us about him since they will not hear his words directly from his lips? What are the essentials of the message?

My Prayer: Teach me how to witness for you, not a canned message from someone else, but the truth as I have learned and experienced it with the essentials to help others to know you, "the Savior of the world." (verse 42)

Day 21
Take Jesus at His Word

John 4:43-54 - What does it take to make people believe?

When Paul wrote to the Corinthians, he said "Jews demand miraculous signs and Greeks look for wisdom..." (I Corinthians 1:22). The "royal official" in verse 47 begged Jesus to come and heal his son who was dying. Jesus seems to have replied very forcefully, "Unless you people see miraculous signs and wonders, you will never believe." Yet when Jesus went on to say, "You may go; your son will live," the man "took Jesus at his word" and discovered that Jesus had, indeed healed his son at the very moment when Jesus had said the boy would live. "So he and all his household believed." What did it take to make the father and his household believe?

What does it take to make us believe? What did it take to bring me to belief? A miracle, an example, Scripture, a testimony, hearing God's voice, realizing his amazing creative work?

When I read the Bible, do I take Jesus at his word and go my way to do what he tells me to do, believe what he says will be true, his promises sure and certain? Jesus always knows us right where we are and knows what we need to hear. He meets our real need and that becomes the place where need and the Gospel intersect. That is the place at which healing, salvation, godliness begin.

Think about three people you are praying for. Define their real need as you see it now, as the Holy Spirit reveals it to you. How can you meet that need? How does meeting their need intersect with the Gospel?

Take a look back – In chapter 3 and 4 Jesus met needs of a

variety of kinds of people – gender, nationality, economic status. What does this say to you?

My Prayer: Show me, Father, where and how to meet the needs of people within my sphere of influence without regard to who they might be.

Day 22
Do You Want to Get Well?

John 5:1-15 - What a question? Wasn't the answer obvious? Well, maybe not! There are excuses – no one to help me, someone else gets there first, I like the attention I get, I have no other means of livelihood except this one, I can't do anything else. Besides the only way I know to be healed is to take a dip in the pool. Is that possible? I don't know! Today we depend on doctors and medicine. Is that how healing comes? Jesus said to the man, "Get up! Pick up your mat and walk," and he did; he was healed. Can that happen today?

What kind of healing do I need? Can Jesus do it? Do I want to be healed? "At once the man (who had been crippled for 38 years, remember) picked up his mat and walked." He left behind his only means of support and did what he had never been able to do before. How about me? Are there things that I could do if I were only free of my fears and doubts, the things from my past that tie me down or my present challenges that paralyze me?

Not everyone understood; some were critical – after all it was the Sabbath and the man was carrying his mat! The man did not know who had healed him!! "Jesus had slipped away into the crowd." But when he needed some reassurance, "Jesus found the man in the temple" and gave him a stern challenge – "Stop sinning or something worse may happen to you." That's the life Jesus wants for us – stop sinning; there is so much ahead when you live the life Jesus has for you!

My prayer: Help me to look deeply into my heart; walk with me through whatever may be holding me back from healing and guide me forward.

Day 23
ROLES AND TASKS

John 5:16-30 - In this passage Jesus talks about what his role and his tasks are while he was here on earth.

1. Verse 17 _____

2. Verse 19 _____

3. Verse 21 _____

4. Verse 22, 27 _____

5. Verse 30 _____

Describe how you respond to each of these claims that Jesus makes.

Jesus also talks about what we should do.

1. Verse 23b _____

2. Verse 24 _____

3. How do you see yourself measuring up to his expectations of you as his disciple?

My Prayer: Lord, how can I best honor you today? I want to hear you speak to me through your Word and by your Spirit and then believing obey!!

Day 24
CONVINCING WITNESSES

John 5:31-47 - Jesus was talking to a hostile group who were trying hard to kill him. He has made his claims quite clear in the preceding verses, but he now turns to more proof through four witnesses, more than enough according to the law, if they will only believe them.

1. Verse 33 _____

2. Verse 36 _____

3. Verse 37 _____

4. Verse 39 _____

What convincing witness does each of them give?

Why do people not believe each of them? What do they miss, not see, refuse to see?

Each of them has left us a record and we have the additional witness of the Holy Spirit. Do you see their witness? Verse 47 may give a clue. Remember all of Scripture, including the stories of Moses, speak of Christ. Don't miss HIM!

My Prayer: I must admit, Lord, that I do not always look for you in all of Scripture, especially the Old Testament. Open my eyes, my heart, my mind to realize your presence and your voice through your witnesses, old and new.

Day 28
BASKETS FULL

John 6:1-13 - This is how I visualize the story:

Jesus saw the crowd that was gathering to hear him teach and hopefully heal some sick folks. He called Philip over and asked him, "Where shall we buy bread for these people to eat?" Philip must have been shocked when he looked at the sea of people headed their way. They couldn't possibly come up with enough money, even 200 days of labor would not earn them enough, and where could they find enough food for that mob? That's a lot of bread!!

Andrew had noticed a boy sitting right in front, getting his lunch out of his bag. "There's a boy here," he interjected into the conversation. "He brought his own lunch, looks like 2 fish and 5 rolls, but that's a drop in the bucket to what we need."

Jesus told the disciples to have everyone sit down and while they were doing that, he stooped down in front the boy and asked him if he'd be willing to share his lunch. "Sure," the boy replied, and handed it to Jesus. I can imagine Jesus sitting on the grass beside the boy, taking his hand and thanking God for the food, then telling the disciples to get a basket each." He began passing out the 2 fish and 5 rolls, breaking them apart and filling the 12 baskets, the boy sitting in companionable silence and quiet surprised, munching on the first few bites Jesus passed to him.

The disciples moved out with their baskets, feeding the 5,000 men plus women and children, coming back as necessary for refills, or maybe their baskets never emptied. Everyone had as much as they wanted and were full when Jesus told the disciples to pick up any leftovers so nothing was wasted. There was enough to fill each of their baskets with bread to eat their fill. I can imagine Jesus sitting there munching his lunch with the boy, talking about soccer and fishing and school while all this was going on.

Now, how do you visualize the story.

Day 28
AFTERWARDS

John 6:1-15 - Read again the story in the Scriptures. Read your visualization of the story, and maybe mine too.

Feeding the hungry was vital part of Jesus' ministry, a way of showing them his concern for the whole person. The church is well-known for its care for the physical needs of people. Jesus has often multiplied our loaves and fishes to feed thousands. We always seem to have enough! When have you seen God perform this miracle?

But if we are to be like him, we must be like him in verses 14 and 15 as well. He is the one who receives the honor for what we do, not us. When we help people, whether individually or as a church, and they want to glorify us, calling us wonderful names, wanting to make us "king," it's time to get out of the way so that Jesus can reign, not as "prophet" (verse 14) or as king (verse 15), but as Lord and Savior.

My Prayer: Lord, I know that you are the one who always provides enough for the needs we meet wherever they are encountered, but not everyone we help realizes that we give you the honor. Help me to remember to tell those who receive help at our hand that is God who saw their need and provided their needs through us.

PHILIPPIANS

LET'S GET PERSONAL

Some sections of Philippians are so personal they need reflection by each individual who reads them. "I thank my God every time I remember you...with joy" (Philippians 1:3,4). There are people in every Christian's life like that, people who have influenced us to follow Jesus.

There are also people who have been "partners with us in the Gospel," people who have worked with us in the church or in the neighborhood.

"I am confident that he who began a good work" in me, in you, in those named and unnamed above who will see that "good work" continue to completion, until the day of Christ. He may even have begun that good work through you!

"Completion" – what a word! We have no idea when that will happen. Today? Tomorrow? Next year? A long time from now? What "good work" has he been doing in me? What is he working on? Is it a negative thing, something I need to be rid of? Is it a positive thing I need to develop? What will I look like when I am complete? I guess none of us will know that "complete" answer until the "day of Christ." My goal is to keep moving forward in Christ, to keep getting better and better by the work of the Spirit in me.

"I have you in my heart" (verse 7). So another list. Who is in your heart? Who shares with you in God's grace? For whom do you long "with the affection of Christ Jesus" (verse 8). Jesus has such a deep compassionate love for us, a yearning to meet all our needs in the way he knows is best for us. For whom do you and I feel that sense of affection, of compassion?

For those people this is my prayer – "May you abound more and more in knowledge and depth of insight" It takes love to gain real knowledge and real depth of insight into the important things in life – into God, for instance, into myself, into the people I love. "So that you may be able to discern what is best." How do I know how to serve God? How do I learn to know and love myself? How do I know what to say or do for others, even in my family, that will be right and pleasing and helpful? It will take love gained through knowledge and insight or it will take knowledge and insight gained through love, love nurtured and growing through my love for God and his work in me.There is a second very profound and beautiful result of love. It will make us pure and blameless until the day of Christ (verse 10). That's the day, that day of Christ when we will be brought to completion. Then we will be "filled with the fruit of righteousness that comes through Christ Jesus, to the glory of God." What a prayer. I need to pray that for myself every day. I need a love like Jesus loves! And I pray it for you also!

HOW CAN THIS BE?

Philippians 1:12 – How am I supposed to respond when someone is arrested or even martyred because of their faith in Christ? It seems so tragic, so "how could this happen?" Where was God and his protection over his people who are doing his work? Then I read what Paul says here – "What I want you to know, brothers, is that what has happened to me has really served to advance the gospel. As a result, it has become clear throughout the whole palace guard and to everyone else that I am in chains for Christ. Because of my chains, most of the brothers in the Lord have been encouraged to speak the word of God courageously and fearlessly." Paul is in prison, a very unhealthy place to be, and how can that be good? Yet he speaks of two incredible outcomes: the whole imperial guard is hearing the message of Jesus and his fellow Christians have been made more confident in daring to speak the Word.

Paul says elsewhere, in Romans 8:28, "And we know that in all things God works for the good of those who love him, who have been called according to his purpose." Paul sees his imprisonment, or whatever ill comes his way, as God working for the good. All things, even imprisonment, martyrdom, things not going the way we planned or at least thought they should go, interruptions, illnesses as God's purposes – purposes we never saw, purposes that could happen only because of what we thought of as tragedies or at the very least inconveniences. How will God use them? How has he used them in your life? The whole imperial guard heard the good news. Other Christians were emboldened to speak up for Jesus!

HINDRANCES, HINDRANCES!

1:15 – Here is another hindrance Paul faced or at least what others saw as a hindrance. There were those who "preached Christ out of envy and rivalry or selfish ambition" in order to stir up trouble. Paul's response, "But what does it matter? The message is more important than the man" (verse 13 Message). If the truth is being heard, the Spirit will work. Some today preach a "gospel" we do not believe but God uses them to bring people to Christ whom we have not been able to reach. Those men and women have gone on to lead godly lives and bring others to Jesus. We may interpret some passages of Scripture differently than another. What happens to those who understand some aspect of Scripture differently than I do? Are they, or am I not a believer? The Spirit works in mysterious ways – let's rejoice.

TO LIVE OR TO DIE – THAT IS THE QUESTION!

Paul knew it was not his choice to live or to die, and he saw the value of both. If he lived, he would live in Christ. If he died, he would die in Christ – in fact, that would no doubt be better. Literally being with Christ would fulfill his heart's ultimate desire. On the other hand, being there in heaven with Jesus would mean not being close by to minister to these Philippians who were dear to his heart. Being here did, however, mean being in prison and he was willing to be in that place if it would help them in their "progress and joy in faith." He would be able to share in their "boasting in Christ."

There are some people with whom it is such a joy to share faith, with whom we enjoy working, with whom we love to worship, and we don't want it to end. But then we think it's probably better for them to "depart" to the better life. There are times when we want to "depart" but we know it would be more helpful to others to stay here. Fortunately, it's not our choice whether we live or die. God knows what is best!!

BE WORTHY

"Conduct yourselves in a manner worthy of the Gospel of Christ" (Philippines 1:27 NIV). "Live your life in a manner worthy of the Gospel of Christ" (NRSV). The challenge is to do that whether someone like Paul or my pastor is watching or not. Remember, Jesus is watching, and he has taught us how to live, shown us an example, given us guidelines, sent the Holy Spirit to help us and give directions and warnings. We can stand firm; we can be in "one spirit, working side by side with one mind," the mind of Christ which we all have. What a need there is for that kind of unity in the fellowship of the church. We won't be intimidated by detractors or detractions. A little suffering from opponents can make us strong! Our unity can make us a formidable force. We need each other; we need each other's gifts. No one of us can do it all. Each needs to be involved. We need greeters and teachers, kitchen help and children' workers, gardeners and mentors, janitors and musicians – all working in unity, side by side striving with one mind to service Christ. If we each see that "all my work is for the Master," and it should be, that will happen. "Live your life worthy of the Gospel of Christ."

SAINTHOOD

Philippians 1:3, 4 – "I thank my God in all my remembrance of you, always offering prayer with joy in my every prayer for you all." What a great way to be able to pray for someone or especially a group of people, a whole church of people – with thanksgiving and joy! There are so many in my past and in my present who are like that. I know they have faced and are facing challenges as were the people in Philippi to whom Paul is writing, but my basic thought, my underlying experience with them is joy and thanksgiving. Thinking about Ken, Gordon, Alastair, Joy, Lisa, Lucy, Jack, Dorothy, Ray, Sveta, Valery, Sasha, Galina, Donna, Bernie, Michelle, Frank, Adrian, Michael, Karen, Bob, Clem, Velma, Brian, Sarah, Jim, Rio, Rachel brings me joy and fills me with thanksgiving. Are they the saints "at Philippi" for me? That's a good question! When does one become a saint? What qualifies one to be a saint? Are all saints alike?

In Psalm 16 David says this about saints who are in the earth. "They are the majestic ones in whom is all my delight." Daniel 7 describes saints as believers, the holy ones. The Psalmist describes them as the ones who love the Lord (Psalm 21:23) and those who sing to the Lord (Psalm 30:4) even in their beds as they rejoice in God's honor (Psalm 149:5). Revelation describes them as those who do righteous acts (Revelation 19:8). Other Scriptures describe them as ones connected in such a way with God that the Spirit intercedes for them (Romans 8:27), the ones he guards (I Samuel 2:9). There are promises regarding what they will do, like judge the world (I Corinthians 6:2). Their death is precious in God's sight (Psalm 116:15), and they will receive the kingdom and possess it forever (Daniel 7:18). And who judges sainthood? Ultimately I'm sure it is God and God alone, but do we not see sparks of sainthood as we look at these Scriptural definitions in the people we live with, work with, worship with.

A definite mark of sainthood is a person's willingness to serve, to be a "slave" as Paul describes himself. He calls the Philippians saints, but he calls himself and his co-worker, Timothy, "bond servants, slaves of Christ Jesus." He uses these terms at the beginning of most of his letters. Somehow we are not surprised. One of Jesus' most repeated directions to his disciples was that they needed to become slaves, servants of all, always looking, he did, for ways in which to serve others. But Paul was not an apostle. He hadn't walked with Jesus for three years. He was not a witness to miracles or to the resurrection, though he did experience an encounter with the Risen Christ. He didn't hear Jesus preach or teach and yet he knew that to be effective in his ministry he needed to serve.

Was it an idea the Spirit gave him during his three years in the desert? Was it often repeated as he related to Peter and other disciples, one they had heard repeated, one with which they struggled? It appeared to be a tough one for them to grasp, for anyone to grasp as a follower of Jesus. Was it just intuitive? Jesus never failed to serve anyone, anywhere. That must have been a well-etched memory for the disciples that became a reality for Paul as well.

Paul had a mission, one Jesus himself had given him and not an easy one. It turned his world upside down. His intent had been to persecute Christians, even in Gentile areas like Antioch, but Jesus instructions to him now were to go to the Gentiles, specifically to tell them about Jesus at whatever cost to him as the servant of Jesus, as the servant of the people, without complaint – it's just part of being a servant.

POEMS OF SCRIPTURE

Acceptable Sacrifices

"What can I render to my God
For all his treasure's store?"
The people of long ago gave sacrifices –
Bulls and doves and goats and lambs -
But, even then, you reminded them,
"I own the cattle on ten thousand hills
And, besides, I do not eat the flesh of bulls
Or drink the blood of goats."
What you really wanted, even then,
Was a sacrifice of thanksgiving from the heart,
A sacrifice of praise from the lips,
The fruit of lips that confess your name.
So what can I offer to my God?
"I'll take the gifts he freely gives,
And humbly ask for more."

"AND I WOULD HEAL THEM...."

They came with diseases and he healed them;
They came with demons and he healed them;
They came with complaints and he healed them;
They came with sins and he healed them.

No, not all of them,
Though he could have,
Though he would have
If they had wanted him to,
If they had believed he wanted to.
If they had believed he could.

We all have wounds,
Limitations,
Broken relationships,
Sins!
And he would heal them!
Healing – what we need!
What we want?
How we want it?

He would!!

BLESSINGS AND CURSES (Deuteronomy 28)

Promises

Hopes and Warnings

God speaks.

Israel heard,

But did Israel listen?

Did they believe?

"If you will only obey...."

You will be above all nations.

You will be blessed everywhere.

You will be fruitful.

You will be blessed coming and going.

You will defeat your enemies.

I will open my rich storehouses,

"If you will only obey."

But if you will not, oh if you will not....!

Did they not hear?

Did they not listen?

Did they not remember?

Do I?

Creation

What a way to start!
Darkness void, nothingness,
No Form and just a Spirit hovering.
Doesn't sound very promising – maybe even scary!

But God said…
And there was….
And look what happened when you spoke!
A whole universe was created
In the midst of that darkness and void
And nothingness, that scary place.
You always see such potential
You always have such hope
You always make such plans.
If you could do that,
You can do anything.
What do you want to do with me?

Day 1

I live way up north these days -
I don't take light for granted any more.
During the winter, daylight hours are very short –
Sometimes only four of them
And the sun never shines.
Of course, in summer we get the opposite.
And we really celebrate then!
And God said, "Let there be light."
I'm sure glad you said that, God.
It's a great invention.

Day 2

When you made something, Lord
You didn't start small!
You created "expanse"
And you called it "sky."
It took a mighty word
A powerful word
A strong word
To move all that "water" around
To settle the chaos and bring about order
To make room for "sky."
Your word could do it.
And You're still at it, bringing order to chaos.

Day 3 Genesis 1:9-13

Did you get excited as creation unfolded?
Did you make a wave crash against the new shoreline –
just for the fun of it?
Did you smile as the fragile blades of grass poked
through the brown earth?
Did you laugh when the tree burst into blossom and the
fruit began to turn red?
Did you revel in digging up the first potato?
I think so!
Oh sure, it was a scientific process,
But it was more!
Oh sure, it was a supernatural process,
But it was more!

It was a joyful work experience –
Like all work experiences should be!!

Day 4 Genesis 1:14-19

What a sky you made, Lord!
A lot of mathematical and scientific
Calculations and equations went into that!

How to measure the hours in a day.
When should the sun "rise" and "set"?
How should the moon travel so that it shines
a bit differently every night?
Where should the stars go and how long should each one
shine?
How will the orbits work so the seasons will be right?

No wonder it took a whole "day"!
But it was good; you said so!

It is good!
I really like what you did on day 4.

Day 5

Everything living and moving thing in the water
and every winged bird.
"It's ready," I can almost hear you say.
"Let's start with water.
And at your word the oceans and seas and lakes and rivers
Are teeming with perch and bass and salmon and blue gill,
With frogs and toads and alligators and crocodiles,
With whales and dolphins and seals and lemmings.
And then you said,

"And now for the sky –
"Let's make things that fly,
"Like eagles and sparrows and parrots and toucans.
"Wee little ones that flutter
"and huge ones that soar."
And then you said,
"Make some more!
"Fill the water; go all over the earth."
I'm glad you did! I wouldn't want one to be left out.
"Enough for one day," you added.
"But tomorrow, ah yes, tomorrow."

DAY 6

Did You sleep last night, Lord?
I think You must have been awake all night
Planning for this day!
It must have been great fun –
Making long-necked giraffes
And curly tailed pigs
Hump-backed camels
And spotted leopards

Did you put the stink in skunks right away?
And about those rabbits that eat my garden –
I'm really fond of dagos of all kinds
And an occasional cat is okay.
Wherever did you get the idea for a mongoose
And a kangaroo?

We could have used a few more koalas,

But then eucalyptus trees are rare in most places,
And such a variety of bears and deer
And then to round it all out, people!

You were really busy on day 6, Lord.
Thanks!!

WHAT DID GOD DO ON DAY 7?

What kind of Sabbath did God have
On the very first 7th day?
The work that he planned was completed.
Now maybe it was time to play.

Did he romp with the rabbits and otters?
Did he swing with the monkeys in trees?
Did he have a long roar with the lions?
Or fly with birds and the bees?

Did he move through the stars and the planets?
Did he check on the sweetness of pears?
Did he count all the ferns he had planted?
Or watch the clouds float through the air?

Did he have a nice long chat with Adam?
Go swimming with dolphins and whales?
What kind of a Sabbath did God have
On that very first 7th day?

Fear

It's a natural emotion, given us by God for our safety.
Fear – it will protect us from accidents, disasters,
and bad choices.
But God says, "Do not fear!"
And when HE says it,
it usually means he's going to do something great
On our behalf,
Through us even!!
He means he is already at work, doing
something unbelievable.

"Do not fear, Zechariah."
"Do not fear, Mary."
"Do not fear, Joseph."
"Do not fear, shepherds."

Did they "fear"?
I wouldn't be surprised –
after all it was an angel or a vision or a dream
Unexpected, not "normal," quite astonishing,
out of the ordinary,
A "give me a minute" moment.
BUT they listened to the message.
They may have expressed some doubt, some astonishment,
Continuing fear, mixed with hope, moving towards belief,
faith, obedience.

I'LL BE THERE

Sometimes thing go wrong –
A broken ankle – little things.
The loss of everything – big things.
"I'll be there!"

Sometimes decisions have to be made –
Answers to a child's desire for ice cream – little things.
Should I move to take this job? – big things.
"I'll be there!"

Sometimes, often times, things go right
I remembered her name – little things.
My comments healed the relationship – big things.
"I was there."

Remember the "I-was-there" moments!
Remember the "I'll-be-there" promise!

Gain the "uncommon confidence": "I will be with you."

IT'S A MYSTERY – Mark 4:10

It's a mystery, hidden,
But it will become known
To those who listen,
To those who hear,
To those who perceive,
To those who pay attention,
To those who ponder,
To those who consider carefully.
Let it "dawn" on you;
Let it become understanding
Let the "Ah, ha" happen.
Sometime!!

LOST AND FOUND

Lost means ending up in the wrong place, but for us it is a choice we make, to want to be away from God, to end up wanting nothing to do with God. That is the ultimate "lost," but for some, that's what they want; for others, even those who have been led away from God by family or circumstances, there is a longing for God even though they may not know it. There is a searching, even a willingness to humble themselves, confident in God and what he can do, accepting the fact that we were not able or worthy on our own. We can come back to God; we can be found wherever we are!

MEET ME

Henri Nowen's friend and fellow theologian Jan Vanier described a scene in which a care worker cradled a dying addict in a park. The addict's last words shook her to the core: "You never wanted to meet me; you always wanted to change me!"

You never wanted to know me; you only wanted to fix me.

You never wanted to discover me; you only wanted to help me.

COME

Come and rest – overworked and weary – and find peace.

Come and follow – bored and despairing – and find fulfillment

Come and abide – confused and fearful – and find security

ON HOLY GROUND

You led Moses to a bush that was ablaze but did not burn, and then you spoke his name. That was holy ground. You said so.

You led Samuel back to bed three times and then you spoke his name. That was holy "ground." You were there so it must have been.

You lead me daily to my "postinia" and there you speak my name. That is "holy ground." You are here so it must be.

Do you speak today? Your words and God the Fathers are in the Bible and they speak quite clearly – if we have ears to hear and minds and hearts that will take in what we hear. We can listen to the Spirit as he gives understanding and then we can respond with obedience. The question may not be, "Do you speak?" but, "Do I hear?"

For Moses, the 40 year old, for Samuel, the 12 year old, you broke through using their names. Do you still speak my name to get my attention? The song says,

> "Speak to me by name, my Master.
> Let me know it is to me.
> Speak that I may follow faster,
> With a step more firm and free.
> I am listening, Lord, for thee.
> Master, speak, oh speak to me."
> **SASB 775**

At 40 Moses responded, "Here I am!" But when he heard

what you wanted him to do, he had a dozen excuses – "Who am I? Who do I say you are? Can I have a sign? How about another one? I'm not eloquent! Send someone else!" God had an answer for every one of them.

At 12 Samuel responded, "Here I am. Speak, Lord, for your servant is listening." The message God had for Samuel was as intense, as frightening as the one he had for Moses. But Scripture records that 12 year old Samuel made no excuses. He simply went back to bed until morning and then opened the doors of the house of the Lord and when Eli asked him about what God said, he willingly told it all.

I think when I was 12, I would have gone anywhere, done anything, said any word God wanted. When I was 40 I made excuses why I couldn't go there, do that or say what he wanted me to say.

Now when I hear my name, I respond, "Here I am, your servant is listening." But I'm still learning to obey.

ON THE PRODIGAL SON'S HOMECOMING
THE PARTY

When the shepherd found his sheep that had been lost,
He threw a party,
And everyone came.
When the woman found the coin that had been lost,
She threw a party,
And everyone came.
When the father found the son who had been lost,
He threw a party,
But....

Why is it that everyone comes to the celebration
When a sheep or a coin is found,
But some won't come
When a man who was lost is found?

IT'S ALL YOURS

He was one glad Dad when the boy came home;
The lost one had been found.
But the other son who was always there
Just would not come around.
"But son," Dad said, "you have to know
That all I have is yours.
Your brother took all he'll ever get;
This rest will all be yours.
The dead is alive, the lost is found
And we must celebrate!
He is my son –
And so are you!!

A MOM'S REFLECTIONS ON HOMECOMING

Where were you, Mom, when he came home?
The story says Dad saw him a long way off
And ran to meet him.
Where were you?
Had you shared in Dad's long watching?
Or did you just know that someday he would come home -
A mother's instinct!
Maybe you headed straight for the kitchen
to bake chocolate chip cookies
And sour cream coffeecake,
And a coconut cream pie.
Maybe you went to the bathroom to have a good cry
Before you faced him with your eyes streaming with joy.
Maybe you stayed in the background,
A little afraid of this new son,
Not sure what his motivation might be for coming home,
Coming now.
Maybe you were right behind your husband,
Maybe you heard the boy,
Now a grown man,
"I'll be a servant in the house
I've done so much wrong."
Maybe you knew his Dad would say,
"Let's have a party, fit for a king.
Not a servant."

Where were you? Where was I?

HOMECOMING

O son your hair has not been cut; your feet are cut and
bruised.
Your cloak is gone; your shirt is torn;
your hands are work worn and calloused.
I see all of this and my heart cries.
What has happened to you, my son?
But no, I don't want to ask that question!
You are here and that is enough.
I'm not sure how to treat you.
Your father reaches out without hesitation.
He holds you and claps you on the back and orders a
party.
But I'm not sure what to do.
How do you feel about me? Why did you want to leave?
What caused this departure from us, from home?
I'm not sure what to do.

PEACE

Peace does "settle over me" in this place and time. It enfolds me in God. I can receive it abundantly and peacefully, with a smile, with joy, in hope. *The disciples had denied Jesus, run off when he was in trouble and three days later he showed up in the room where they were hiding, and what was the first thing he said to them? "Peace be with you."* In spite of anything I might do, like denying him or running from him, he comes to me and says, "Peace be with you" and you are still going to use me, send me. WOW! (John 20:21)

Of all the things he gives us, he mentions peace often, peace that comes through the Holy Spirit, peace, sent to guard our hearts and minds in Christ (Philippians 4:7).

The Rock

Deuteronomy 21:31

Rock solid, stable, unmovable;
Crumbling, toppling, crushing
Their rock is not like our Rock

Thinking about God

My devotions asked this question today –
>   Which is harder for you to comprehend –
>   God's transcendence or God's immanence?

First, a definition –
>   Transcendence – above, beyond, great!
>   Immanence – present, active, near, accessible

God is transcendent – He created the entire cosmos.
God is immanent - He knit me together in my mother's womb.

God is transcendent – He has always existed.
God is immanent – He is with me now.

God is transcendent - He fills the earth with his glory.
God is immanent – He fills me with his presence by the Holy Spirit.

God is transcendent – He knows everyone's name.
God is immanent – He knows my name.

God is transcendent – He knows everything about everything.
God is immanent – He knows all about me.

God is transcendent – He is strong enough to move mountains.
God is immanent – He is my refuge, my shield.

God is transcendent – The highest heavens cannot contain him.

God is immanent – He gives attention to my prayer and plea for mercy.

God is transcendent – He is sovereign.

God is immanent – His eyes are open to me and his ears hear me.

I like to think about God as near, with me, Immanuel.

I need to realize that God is immense, able to do anything, to be everywhere, to know all there is to know.

THOUGHTS ON THE WORD

Benedictine monks memorized most if not all of the Psalms. That was partly because many of them could not read. They would repeat them over and over until they were firmly in their minds. Benedict chose Psalms that remind us of the things of God that will challenge us, sustain us, remind us to praise. God delivers; God is our refuge; God saves; God brings us home. We can move from hard times to joy, from feeling like a captive to liberation, from depression and despair to trust as we read these wonderful passages, some of which we should memorize, know by heart, so that they are on our minds when we need them.

TOO HARD?

Deuteronomy 30:11 – "Surely this commandment that I am commanding you this day is not too hard for you, nor is it too far away…No, the word is very near to you; it is in your mouth and in your heart for you to observe."

This commandment – just one, Lord?
Not too hard – if you want to, if you choose to.
Not too far away – check your mind, your mouth.
In your very heart!
You can see it; you can hear it.
Are you looking; are you listening?
This commandment – it is knowable!
This commandment – it is doable!
Now what's your excuse?!?

WHAT WILL FIT?

How much will fit in the suitcase?
> How many suitcases will fit in the trunk?
>> How much can I carry on the plane?
>>> How much can I take through the gate?

I'd like to at least have my gold watch – it was my grandpa's.
> And my new car – it's just a few months old.
>> Oh, and enough money,

Maybe even plenty since I don't know what might happen.
> Good quality clothing for all seasons which will last.
> Some good friends, the "right" ones to pal around
with.

"You'll have to leave most of it behind."

I'd also like to know about scary ledges along the way,
> Will the scenery be pretty?
>> Are there rocks to climb over?
>>> Will there be others along the way.

"You'll love it, though you never know what you'll
encounter."

What will fit through the narrow gate?
> "Just you, my friend. Not many will find it.
> It's small,
>> But it leads to life, LIFE!
>> It's worth it!!"

YOU SHALL NOT BE AFRAID OF THEM!

Horses and chariots
And armies larger than ours
O Lord, how could you send us
Into this battle so ill-prepared
So out-numbered
So unequipped

"You shall not be afraid of them.
For I, the Lord your God, am with you
Remember, I brought you from the land of Egypt
I can do it.
Do not lose heart
Or be afraid
Or panic
Or be in dread of them

It is the Lord who goes with you
To fight for you.
Against your enemies
To give you victory."

Lord, my enemies don't have
Horses and chariots;
They have backbiting and gossip;
They have pride and power;
They seem so strong,
So powerful,
And I don't know if can be an overcomer.

"You shall not be afraid of them."
"Lo, I am with you always."
"We can be more than conquerors."

And you will give me the victory!
I remember, Lord!
You've done it before!
You can, you will do it again!!

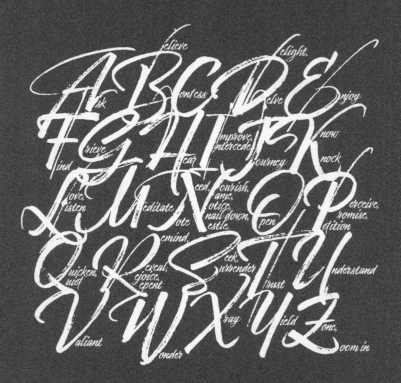

A — Ask
B — Believe
C — Confess
D — Delve, Delight,
E — Enjoy
F — Find
G — Grieve
H — Hear
I — Improve, Intercede
J — Journey
K — Know, Knock
L — Love, Listen
M — Meditate
N — Name, Notice, nail down, nestle,
O — Open
P — Perceive, Promise, Petition
Q — Quicken, quiet
R — Remind, Reveal, Rejoice, Repent
S — Seek, Surrender
T — Trust
U — Understand
V — Valiant
W — Wonder
X — Xray
Y — Yield
Z — Zone, Zoom in

REFLECTIONS ON PRAYER

Is there a way to pray? A way to address God? A way to voice my feelings, my concerns, my love, my praise? I have found through the years that there is not a way, but many ways. You will find some of them listed in the following pages because I have experimented with them, tried them, changed the way I pray many times in my 80 years of living. It's been a great adventure and journey with God.

AN ACROSTIC FOR PRAYER

Ask

Believe

Confess

Delight, delve

Enjoy

Find

Grieve

Hear

Improve, Intercede

Journey

Know, knock

Love, listen

Meditate

Nourish, name, nail down, need, nestle, notice, note

Open

Perceive, promise, petition

Quicken, quiet

Remind, reveal, rejoice, repent

Seek, surrender

Trust

Understand

Value

Wonder

Xray

Yield

Zone, zoom in

Healing

Jesus' healings were often instantaneous – Peter's mother-in-law got up from her bed and began serving; the sick and demon-possessed were healed when they showed up at the door. Some of them might well have recovered over time – an aspirin and a good night's sleep but Jesus often took care of them then and there.

At times he does it quickly when we ask, when there is a good reason like when something needs to be done, but most often today God uses an "aspirin and a good night's sleep." That's Jesus still at work! He has helped human beings to create all the medicines we use today, all the surgical procedures that save lives.

The primitive people discovered leaves and bark and plants – You guided them. The researchers discovered xrays and amazing treatments for all kinds of diseases – how?

You guided them. We praise you for doctors, surgeons, therapists, nurses, and for aspirins and a good night's sleep!

HEARING

"Hearing but never understanding, seeing but never perceiving," having calloused heart – the reason they don't get it - dull ears, closed eyes. I think it works both ways – there is a choice not to see or hear and the heart becomes calloused and then ears and eyes cannot perceive because the heart is calloused. And God would love to heal them. I think of people, not closed to him, but refusing, I think, to turn. There are others who have not only dull ears and closed eyes, but deaf ears and blind eyes. How many people see the beauty of the world and do not perceive God or hear the morning stars singing and don't get it! Thank you for my growing perception, my growing understanding of what there is to see and hear that reveals you, the Lord. I see and hear the changing of the seasons, the color of the leaves, the lakes and rivers that flow so profusely, the tastes of food of such variety; the birds that sing and tweet and chirp each with their own song, the squirrels and chipmunks, deer and bear! What wonders! And people, Lord, some of whom are such a blessing - and such a challenge.

I am ready to listen with my heart, uncalloused and ready to hear more than the surface, to realize the depth, to enjoy the humor, to hear the pain and joy and cries of need beneath the talk, talk, talk. I want to perceive and understand, to listen with an uncalloused heart.

HO!"

Not "ho, ho, ho." God is using this strange greeting to get attention, like "Hey!" is for us. He has good news and he wants the people to hear it. The thirsty and the hungry are invited, encouraged to come without money. "Ho" may get their attention, but then the familiar, "Listen carefully; incline your ear and come, listen so that you may live." And here are the steps for them to take – listen, seek, call on him, return so that he may have mercy on you, pardon you. That's a word for us as well.

God's thoughts are so much greater than ours; his ways are so much greater than ours. His Word waters the earth in the same way as the rain waters the earth. It will accomplish its intended purpose. We can be led home and everything will rejoice. All these blessings are available to us as we learn to follow him.

HOW DO I KNOW THAT I LOVE YOU ENOUGH?

"Love the Lord your God with all your heart, soul, mind and strength." (Mark 12:30 -NIV)

"So love the Lord God with all your passion and prayer and intelligence and energy." (Message)

How do I know I love you that way? How do I know I love you above or more than anything or anyone else? I know I should love you first! That's the greatest commandment. You said so, but do I? I think so, but if that love were really challenged, how would I do? I realize how much you love me – you are so good to me in mercy, in grace, in provision, in redemption. You are worthy of all my love, with my whole soul and body, mind and heart. Maybe that's enough for now to show, to tell you that I love you. Do you need to test that love today?

IMMENSE LOVE

When I think about the immensity of God's love, I cannot bear to be 'out of that love' even for a moment! Consider whose love it is! You, Lord, don't need me or my love, but you long for it, not for your own sake, but for my good, my satisfaction, my peace. And that love, best described as mercy, undeserved love extends to everyone. Even the worst of sinners. Amazing!!

IN THE STILLNESS

"Be still and know that I am God." Where can we find stillness enough to know God?

I had an experience in the doctor's office that helped me to find it. My eyes were dilated so that I could not read, and the conversation going on around me – first distrust of the government and then about bar hopping – was loud and there was no room for a quiet witness. So I leaned my head back, closed my eyes and heard, "Be still and know me." I thought about what I know about God and then I heard, "No! Be still!" And then I knew God. Being still is not easy but in the stillness he comes; he makes himself known; in chaos, including loud conversation going on around us, God can come and we can know it is him and we can know him.

THOUGHTS ON PRAYER

Picked up from here and there along the journey

Bunyan defines prayer as an "affectionate pouring out of the soul to God."

Many verses in the Psalms talk about a longing for you and sometimes that is true, but at times it's just a quiet, affectionate conversation that expresses love and experiences joy and peace in your presence, loving to be with you.

"Those who persist in knocking will succeed in entering ."
Moses Ibn Ezra

"Sing praise wisely" Psalm 47:4

Praise cannot be repetition without meaning, not more words for the sake of more words, not to gain merit points or to do penance. Prayer of all kinds should be short and brief, for the purpose of relationship, not "to say our prayers," but to become a pray-er, pure of heart, one with God. Swift, strong, quick, deep, soul-shaking! Inspiration, challenge, conviction forgiveness, insight, guidance. That's what happens to a pray-er.

The issue of prayer is not prayer; the issue of prayer is God. Do I have faith in my own ability to really come boldly before the throne of grace, to pour out my needs and those of others to the infinite, merciful, eternal God? John says in I John 3:18-22 that we will love in speech, in truth, and in action and that when we do, our hearts will not condemn us and we have boldness before him, and will receive from him whatever we ask. The key words are <u>believe</u> in Jesus and <u>love</u> one another. "The one who is in you is greater than the one who is in the world." Sometimes we have a hard time seeing that as in the situation with the grandson who is a drug addict, consumed by his addiction. How can those grandparents, or we, see and believe that you are greater? How do we believe that we will receive whatever we ask? You have given us your Spirit, Lord, and know he abides in us. Am I too hesitant to come boldly before you? Does this apply to all prayers or only to prayers for myself? Each person has to make some decisions for themselves; I can't make it for them. So how do I pray? How do I come boldly to you who is merciful on behalf of those in addiction? I can pray for peace of mind for parents and grandparents, faith and strength to endure, wisdom for words to guide and lift the caregivers, breakthroughs of some sort that will hold.

"Prayer depends on a mind in which God is at home." Trust in a merciful, infinite, eternal God is essential.

"Watch and pray. To watch without praying is to rely on our own strength. To pray without watching is to presume on the presence of grace." (Puritan Father)

DAY DREAMING
WITH POETRY

Some thoughts, even about the Bible and its stories and messages just can't be expressed in prose; so they take on poetic form, sometimes rhyming, but, for me, more often not in rhyme. Some of these are for fun; some are from everyday life; some are my imagination let loose. They were mostly fun to write, although sometimes they tore my heart. Sometimes a squirrel caught my attention and sometimes a verse or story from Scripture, sometimes a row of haystacks and sometimes it was something Jesus said. It's just me pondering!

558 DAYS – a book

By Yolande Korkie
Christian Art Publishers, PO Box 1599, Vereeniging, RSA
2016

I finished reading a book yesterday –
It was about a couple who were taken
hostage in Yemen.
I read about deprivation and discouragement,
About hunger and filth,
About discomfort and lack of sanitation,
About no chair and a thin mattress,
About sickness of mind and body,
About reality and dreams,
About fear and anguish,
About separation from children and then from each other,
About cruelty and subjugation,
About hopelessness and wavering faith,

I'm glad I read the book; I'm glad I finished the book!
I'm glad I finished the book –
but it's not finished with me!

I read about holding on and holding up;
About being held, being loved and knowing it;
About faith that is tried and comes through;
About hope that doesn't give up;
About Scripture that we don't know we know;
About the value of paper and a pen;
About songs in the night;

About kindness from unlikely people in unlikely places;
About choosing right attitudes including forgiveness.

I'm glad I read the book.
Help me never to forget the book.
Help me be like the people in the book
No matter what my circumstances might be!!

A CELEBRATION OF BORIS SHULYANSKI

Boris was a beautiful man
    like the mountain as the rays of morning sun light it.
Boris was a deep man
    like a deep lake full of internal, real life and beauty.
Boris was a sensitive man
    like a small tundra flower that has survived winter
storms.
Boris was a gentle man
    like a river cutting the deepest Canyon, patiently.
Boris was a rich man
    like a king who, looking, sees there is nothing he needs.
Boris was a spiritual man
    who is now singing with the angels, "Holy, Holy, Holy."

Thank you, Lord, for Boris Shulyanski.(Boris was a student of ours at The Salvation Army Seminary when that seminary was in Finland. He died about 8 years after he was commissioned and ordained as a Salvation Army officer. His wife continued to serve in Moscow until her retirement. One daughter is a Salvation Army officer serving in Moldova.)

A MEMORY

I washed the glass in the door today.
It didn't take long at all –
Some dust, some rain drops, a fingerprint or two.

It used to take a lot longer –
Handprints sticky from peanut butter and jelly,
Mouthprints from making faces at big brother on the other
side,
Or Daddy coming home.
Noseprints from the dog watching
an intruding squirrel in the yard
Or anticipating a walk around the camp.
It used to take a lot longer.

I washed the glass in the door today,
It didn't take long at all.
Some dust, some rain drops, a fingerprint or two,
I haven't washed those sticky handprints
or mouthprints or noseprints for a long time.
I knew there would be no more.

But today I washed the glass in the door
And I remembered.
I rejoiced in the memories;
I laughed; I smiled; I was glad.
And I said, "Thank you,"
Not just for the memories
But for who and where we are now -

The boys, the Dad and me, and even the dog.
Thank you, God, for handprints and mouthprints and
noseprints,
For memories and for your faithfulness.

A SEED

A seed needs soil, light,
Warmth, moisture, time
To unlock its vitality.

What do I still lack?

BUT I WANT TO WRITE!

I really do
But writing is so hard to do.
I sit here and I wonder how
To write a word –

Do I use a pencil or pen or input right into the computer?
On scratch paper or in my journal or a notebook?
From old journals or only new thoughts?
Poetry or prose or some of each?
Inspiration or studious thought?
Observation or scientific research?

Writing is so hard to do –
Or is that an excuse?

BUT IT HAPPENED

Incomprehensible! Yet I grasp it.
Unbelievable! Yet I believe it.
Unexplainable! Yet I know it.

The King of Kings,
The Lord of Lords,
The Sovereign God,
The immortal One
Who is invincible and invisible
Met with ME,
In my room,
At my rocking chair
This cloudy, damp March morning!

CHANGE

I've got a new boss!!
How does he work?
How does he manage?
How will I feel?
How will he treat me?

I'm worried
And maybe I'm scared.

The old boss and I got along really well,
Except once in awhile, here and there.
Now I want to defend him and his history here.

But this boss is an unknown
And all of these questions
And feelings
Keep struggling for my attention.
It's so hard to focus, to learn new ways.

He's only been here a short time –
So maybe I shouldn't have all the answers, yet.
Maybe I should give him a chance.
Maybe I should give me a chance

DOES OUR HOME SPEAK OF YOU?

When the front door is open
And guests walk in,
What do they see
To remind them of Him?
Do the walls tell His story?
The plants speak His praise?
Are the magazines helpful,
The books on display?

Is the atmosphere friendly
And warm to the touch?
Does peace seem to reign here
Not sometimes, but much?
Does a hug express welcome,
Invite them to stay,
Feel safe in our home,
Not sent quickly away?

Is a feeling that Jesus
Might dwell in this place
Conveyed by the things
They can see, smell, and taste?
And can they see Jesus
In the ones who live here?
Oh, Lord, may it be so
Each day of the year!

HAYSTACKS

Where are they?

In the sunshine	In the Snow
In the fog	In the rain
At sunrise	In deep snow
At sunset	By moonlight
At a distance	In the fields

Someone worked really hard to get them there!

IT'S TIME TO PRAY!

To Contemplate   To Listen
To Meditate   To Hear
To Praise   To Resolve
To Give thanks   To Obey
To Confess   To Trust
To Intercede   To Be Bold
To Rest   To Invite

How will I pray today?

My Little Bits

But this is all I have, dear Lord!
How will I survive?
Look at all these needy folk
You want to keep alive.
My little bit won't help at all;
It's such a small amount.
He said to me, "Just bring it here; I'll make your small bit
count."

He took the loaves and little fish,
'Twas all I had to give.
And with them fed both them and me.
And so we all could live.

If I had kept them to myself
I still would be alive,
But he could take my little bits
A banquet to provide
For thousands who are hungry
In a needy world today;
So take my bits again, dear Lord,
And use them in your way.

Yes, this is all I have to give,
But I know that I'll survive
And care for all the needy folks
That WE can keep alive.

MY MORNING SQUIRREL

Every morning,
And it seems no matter what time
I come to my quiet place,
My morning squirrel runs across the yard,
over the edge of the sandbox
and into the trees.
Sometimes he sits on a broken limb,
shaking his tail
and observing life in his acreage.
He's brave – we do have a neighborhood fox
and bear have been seen
and mountain lions have been heard.
But he needs to get out
to get his daily bread,
to play with friends

He teaches me important things –
Have some routine,
Observe what's around you,
Get out in spite of the danger,
Work and play,
And leave the rest to God

MY PRAYER LIST

I have a prayer list, Lord,
A pretty long one.
People who need or would like to be healed.
People who are out of work and need a job.
People who are carrying burdens, sometimes heavy ones.
People who are captives of terrorist groups.
People who are adjusting to new challenges.
People who are traveling by car or by plane.
People who are struggling with relationships.
People who are moving house, city, even country.
People who are dealing with wayward or needy children.

How do you want to answer my prayer today?
How will you "heal" them all?
I know you want to "heal" them all.

Can my faith make a difference? Can theirs?
Wait a minute -
Am I supposed to answer their prayer?

ON WEARING A HALO

I tried on a halo the other day
(Someone told me I was wonderful
and I liked the way that sounded.)
I decided to wear it home
Try it out
Show it off
Just a bit

Boy, it was hard to keep it clean
And harder yet to keep it in place
And no one seemed to notice it!

Maybe because it kept slipping down around my neck,
Maybe because the shine had already worn off,
Maybe because it wasn't a halo kind of day,
Maybe because I wasn't a halo kind of person.

I've decided to return my halo.
I'll just wait until Jesus gives me one
-If I deserve it.

QUESTIONS AT THE END OF THE DAY

What did I miss as I walked with you through your world
today?
What did you want me to see?
What could have increased my faith in you-
Faith that could have dared to believe?

I don't want to miss anything and not be ready for what's
next!
You might want to work through me;
I'll need to be strong!
There could be a storm up ahead.
You might need me to help another,
For whoever is in the storm with me;
Whatever that storm might be.

REMEMBER!

To the Israelites God said,
REMEMBER

What your eyes have seen and make that known to your
children –
The Red Sea Crossing
The Ten Commandments and all the law
The victories that were won by Me, not you
Og, king of Bashan,
Sihon, king of Heshbon
The Great Commandments
My protection and provision for 40 years of wilderness
journeys
And how you provoked me to wrath

To me God says,
REMEMBER

Deliverance
Healing
Protection
Guidance
Faithfulness
Provision

Do not fear for I am with you!
Still
Always
Everywhere
In all situations!
Remember and go on!!

SOMETIMES

Sometimes I need to lift my eyes
Above the fence and the roof top and the trees,
And even way out beyond the clouds
Where I catch a glimpse of glorious blue
Above which I cannot see,
And there I see God!

SOMETIMES – 2

Sometimes I forget
To look at the Majesty of the mountains,
To see the beauty of a spring crocus,
To listen to the chirping of the chickadees,
To feel the soft touch of the breeze going by.
Lord, remind me that you are in them all!

Sometimes I forget
To notice the despair on the teenager's face,
To hear the joy in the voice of the proud parent,
To understand the tears of the troubled child,
To care for the burdens of the aging friend,
To share in the victory of the recovering alcoholic.
Lord, remind me that you are in them all!

THANKSGIVING

As we gathered round the board to offer thanks to God
For home and family and friends
And good food from His sod,
My thoughts especially were stayed on blessings which are
new
Which just this year God gave to me,
Among them, Sweetheart, you!

We met, and God began to show a plan we had not seen.
We loved, we love, and as we love,
We find just what God means.
His plan unfolds as day by day we walk wrapped in His
love,
And as we closer grow to Him
Our pathways meet above.

Those beams across a moonlit lake He's bringing close
together.
Some day they'll merge, if that's His plan,
And I'll be yours forever.

THE LONG WAY

I walked a long way today,
A different way -
Saw some new places,
Smelled some new flowers,
Collected some rose petals for remembering,
Grieved with a child who showed a picture of her lost dog.

I was gone a long time .
Passed houses hidden in the trees,
Through the cemetery blanketed with flowers and
memories I don't share,
Passed the swimming pool giddy with families,
Along the soccer field raucous with boys and their dads at
play,
Around the swamp overgrown with jungle green,
Up the hill rutted from the rain
And home again.

You might think I was lonely, but I wasn't.
Maybe we'll go that way together sometime;
I'll show you what I saw
And why I wasn't lonely.

Or maybe not.

The SAGA OF THE SWING

4/15/18

The outdoor swing is beckoning from the alcove window
On this sunny early spring morning;
But it has a winter's worth of bird droppings all over it
And a tree branch has fallen across the seat.
I might scare away the grosbeaks who have just returned,
And the wind is pretty strong.
I think I'll wait a day or two.

4/21/18

The outdoor swing is beautiful this morning –
Covered with snow, deep, heavy snow.
I don't think I'll go out and sit there today.
I'll leave it to the birds and squirrels as their playground.
But it won't be long now.

5/11

Harry moved that pesky branch off the swing yesterday
And scrubbed off a winter's worth of bird droppings.
The sun is brilliant; the birds are singing.
A hummer stopped by briefly.
It would be a good day to sit in the swing.
Maybe I'll get out there today, if....

THE SAGA OF THE BIRD FEEDERS

4/15/18

There's not much seed left in the finch socks
Nor in the bin in the garage
The poor little guys are having to fight for a spot
Just two or three at a time.
There's no doubt food for them somewhere
Out there in the wild.
But I like them here where I can see them.
There's not much see left in the socks or the garage.
I think I'll wait a day or two.

4/21/18

There is seed in the finch socks
And in the bin in the garage.
They've been feeding voraciously, 10 or 12 at a time.
It's a good thing we bought it when we did.
It's hard for them to get to the wild stuff
When it's covered with a foot of snow.

5/11/18

The finch socks were full yesterday.
And the bin in the garage was too.
They're still feeding voraciously - 22 at a time.
So not much left today.
I guess that means filling them again.
But that's okay.
It's what we put them up for.

THOUGHTS ON THE SABBATH

God planned a pattern.
He blessed the Sabbath day, the seventh day
And hallowed it.
And on that day he rested
from all the work that he had done in creation.
And then he said through Moses,
"Remember the Sabbath Day, to keep it holy."
Rest for everyone – me, my children, my servants,
Even my animals and the strangers among us.
Remember the Creation story
And the Exodus from Egypt,
Remember the times you have been blessed;
Remember the times you have been challenged.
Remember God.
It's a command and it's good for you!!

In the New Testament there is a shift –
A shift to a daily relationship,
More personal, more one on one,
With God through the Holy Spirit,
In remembrance of creation,
In remembrance of Christ,
In remembrance from sin and from sinning.

We observe the Lord's Day -
A celebration of Christ's resurrection
A time for soul rest –
"Take my yoke,
Learn from me,
And find rest for your soul."

It's a bigger perspective –
A personal relationship,
A way of life
A sacramental life,
A life of worship, of caring, of fellowship

TO BE HEARD

Maybe in the world a voice like mine is hardly heard
But God hears.
I may think within my heart the greatest thought
unvocalized
But God hears.
And so I know that all my speaking is surely not in vain
Nor do my thoughts just go around and die unvocalized
For God hears – and He understands
And maybe others hear too.

USUALLY

When friends leave after a visit
We usually go into the airport with them,
See them to the right check-in desk,
Make sure everything is in order,
Walk with them to passport control,
Hug and maybe even kiss them one last time,
Watch them through to the other side,
Wave at them through the glass,
Leave when they are out of sight.
Sometimes I cry – especially if it's my kids,
Or a really close friend
Or someone I won't see for a long time.
That's Usually -
When you left
I went into the airport with you
Saw you to the right check-in desk
(You had forgotten where to turn on the way to the airport
and you couldn't seem to see your flight listed).
And then I left.
Oh, I hugged and kissed you.
I said, "Hurry home"
I said, "I love you."
But I left.
Today I cried,
All the way home,
Not bitterly, nor remorsefully,
But with sadness and longing for you – already.
I did not want you to know
How much I wanted to cry;
So I left and then I cried.
Now I want you to know.

WARNING!

When you spoke to Abraham, Lord,
>You warned him that his "family"
>Would fail and be sent into slavery,
>>Slavery for 70 years,
>>And they were,
>But you would deliver them
>>And you did.

When you spoke to Moses
>You warned him that his people
>Would fail and be sent into exile,
>>Exile for 70 years
>>And they were,
>But you would deliver them
>>And you did.

Was there another warning
>Or just the promise of the Messiah
Who would leave that family, those people standing in
history
>While you created a new family, a new people -
>The church.

And are you warning us –
>It won't be slavery
>It won't be exile
But if we don't love and serve you,
>If we fail you, there is only one alternative -
>>And from it there will be no
>>deliverance.

WHAT ARE THEY DOING?

Aspen leaves have been said to tremble –
I think they are
Waving at one another
"See, here I am and feelin' fine
This fine Colorado morning."

And then again they could be
Clapping for joy
In the dappled sunlight,
Praising their Creator.

But then again they might be
Trembling in awe
Before their Creator
Reveling in His presence.

Me too!!

WHERE TO WORSHIP

You chose the place where Israel would worship –
First it was one they could carry during their desert
wanderings,
A tent with elaborate hangings
And golden furnishings.

When they were settled it was an elegant building
on a site you chose,
Filled with items to receive sacrifices,
Altars for bulls and for grain,
Tables for bread all gilded with gold.

When your people sinned gravely and were sent into exile,
When they continued to live far from the site
you had chosen,
You told them to come together in synagogues
Where they could at least hear your word
Though they could not sacrifice bulls or grain.

Temples were built and temples were destroyed
And over time you seemed to say,
"What is important is worship;
What is important is thanksgiving;
What is important is acknowledging me;
What is important is knowing me."

Then you came to earth in your son, Jesus.
The fields became the place of worship;
The sea became the place where they would find you;
The shore would be a gathering place for hearing your
word;

The place became less important than the acts
Of worship and learning and fellowship.

You left us, Jesus, but your Holy Spirit came
And people who loved you
Gathered in homes to continue
To worship and learn and fellowship.
Homes weren't big enough
So halls were rented, then churches were built.

And now how do I choose a place
For worship, for learning, for fellowship?
You were very directive with the Children of Israel
You told them what, when, and where.

Today you seem to offer a myriad of choices.
Lord, help me make the right choice for me,
a place and a people
For worship, for learning, for fellowship.

WORDS

I'm home alone –
    Alone is a country where I don't know the
language.
Yesterday I said, "Keittos" twice.
    (That's "thank you" in Finnish.)
    And that's all I said,
    All I said for two days.
    At least that's all I said out loud
        To another human being.

But I've talked with God a lot.
    I'm not sure you'd call it "praying" –
    Just talking, listening,
    Really being in communion with God.
I've heard him respond, ask questions, share his thoughts.
    I've responded, asked questions, shared my
thoughts.

It's really been a neat experience,
    A growing experience,
      An enlightening experience,
        A frightening experience,
          An intimate experience,
            A peaceful experience.
              It's been a good experience.

But I hope the silence doesn't last too long!!

HOLY GOD

You are God of the dog that barks
Of the squirrel that chases
Of the bird that flies

You are God of the woman who prays
Of the man who listens
Of the church that obeys

You are God of the past that has happened
Of the present that is happening
Of the future that will happen

You are God; holy is your name.

FAMILY

The first poems in this section relate to our ownership of the Sundune, the cabin we built with Dallas and Phyllis Raby on Lake Michigan just up the beach from Jack and Lucy Thomas. We spent many delightful vacations there with the Rabys and with many other friends who loved the place and found joy and peace there.

Each year for several years I have written a poem for Harry, Steve, and Kevin for Valentines' Day and some for other occasions. These are pretty personal and from my heart. They are "love songs" to the three most important people in my life.

OUR SUNDUNE

Conceived in Harry's fertile mind,
Designed by Dallas' hand,
Built by nine who gave themselves
To make this dune of sand,
Where bodies wearied by life's toil
Could stop and rest awhile,
Where minds exhausted by life's stress
Could learn again to smile,
Where souls, sore troubled by life's woes
Could find the burden light,
Where God could come to all life's woes
And darkness change to light.

The sand was moved; the footings poured;
Cement laid on cement.
The walls were raised; the paneling nailed;
We moved in from the tents.
The waves came in; three walls were built;
We held our breath in fear;
But sand built up; the walls are hid.
We'll come again next year.
Our bed was made; a mobile built
Of driftwood, what a sight!
It hangs right over someone's head
When sleeping every night!

We've launched our boats and sailed the waves,
Becalmed a time or two;
We've talked and swam and built in sand
And played games, quite a few.

We built a shed, or maybe it's
Bunkhouse – nope, a shed!
And next…well, with these guys in charge
I think that's enough said!
Our children have grown up and gone
From our homes one by one;
But this will always be the place
They come to – it's our home.

We've seen God's grace expressed in waves
That never seem to cease –
Sometimes in storm; sometimes quite calm,
But always speaking, "Peace!"
We've seen God's presence in the sun,
His glory in its set.
We've marveled as its silvered waves.
He always says, "don't fret."
We've see God's presence as we've walked
The beach in joy or woe.
He's walked beside us all the time –
His footprints tell us so.

We shared this place with many folks,
Some came, year after year,
We only met a few of them –
But they, too, like it here.
There is a reverence in this place –
This place of calm retreat,
Where God has cleansed and freed and calmed
And brought to us his peace!
When comes the time to leave this place

We always feel sad.
We've found some rest, some peace, some hope –
Our lives have been made glad.

The Sundune, built in 1979
Poem written in 1992
The cabin was sold in 2015

25 YEARS AT THE SUNDUNE

If walls could talk
    Revealing the secrets of years
    Telling us what went on in this place,
What would we hear?

Children screeching in the waves;
Laughter ringing over table games;
Adults reminiscing about years gone by –
    It was they who were children here once.

Now it's grandchildren screeching in the waves;
Now it's children, all grown up, laughing over table
games;
And grandma and grandpa sitting by
    Remembering and smiling.

FOR OUR 37TH ANNIVERSARY

That never seemed like a particularly significant number -
Thirty-seven – three ten times plus seven,
But every year seems like another miracle;
Every year is another miracle.
And that makes 37, thirty- seven, three times ten plus
seven
A very significant number.

Thanks for another miracle –
For our trip to Italy
For lunch and the beauty of Porto Fino
And the climb and the beauty of Barbara's refuge
And the rest and beauty of Bobbie Pellics
For our year of working together
For teaching Pastoral Care together
For pre-marital counseling together
For administrative duties together
For our visit "home" at Christmas
For caring for me on the journey
For giving me our boys to enjoy
For loving me with understanding
For our shared trials
For helping me understand
For showing me the "other side"
For guiding me through the tough issues
For our mutual and growing love

May the miracles keep on coming!!

For Harry 2009

Valentine's Day has become for me a day to remember -
To remember our years of love
and challenge and growth and change
of getting to know each other
of becoming a family of 3, of 4
of working and ministering together
of finding how strong our love could be
of learning to love in spite of....
of growing older together
of developing now ways of ministering together
And now after 43 Valentine's Days together it is just better
than ever!!
I LOVE YOU!!

For the boys

My boys were
fun, great,
challenging, worrisome, exciting.

My men are
more joy than fun
great friends (of each other and us)
occasionally a worry, mostly exciting

Thanks for letting me still be Mom
and for adding all these things and so much more to my
life.
On this Valentine's Day, know that I love you and remind
you
that God loves you even more than I do.
Let me love you and let God love you too.

YOU LOVE ME!!

It isn't as if I still have to ask, "Do you love me?"
Because I don't.
I know you love me!!
How do I know?
It isn't just because you create a laundry room,
Or remodel my end of the closet,
Or even feed me when I have surgery.
While these, and so many more things you do are
wonderful,

I know because
You look at me with love,   ♥ ♥ ♥
You hold me with tenderness,
You touch me with gentleness,
♥ ♥ ♥   You hear me with patience,
You give me with joy,
Your presence brings me peace.

And you know what?
I love you too, because when I am with you
I know love,   ♥ ♥ ♥
I experience tenderness,
I want to be gentle,
I strive to be patient,
I feel joy,
I am at peace.

Thank you!!

For Steve:

I guess I'll never stop being a mother –
I hope you don't mind!
You're kind of stuck with me
And I love it; do you?

I don't have to wash and bandage skinned knees
Or help with homework;
I don't need to sing you to sleep
Or read stories in the car as we travel.

But I do have to think about you and wonder,
And offer a bit of advice as necessary;
I do need to pray for your peace of heart and mind
And make suggestions now and then.
And maybe shed a tear.

I guess I'll just keep on being your mother –
Whether you know the times
I think about you and wonder
Or pray for you and hope.

You'll know when I offer advice
And make suggestions,
But remember, it's because I love you
And I'm still your mom!

On this Valentine's Day 2010, and every day
With love,
Mom

For Kevin with a mother's love:

Looking back –
Such joys to remember
Such pride to enjoy
Such sorrow to share
Such experiences in which to revel
Such growth to reflect on
Such love to contemplate

♥

But looking ahead –
Such a future to anticipate
Such hope to contemplate
Such love to rejoice in
Such experiences to prepare for
Such pride to enjoy
Such joys to revel in

♥

What a privilege it is to be your Mom,
To look back and remember,
To look ahead and rejoice

♥

With love – and prayer
On this Valentine's Day, 2010

YOU ARE WORTH CELEBRATING!

For a "found" son

Sometimes my joy is so complete
When thoughts of you run through my mind;
My day is light; my heart can sing
With praise and gratitude sublime

But sometimes I am so concerned
And just don't know what's going on –
A darker feeling, sad, forlorn
Comes crashing in and I am torn.

But then I turn to God and share,
I know that you are safest there.
The darker feelings, lost in love,
Are given up to God in prayer.

You are our gifted, talented son;
Your way has not been easy,
But ahead are possibilities
And chances to live freely.

So look to God who knows the way;
And the trial's end has come,
He'll show you how he loved you too,
And with us say, "Well done."

With much love and prayer today.
Love, Mom

TOGETHER IN LOVE

Computers, lists, long calls by phone
Can sometimes drive me crazy!
But then come snuggles, walks and naps
And drives and being lazy.

You are my love through all of that,
My help, my best dishwasher,
My steady source, encouragement,
To do just what I "oughter."

So thanks for all these years of love,
Of sticking close beside me;
For "putting up," and bringing forth
The very best that's in me.

With an abundance of love
More than you can imagine!!

Me

Steve:

Today you are on your way to spend some time with Anita. You are always geographically far away, close by phone or text or e-mail, and closer yet in my heart.

We tease about the night you were born; I think about the quiet moments of nursing you, of singing you lullabies, of praying over you in your crib, of later kneeling beside you as you said your prayers.

Those days are gone and you are far away, but still close at heart! I don't feed you very often or sing you lullabies. I still pray for you more often than just at night over your crib or by your bed. Now, as then, I thank God that you are my son and that God is still watching over you, loving you more than I do and planning for you in love.

Enjoy spending time with your Valentine, and remember how much you are loved!!

WHO ARE WE BROCKSIECKS?

We are a very small family –
a dad, a mom, two sons and one grandson.
But we are special –
We love each other;
We care for each other;
We don't talk a lot –
After all, four of us are introverts!
We enjoy being together
Even in silence and then enjoy the contrast
When Dylan is around.

We've been through tough times
And separations
And being lost
And being found!!

We're a mom and dad who will never stop
Praying for our three boys
Believing in each of you
Hoping for good things for each of you
But mostly loving you.

You are our delight and joy!!

HAPPY VALENTINE'S DAY!!

Valentines 2015
Steve:

You're far away and I don't see you with my eyes each
day,
But in my heart you're always close
You're just a thought away.
I have great memories, mixed with tears that on occasion
come
But you've made choices, grown so much –
I love what you've become!
So on another Valentines' I'm sending lots of love
And thanking God for being close to, my older son
I'm praying, too, that you will know that Jesus loves you,
too.
His love is even greater than the love I have for you.
BE LOVED, REALLY LOVED, TODAY!!

2015 – Kevin

How does Mom express her love for one whom she calls,
"son"?
Sometimes it's tears, just buckets full,
And sometimes laughter by the ton. (Had to make it
rhyme!)
But mostly for this mom of yours, it's having you around,
It's knowing that you're safe with us,
Until we know you've found
The place to work, the love to share what God has planned
for you!
With patience we'll help all we can –
At least we're trying to!

So on another Valentines' I tell you from my heart
How very much I love you, Kev!
With joy, though tears may start!
BE LOVED – BY GOD AND ME TODAY – LOTS AND
LOTS!!

GROWING OLDER TOGETHER

Hey, let's grow old together! Does that sound like a plan?
I think that's what God had in mind by joining woman and
man.
I like it; so let's do it; I think we're on our way!
We'd better take advantage and not miss a single day!
A snuggle in the morning; lie closely every night –
Let's take a trip, don't give a rip, and never get uptight!
Just so you're close where'er we are or who might come
along.
I need you now; I'll need you then;
Now where was I – I can't remember....
Oh, I remember
I LOVE YOU!!

LOVE IS PATIENT

Like when you are willing
to help me do the prayer bulletin, again;
And even when I am not patient with me.
LOVE IS KIND
Like when you find something I would really like to have
or do;
Well, maybe except a portrait of me for me.
LOVE IS <u>NOT</u>, according to Paul lots of things,
And you are none of them, like rude or easily angered,
Although sometimes you keep a mental record of hurts.
BUT love lets that all go and with me, at least,
you always do.

No wonder I love you, "not only for what you are [and
there is no one better than or even like you], but for what I
am when I am with you" [and that is so much better than
just me].

I hope that lasts a long, long, long, time!!

Dear Kevin:

I am so proud of who you are becoming –
You have overcome so much;
You have been through so many challenges;
You have faced so many mountains;
You have accepted work to be done on yourself.
And you've done it!!

Now I am anticipating completion of some of the work –
Victories over challenges;
Reaching to top of some mountains;
Realizing some hopes and dreams fulfilled;
Making progress towards all you can be.

As Bill Himes said in the midst of his tragedy –
"All that I am; all I can be; all that I am; all that is me,
Accept and use, Lord, as You would choose now,
Right now, today.
Take every passion, every skill; take all my dreams
And bend them to Your will.
May all I give, Lord; for you I'll live, Lord,
Come what may."

God still has a plan for you, for good and not for evil; to
give you a hope and a future, a good plan, designed just
for you!!

A 50TH VALENTINE

Do you realize that some 50 years ago, you were formed in
me, woven together to become you in my inward parts?
I loved you then for nine wonderful months!
I loved you as my very son for 18 challenging years as you
grew up!

I loved you when we went away.
I loved you when you came "home."
I loved you when we took you to California -
And now that we have lived apart for 25 years or so, I love
you still -
Differently, but unconditionally.
I've loved you a long time!

And I always will!!

Love, and lots of it!
Mom

OUR ANNIVERSARY

It really is a miracle,
to be married for 52 years,
to be in love
and to grow in love,
to be able to share times of joy and excitement,

to be at peace when we are together or apart,
to know that we can forgive and be forgiven,
to experience forgetting things that have hurt, to long for
moments of being together,
to enjoy snuggling,

to love watching TV, listening to CDs, as long as we do it
together,
to be together when we aren't doing the same thing,
to be parents and grandparents of wonderful young men,
to celebrate their lives and their accomplishments,
to feel as if we did not fail though at times we might have,
to travel together or with friends whom we enjoy,
to find people we want to be with because we both find
pleasure in their company,
to think through these things on this day!

All of this and so much more I am celebrating this day,
looking back
And looking at all we have had,
all we have
and all we look forward to.

"I love you not only for who you are
but for what I am when I am with you."
We are already growing older together,
and I long for more of that –
"The best is yet to be."
**If it weren't for Valentines' Day,
would we think about love,
especially in February**
When it's cold and often snowy – though not today –
And in some places the sun doesn't shine – though not
here?
Well, I would!! Whenever and wherever I am
and you are nearby,
I think of love a lot, and not just on Valentines' Day.
And that's because I love you and I know I am loved by
you.

How do I know that? First of all, you tell me.
And second of all you show me –
You care about me and for me.
You make love to me, whether that includes sex or not!!
You hold me close; you touch me during the day
and especially at night and in the morning.

You are my hero – taking care of cantankerous neighbors,
knowing everyone at church,
Snow blowing for anyone who needs it,
dealing with the grocery store clerk who is unhappy,
Looking for church folks who need a job to do,
proof reading the prayer bulletin, etc. etc.

You bless me! God arranged our marriage –
what more could we ask!!

With all my love – and God knows just what I mean,
ME

FOR A SON

In my mind and my heart, I love you every day –
And not just on Valentines' Day.
I'm not a very demonstrative person,
And sometimes I don't show you a lot of love
At least not by hugging and kissing –
Or maybe I quit doing that when you were 8 or 10.

But believe me, I love you as only a mother
Can love a son. I have since the day you were born
And it keeps on growing as I watch you become
The man God wants you to be.
So don't quit now, and I promise I will love you –
Even more tomorrow and in the years to come.

Love, Mom

"Love is...."

Patient – even if I don't want you to help me figure out how take a shower.

Kind – even when I ask you over and over again what the password is.

Does not envy – even when I go to breakfast with Bernie instead of eating with you.

Does not boast – even when you have to help me put on my nightgown.

Is not rude – even when I am impatient with you and verbally strike out.

Is not self-seeking – even when I take up all your time with my "needs."

Is not easily angered – even when I become angry or upset with you.

Now, that's love, and that defines YOU, especially over these last seven weeks! And I am so grateful!!

"Love is...."

Patient – always ready to help with the computer.

Kind – fixing meals when we are coming home.

Does not envy – willing to be home alone.

Does not boast – what is there to boast about?

Is not rude – listens with kindness even when we disagree.

Is not self-seeking – ready to lend a hand when you can.

Is not easily angered – sometimes, I'm sure, holding it in so that we can maintain peace.

"Love never fails."
Sometimes I think we fail you,
Fail to understand,
Fail to say or do the thing you need.
But it is our aim to protect, to trust, to persevere
And never to give up hope.

I hope you see us that way.
We want to "follow the way of love."
We love you!!

To Kevin

And here we are wishing you a happy one.
We really do wish you had someone really special
to share it with – But then maybe you do.
You are one very special guy – Just ask us, we know!!
You were a very special child, a very special teenager,
And have become a very special adult –
Sometimes far more independent than we would like,
But exactly right, right now!!
God loves you and so do we!
Be all you can be – and you can with God's help!!

IF YOU DIDN'T LOVE ME

If you didn't love me –
    I'd turn into a prune
        And then a raisin
        And then I'd just dry up
        And blow away.

If you didn't love me –
    I'd melt away like a snowman
        And I wouldn't be able to come back again
        Like Frosty.

If you didn't love me –
    I'd be like a tree with no leaves
        And there'd be no promise of spring
        Or hope for new life,
           Chopped down.

If you didn't love me –
    I'd be like those chocolate Easter bunnies,
        Looking pretty good on the outside,
        But hollow on the inside
        And soon gone.

But you do love me
    And so I am like a seed
        Full of potential and promise
        Full of life and hope.

But you do love me
    So I will not melt away

But continue to gain fullness and fulfillment,
Wholeness and completion.

But you do love me
    So I will blossom and bear fruit
        In season and out of season
        Being nourished and giving nourishment

But you do love me
    So I will be filled with good things
        Like joy and peace and love,
        Looking good on the outside
        And full and rich on the inside.

What love can do!?!?

WE ARE BLESSED

God blessed us so much
On the day you were born –
A son who got better each year.
A worry or two
Which God sees us through
And for a wonderful year.

BETTER AND BETTER

It keeps getting better and better,
These years of this marriage of ours.
Each Valentines' Day
In its own special way!
I want to tell you how.
You mean more and more
As I think of our love
It's grown and developed with time.
It's mature
And it's sure
It will pass any test; I'm sure it's the best!
And to me it is simply divine.

WHILE I WAS PRAYING

While I was praying this morning,
The phone said, "A message."
God said, "You'll want to read this."
And I know why!
It was a message from someone I love.

While I was praying this morning
A person crossed my mind.
I wrote their name down and prayed for them
And waited for God to tell me
What to do for them.

While I was praying this morning
The sun burst over the horizon.
I couldn't just let that go by
So I burst into praise
And thanksgiving for a beautiful day.

While I was praying this morning!

CPSIA information can be obtained
at www.ICGtesting.com
Printed in the USA
FSHW011439141120
75801FS